*To my mum, Chaz Queen,*
*because of all the things,*
*too numerous to write,*
*but mostly the love.*

*The author and Hardie Grant acknowledge*
*the Traditional Owners of the country on*
*which we work, the Gadigal people of the*
*Eora nation and the Wurundjeri people of the*
*Kulin nation, and recognises their continuing*
*connection to the land, waters and culture.*
*We pay our respects to their Elders past,*
*present and emerging.*

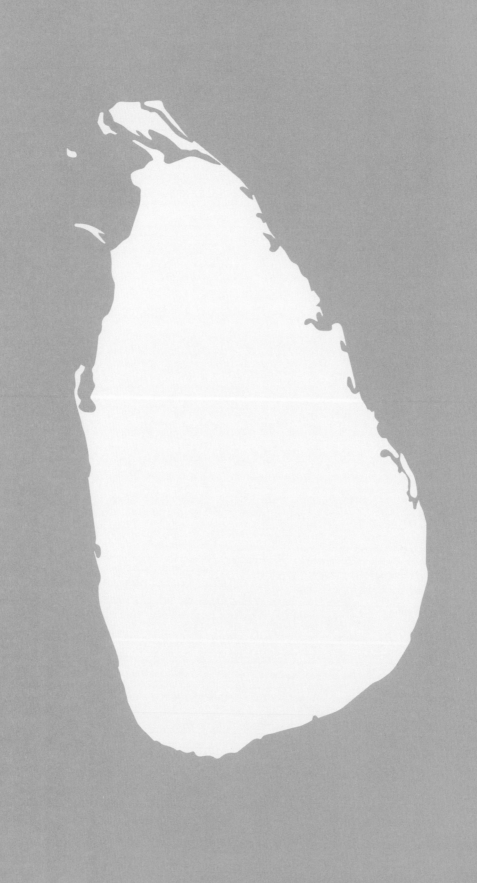

O TAMA CAREY

ආහාර

# Lanka
# Food

உணவு

Photography by Anson Smart

Hardie Grant

BOOKS

*If one does not eat his life ebbs, he becomes a non-thinker,
non-seer, non-hearer, non-speaker and finally, as the virtual breath departs,
non-existent ... Food truly is the source of this world.*

Translated prose, Pushpesh Pant,
from the *Maitri Upanishad*, an ancient Sanskrit text

*The island seduced all of Europe. The Portuguese. The Dutch. The English.
And so its name changed, as well as its shape – Serendip, Ratnapida ('island
of gems'), Taprobane, Zeloan, Zeilan, Seyllan, Ceilon, and Ceylon – the wife
of many marriages, courted by invaders who stepped ashore and claimed
everything with the power of their sword or bible or language.*

Michael Ondaatje, *Running in the Family*

අන්තර්ගතය

# CONTENTS

பொருளடக்கம்

# INTRODUCTION

*Ceylon falls on a map and its outline is the shape of a tear ... it is so small. A miniature. Drive ten miles and you are in a landscape so different that by rights it should belong to a different country.*

Michael Ondaatje,
*Running in the Family*

Sitting on the edge of the Indian Ocean, just below India, is a tiny teardrop-shaped island called Sri Lanka.

It's a place often described as a tropical paradise and, at its best, it is. There are beautiful coastlines: some calm and blue and edged with white sands and palm trees; some rugged, wild and unswimmable; some with dolphins and phosphorescence. There are rain forests, lush hill country and delicious fruits. The weather is glorious, the heat broken at intervals by cleansing monsoonal rains. The air is muggy and warm and feels close to your skin. There is a constant wafting of spices, the smell of onions cooking, of the briny ocean, and the vegetal greens of gardens and forests. You'll find elephants, leopards and monkeys, amazing ruins, beautiful architecture, stunning Hindu kovils, and more statues of Buddha than you can count. There are women draped in beautiful saris, hordes of school children in pristine white uniforms, and village men wandering around dressed in nothing but a tied sarong. It's an easy place to travel, full of excellent humans who are welcoming and friendly.

There are also bits that are not so great. In some areas the poverty is extreme. The capital, Colombo, can feel too crowded, dusty, busy, oppressively hot and polluted. In fact, pollution is a real problem that is sadly cloaking the island's natural beauty. Politically it's had to battle, with a long history of foreign rule, a violent civil war, and sustained corruption. There is still a caste system, which doesn't sit well in the modern world, and sadly women still have a hard time of it, despite the country's proud claim of having the world's first female prime minister. Add to this a devastating tsunami which, apart from all the damage to the people and the land, was a major set-back for the tourism industry, an important revenue stream.

This small island, similar in size to Tasmania, is rife with contradictions: you're usually too hot until you get to the hill country, where you may need a fire; rural life can still seem stuck in the last century yet in parts of Colombo you are in the midst of a bustling modern metropolis; and it can be in the poorest of areas that you receive the most generous hospitality. Despite its diminutive size, Sri Lanka has had more than its fair share to deal with, and to dwell on the country's beauty alone does it a disservice, because it's so much more.

Just as Sri Lanka slowly starts to find its post–civil war independent voice, it seems like the entire world is rediscovering the island – and its food. But while the flavours and dishes are becoming more recognisable, the foundations and building blocks of this unique cuisine are seemingly still not entirely clear. It is a food culture very much cooked at home, with recipes handed down verbally through generations, which means there is very little written record. So many peoples, flavours and ideas overlap and blend to create a cuisine that is distinct, yet difficult to define.

The food of Sri Lanka is almost impossible to understand without looking at this tiny island's fascinating story, its complex cultural context and diverse communities. The Sri Lankan population is made up of Sinhalese, Tamils, Malays, Moors and Burghers, each with their own food heritage. The religious mix of Buddhist, Hindu, Christian and Muslim adds another layer in terms of food restrictions and traditions, along with the dishes prepared for their festivals and celebrations. And the country's history is dotted with foreigners, both from international trade and invaders, resulting in a cuisine that is inclusive of non-native ingredients.

In my quest to understand Sri Lankan food, I am constantly discovering new recipes, as well as knowledge and ideas. This book will hopefully bring you all three.

The snippets of information and history are by no means exhaustive but offer an overview through a lens of food. The recipes are bits and pieces from everywhere. Some are my nan's, which I learnt while cooking with her in Perth (Lankan food with hints of suburban Australia). Some dishes are from my mum, who cooks the food of her remembered childhood and still tweaks it. Some are inspired by things I have read, some are strictly traditional. Others are collected from my travels through Sri Lanka: my versions of dishes I have shared at family meals or discovered through questioning people in their kitchens. And there are also dishes that evolved because of the produce we have available in Australia and the fact that my culinary training has taken me all over the place.

I want this book to be multi-purpose: a guide for those seeking a deeper understanding of Sri Lankan culture through food, a way to demystify the cuisine, and a starting point for you to cook Sri Lankan food and share it with your favourite people. But mostly I just want it to be a cookbook that you use so often it gets messy.

මා එහි ගිය ආකාරය

# LANKAN FILLING STATION
# (& HOW I GOT THERE)

என் பயணம்

*Lankan Filling Station
is one of many incredible
Sri Lankan restaurants
in Australia, but it is also
writing a thrilling new
chapter in what that cuisine
means here and now.*

Besha Rodell, *The New York Times*

I distinctly remember the first time I tasted a hopper in Sri Lanka. While I can't remember any of the accompaniments, I clearly recall being presented with this beautiful bowl-shaped pancake, with crisp edges, a soft and fluffy interior and a slightly sour tang to its flavour. I was beside myself with joy. It was the start of my hopper obsession.

I was 18 at the time. I'd just finished high school and set off to travel the world, starting with six weeks in Sri Lanka with my mum and a mate. Sri Lanka was still in the throes of its civil war and the Australian government was warning travellers against visiting, but we were determined to go. This trip was only the second time Mum had been back in 25 years. She and I had lived there for six months when I was one, but all I remember from that time is what I'd been told – apparently I ate nothing but bananas and pappadums and my mum had a pet monkey.

My mother's family are Sri Lankan, a mix of Tamil and Burgher going back many generations. Charmaine Moldrich (my mum) was born in Colombo to my grandfather (Poppy) Aloysius Granville Elmo Moldrich (a Dutch Burgher) and my grandmother (Nan) Ranee Sakuntala Palissundurum (whose dad was Tamil and her mum Burgher). My mum was one of seven children and the family was considered middle class. Granville worked in a bank, Ranee was a housewife, and the children were brought up as Catholics in the city, speaking English at home and Sinhala with the servants and in the street.

Like many Burghers in Sri Lanka in the 1960s or '70s, Mum grew up knowing that there would come a time when the family would leave. Burghers had been migrating out of Sri Lanka since independence in 1948, and this was accelerated by continuing political unrest and an impending civil war. And so, when my mum was 13 (her youngest brother was seven and the oldest sister was 23) the whole family packed up and moved to the suburbs of Perth in Western Australia. To go from sophisticated living in a cosmopolitan city, being looked after by servants, the lifestyle of the tropics, amazing food, and holidays and festivals of a plethora of religions, to white, bland, sometimes racist, suburban Australia at a time when you couldn't even buy fresh garlic was undoubtedly a shock. But they stayed, they assimilated, they contributed and they thrived.

I was born in Adelaide, South Australia, a small capital city with a country-town feel and a mostly white population. My father's family are white Australians with the usual ancestral mix of English, Irish, Scottish and Welsh. While my mum left Perth, all her siblings stayed put, so apart from the occasional visit I grew up without any close relatives on that side, although there was always a cousin or aunty nearby as the diaspora of Lankans is far flung and ever prevalent. (No matter what country I travel to, there is generally a Lanky relative to be found.) Sometimes we would receive a parcel in the mail from my nan, with love cake for my mum and milk toffee for me. Mum would occasionally but brilliantly prepare Sri Lankan feasts (my job was making the pol sambol and frying the pappadums). The idea of Sri Lanka was always there, but the strongest connection was through food.

But when I first landed on the island as a teenager, I felt an immediate ease, a sense of familiarity and connection. We had arrived at Bandaranaike airport outside Colombo at some ungodly hour (for some reason every flight I've taken there has landed between midnight and 2 am, an unsettling time to arrive in what is essentially a different world). We were collected and taken to a friend's house, West Winds, along the coast in Negombo (still the first place I go when I land), and awoke to the first of many excellent eating experiences.

We had the most amazing trip, travelling around the country, exploring far more historic ruins than I thought necessary, spending time with family, shopping, and lounging on beaches. When I told tuk-tuk drivers I was half Sri Lankan they would laugh in disbelief, then immediately ask when I was going to get married. But mostly we ate. I had always been a fussy eater so it was a real shock for Mum to see me devouring the food with such obvious pleasure.

This was the first of many more trips to Sri Lanka, all of which have involved eating too much (and lying on the beach and buying things). But the path from eating my first hopper to having a Sri Lankan restaurant was in no way a straight line. Just like Sri Lanka's history, it was dotted with many international influences.

From that visit to Sri Lanka, I flew into Paris and immediately almost got myself killed by stepping in front of a car driving down the wrong side of the road. Alone for the first time in my life, I thoroughly enjoyed an adventurous weekend before heading to London, where I hoped to find work so I could continue travelling (I had grand plans but little money). And although it happened in a roundabout way, I landed my first job in a kitchen. After turning up for what I thought was a kitchen hand job, and despite having zero training, I was suddenly cooking in a modern British restaurant in Notting Hill run by a woman called Allegra McEvedy. Instead of travelling to Spain, I found myself very happily stuck in that kitchen. It was a crazy time, as exciting as it was educational.

Less than two years later I was back home (heartbroken, still penniless and this time with no grand plans). Practicalities soon

found me back in a restaurant kitchen, at Sydney institution Bistro Moncur. It was the complete opposite of my first kitchen job: strict, rigid, highly competitive and testosterone heavy. But it gave me a good grounding in terms of technique, and the food was delicious. After that I had a brief stint at Uchi Lounge, a super-cool Japanese place. It was the first time I had a job that I'd actively pursued and I was desperate to learn, but there was no one to teach me.

So I jumped cuisines again and started working at another place I'd always admired: Billy Kwong, Kylie Kwong's modern Chinese restaurant in Surry Hills. Like my first kitchen, it was small, interesting, produce driven and run by a woman. I stayed for nearly five years, and during that time gained a proper appreciation for ingredients and for balance. I also met my partner Mat (nicknamed by Kylie as Muu, a name I continue to call him) and other excellent humans, many of whom are still my closest friends. In this positive environment I realised that I not only loved cooking, but I loved working in a restaurant. I finally knew what I wanted to do.

I promptly resigned and spent the next few years figuring out my next step. I kept myself busy with bits and pieces of cooking, until I was offered the chance to be the boss of my own kitchen, cooking my own food at a new restaurant – the only rule was it had to be Italian. My time at Berta was such a great period of creativity and learning. I read a million Italian cookbooks, I experimented, I travelled to Italy a couple of times, I worked too hard (and drank too much), I was highly emotional and had too much fun. (Once I accidently set fire to a whole lamb on a spit in the alley behind the kitchen, which was kind of fun now looking back on it, but it wasn't at the time.) Despite all the madness, or perhaps because of it, this remains one of my favourite cooking experiences.

Post Berta I had another longish moment of (mostly) unemployment that included more travel and stray cooking projects. Much as I loved pottering about, Muu was working hard and I knew his patience would eventually run out. I had to act. So I decided to open a hopper shop.

I knew these exceptional food items were relatively unknown in the mainstream and thought they deserved a moment to shine. Also, on a more personal level, hoppers had long been one of my favourite foods and to eat them I needed to journey to Sydney's outer suburbs or hop on a plane to Sri Lanka, so I decided it would be easier (ha) to open a restaurant and make them myself.

Lankan Filling Station (LFS) opened in Sydney's Darlinghurst in July 2018. I never intended LFS to be a traditional Sri Lankan restaurant, and I have never claimed that it is; rather, I cook with the flavours of the island. And even though I'd never cooked Sri Lankan professionally, and actually hadn't cooked it nearly as much as I had eaten it, I was suddenly in a position where I was meant to be the expert. I had to teach my kitchen staff what the food was and how to cook it, I had to describe it in great detail to my front of house staff so they would know what to tell the customers, and I also had to explain myself to the media to help publicise the opening of my first restaurant. I was often required to somehow distil the essence of a complicated food culture into a few sentences.

The concept of authenticity has been much debated in food. It's a twisty topic with many angles and I often find more questions are raised than answered when I talk about it. Being authentic means being genuine, but in terms of food the concept is often inextricably linked to tradition. And while tradition certainly deserves respect, it doesn't always mean delicious food. All food cultures are subject to innovation, interpretation and influences from others through travel and exchange of ideas and ingredients. In the modern world this can happen instantly, which is why I think more and more people are searching for an 'authentic' experience, but the reality is, no culture is static and neither is their food. Tradition and recipes change from place to place, family to family, and taste is completely subjective.

During the time between my jobs at Billy Kwong and Berta, I was lucky enough to spend a month or so cooking with my nan in Perth, learning her recipes and traditions. She showed me how to make her love cake, sharing a recipe that had been handed down through the generations. She also taught me several other recipes that were littered with ingredients like French onion packet soup mix and Deb mashed potatoes. Does the inclusion of these ingredients make her food less authentic? Or does this just show how traditional foods are subject to time, place and social status?

Since opening a restaurant serving food from my own heritage, I have had to defend myself and my cooking far more than when I was preparing French, Japanese, Chinese and Italian food. Is this because integrity is more of an issue now? Is it because Sri Lankan food is still relatively unknown and those who are in the know are protective? Or is it because I don't really seem 'Sri Lankan enough'? I am only the palest of brown (though of course skin colour is by no means the only mark of ancestry), I don't sound Sri Lankan, and my pronunciation of Sri Lankan words is very much Australian. Yet it is a hugely important part of who I am. On the other side of the coin, I bring an outsider's perspective. I know the flavours and I have an understanding of the cultural references, but I am not tied to tradition and perhaps feel freer to take liberties and experiment. LFS is a product of my own learning and travelling, and a constantly expanding understanding of food and the way I want my restaurant to be. I like to think we are respectfully cooking an authentic cuisine – with intention, care and knowledge – in a modern Australian context.

LFS survived the initial vagaries of opening a new restaurant, and we are also currently surviving COVID. The hoppers were meant to be the centrepiece, but they are now surrounded by a full menu that continues to evolve. But what has been consistent from the beginning is the aromas wafting from the restaurant. As soon as you enter our tiny space, or even just walk past, the scent of spices and curry leaves envelopes you. And on the best days, I walk in and it really smells like a little bit of Sri Lanka.

# SERENDIP

සෙරෙන්ඩිප්

**SERENDIP**

இலங்கை

සෙරෙන්ඩිප්

*But remember,*
*this was also known as*
*the Garden of Eden.*
*It panders to anyone's*
*chauvinism, you know:*
*Sinhala, Tamil, aboriginal.*
*Choose a religion, pick your*
*fantasy. History is flexible.*

Romesh Gunasekera, *Reef*

Eating the food of any country can be a simple delight. However, if you delve deeper into the place and the people, things become a bit more interesting, and you can gain a deeper understanding of that food. Sri Lanka's history is fascinating, tangled and full of legends. We can only take a little look at it here, but I would encourage you to dig deeper and discover more (perhaps start with the reading list on page 281).

First up, the name – or names. Lanka is Sanskrit for island, and in Tamil it means glittering. Arabs and Persians called the island Serendib or Serendip, linking it to the word serendipity. The Ancient Greeks called it Taprobane and the Portuguese knew it as Ceilao, which led to the British, Ceylon. It is now officially the Democratic Socialist Republic of Sri Lanka, or Sri Lanka for short – sri meaning resplendent.

So here we have a glittering, serendipitous, resplendent island.

Sri Lanka was first inhabited by the Vedda, the country's indigenous people. They are traditionally hunter gatherers, with a diet rich in meat and seafood, wild honey and traditions of preserving. Like many indigenous cultures they believe in animism, the idea that everything possesses a spiritual essence. Their culture has been slowly disappearing for a long time now, swallowed by assimilation and the modern world. Despite this, there are some remaining peoples interspersed in Sinhala villages in the south-central jungles of the island and there is one village, in Maduru Oya National Park, named a Vedda reservation site, where there is a tribe still adhering to traditional ways.

From as early as the third century, there was a lot of movement between India and Sri Lanka. The close proximity of the two countries (an almost walkable distance) meant there was always trade, migration and the occasional invasion.

In the fifth century, a disgraced prince from northern India was banished to the island, along with hundreds of his followers. Prince Vijaya converted to Buddhism, established a kingdom and became the first 'traditional king' of Sri Lanka. While the many versions of this particular tale are classified as legends, it seems to be generally accepted as the origin of the first Sinhalese people.

In among these two distinct peoples was the constant trickle of Hindu Tamils from south India, but it wasn't until the 1200s that they began establishing their own kingdoms, while keeping strong ties to southern Indian culture and food. At this stage, the Sinhalese kings were making themselves comfortable ruling in the south, with the Tamil Sri Lankans ruling a kingdom in the north and in Kandy, in the interior.

Although trade routes were established as early as the first century, it wasn't until the seventh century that the spice trade became firmly established. Due to its position in the Indian Ocean, and the fact that the country was bountiful in spices, jewels and ivory, Sri Lanka became very important. It attracted Arab traders, who are still a part of the population today – and with them came a whole strand of food traditions. There were also Malay and Chinese merchants to-ing and fro-ing, and Sri Lanka, as a great port city, welcomed them all, adding them to the melting pot of cultures and foods.

The Portuguese arrived on the scene in the early 1500s and decided they wanted to be in charge. After a lot of trouble and violence, they eventually got their way and ruled most of the island for a good century and a half. The Portuguese brought firepower, chillies, semolina, tomatoes, breads – and Christianity. They married locals, made fish patties and left behind surnames like Fernando, De Silva and Pereira.

After that it was the Dutch. They wanted power through trade (it was the time of the formation of the Dutch East India Company), and at first it seemed they wanted to make friends. But this quickly turned sour, and the Dutch ousted the Portuguese in the mid 1600s with the help of the Sri Lankans – who thought they were going to be done with foreign rule.

Alas, the Dutch stayed on. They never quite conquered the whole of the island, but they did create a lot of commerce, planting coffee and tobacco and selling ivory, cinnamon and jewels. This was the beginning of the Burgher people (again the result of some intermarrying) and what was to become another distinct strain of food: richer, using ghee and more meat (Dutch Christianity allowing for any animal to be fair game).

Then came the British, in the early 1800s, and Sri Lanka was swallowed into the Great Empire. For Sri Lanka, this marked the end of its monarchy and kingdoms; for Britain, it was all part of their grand colonial hopes to 'civilise the natives' of the world. The British legacy is noticeable in the island's architecture, education, rail network and proliferation of English speakers.

The British put a lot of energy into the coffee trade before a coffee blight hit, then they moved to tea. This became quite prosperous, but unfortunately on the backs of Tamils forced to migrate and work under appalling conditions – this population became known as up-country Tamils as a way to distinguish them from the earlier Tamil migrations.

At the time, Sri Lanka was a trilingual society – Sinhala, Tamil and English– the official language being English, with the British favouring the English speakers of the island. This was an issue for the majority Sinhalese population because it meant favouring some minorities: the educated and predominately Hindu Tamils and the Burghers.

In 1948 the country gained independence. The British departed, leaving behind the name Ceylon and a power vacuum, where language became a point of contention. This led to what is now known as the Sinhala Only Bill, passed in 1956, declaring Sinhala as the official language of Sri Lanka. This shift changed the power balance and would come to have great repercussions. It was a period marked by a push for nationalism aimed at appealing to the Sinhalese majority.

Riots began in the late 1950s and led to the further erosion of Tamil rights; Ceylon became the Republic of Sri Lanka in 1972 and security forces imposed numerous discretionary laws against the Tamils. Mounting tensions exploded into a violent civil war between the Sri Lankan army and the Liberation Tamil Tigers of Elan (LTTE), who formed in 1975 and fought for the right to have their own land, Tamil Elan in the north. Officially starting in 1983, this was to become Asia's longest-running insurgency: 28 years of extreme violence from both ends. Finally, in 2009, the war came to a bloody end with the death of the leader of the LTTE, Velupillai Prabhakaran.

I happened to be there in January the following year, when the first post-war election was held. The mood was apprehensive and rumours of corruption were rife, with tussles breaking out between people of opposing parties and stories of election scams.

Since then, the country has been re-building and coming to terms with the years of devastation. Tourism has picked up, as has trade. Foreign investment is gaining a foothold, for better or worse. Expressways are appearing and buildings are being restored. Even though you still need a special permit, travelling north to Jaffna is allowed. Progress has been slow, hampered by the 2014 tsunami, and along the coast and up towards the north, the scars of this and the war are still visible.

Adam's Peak, a mountain in central Sri Lanka (pictured on page 16), is a good symbol of the country's interconnected peoples, religions, legends and histories. This spot is considered sacred to Buddhism, Hinduism, Islam and Christianity. On top of the peak is an indent which, depending on who you ask, is either an imprint of the foot of Buddha, Lord Shiva or the prophet Adam – and was perhaps where the latter (prophet or not) first set foot on earth after being cast out of the Garden of Eden. Adam's Peak is a place of worship with meaning and relevance to all of these people who share the island's history.

Even though this is barely scratching the surface, understanding a little of this background will give you an even greater appreciation of the country's beauty and the resilience of its people. It also shows how much cultural mixing there has been and how it has not only been tolerated but embraced (for the most part). And once you step away from politics, the most obvious reflection of this is the food. The cuisine is distinct and particular and unlike anything else, but dig a little deeper and you can see and taste the influences that have so seamlessly melded on this very special island.

lemongrass
1 tsp = 2 g (¹⁄₁₆ oz)

pandan
8 cm (3 in) = 1 g (¹⁄₃₂ oz)

ginger
1 tsp = 3 g (¹⁄₁₀ oz)

curry leaves
1 sprig = 1 g (¹⁄₃₂ oz)

curry powder
1 tsp = 3 g (¹⁄₁₀ oz)

garlic
1 medium clove = 3 g (¹⁄₁₀ oz)

1 medium onion
= 200 g (7 oz) prepped weight

*measurements are approximate

සටහන් සහ මිනුම් සහ පැහැදිලි කිරීම්

# NOTES & MEASUREMENTS & EXPLANATIONS

குறிப்புகளும் அளவுகளும்

*Like everything on earth, foods are mixtures of different chemicals, and the qualities that we aim to influence in the kitchen – taste, aroma, texture, color, nutritiousness – are all manifestations of chemical properties.*

Harold McGee,
*McGee on Food & Cooking*

◆ My hottest tip for cooking the recipes in this book (in fact, for cooking any new recipe) is to have all your ingredients chopped, measured and ready.

◆ Generally speaking, the way you cut your ingredients matters in the mouth in terms of texture, overall appreciation and correctness of a dish. This is true for most chopping but not all. In the recipes I give clear instructions when it's important; when it doesn't matter, I give a looser guide.

◆ On the subject of cutting, in most Sri Lankan recipes the food is prepared to accommodate the traditional method of eating, which is with the fingers – no knives at the table.

◆ Traditionally Sri Lankan food is cooked in chatty pots over an open hearth, but it is unlikely that you or I will do this. Obviously everyone has different saucepans, tins and cooking equipment, which will affect the recipes, so it is a matter of adapting to your circumstances.

◆ Many of the recipes in this book are designed to feed a group as part of a banquet, with the idea that each dish will be part of a larger rice and curry meal. For ideas on what dishes go best with each other, see page 266.

◆ On their own, each dish should be enough to satisfy a couple of people for dinner with leftovers. Most dishes will last for a good week in the fridge (and generally improve in flavour over a few days), and they also freeze rather well. But if it still seems like too much food, nearly all the recipes will work just as well with the quantities halved.

◆ Most commercial kitchens use grams to ensure accuracy. To this end, I have given gram weights for all spices and many other ingredients. This can get tricky for very small amounts and may feel fiddly if you are not used to weighing everything, so if you'd prefer, use the facing page as a visual guide for approximate measures on common ingredients.

- If you don't have scales, then I do encourage you to make that little investment. There are plenty of good inexpensive scales that measure tiny amounts, and it really is the most precise way to follow a recipe.

- While you're at it, buy a probe thermometer – these are also fairly cheap and easy to find these days, and certainly the most accurate way to measure temperatures.

- Seasoning is one of the most important things in cooking. I usually season a little at the beginning, then again near the end, and always check just before I serve, particularly if the dish has been stored for a day or two. I nearly always use salt flakes and freshly ground black or white pepper (don't worry, I specify which one works best in the recipes), as well as lime juice. The simplest thing is to get in the habit of tasting and checking the seasoning every time you cook, even if it's not included as a step in the method.

- Tempering is a technique used in Sri Lankan and Indian cooking. The word comes from the Portuguese temperado, which means to season. In this practice, ingredients (usually spices, but sometimes onions and curry leaves too) are fried or toasted separately to release their flavour and then added to a curry or dhal at the end to give an extra kick. It also refers to the act of frying these ingredients at the beginning of cooking. It's all about adding more flavour – extra seasoning, you might say.

- In each recipe I say which type of cooking fat to use, but it will not be disastrous if you swap one for another. All it will do is change the flavour a little.

- Recipes have been made using fan-forced ovens except for the dessert recipes; adjust temperatures as required.

- I give a loose idea of heat levels in most recipes but this is totally subjective so don't get too caught up in this. As always, adapt so it works for you.

- Notes on specific ingredients and spices appear in the following pages. Also check the recipe ingredients list for suggested variations. If I haven't provided one, it's because I really can't think of a suitable replacement. Maybe you will think of something I haven't?

මිශ්‍රණයක අඩංගු ද්‍රව්‍යයන්

# INGREDIENTS

தேவையான பொருட்கள்

*In a well-blended curry all the ingredients should be added in such a proportion that the flavour of the meat, fish or vegetable is not killed by the use of condiments and spices.*

Chandra Dissanayake, *Ceylon Cookery* (the ultimate how-to for Sri Lankan cooks)

Here is a list of key ingredients that feature in Sri Lankan cooking. I haven't included all fresh produce and ingredients that are specific to the island as most of us will not have access to them. In Australia, I source what I can and substitute what I can't find. The advent of online shopping has made it much easier to get many hard-to-find ingredients and you should be able to find most of the things you'll need without too much trouble. As long as you are armed with some Maldive fish, fresh grated coconut, curry leaves and jaggery you should be fine.

## Bananas, ash plantain & their leaves

කෙසෙල් | *ke-sel*
வாழைப்பழங்கள் | *vaazhaipazhangal*
Sri Lanka is abundant with many varieties of this fruit, with ash plantain (their starchier, less sweet relative) used in numerous ways. I have a strong dislike of bananas, although I am told they are all I would eat when I visited as a child (along with rice and pappadums). As a result, this is the only mention of the fruit you will get in this book. Their leaves, however, are another matter and very useful for cooking, wrapping and serving food.

## Bitter gourd

කරවිල | *kara-wila*
பாகற்காய் | *paahatkai*
Used in southeast Asian curries and sambols, this vegetable looks like what I imagine the snozzcumbers from Roald Dahl's *The BFG* might look like: pale green, shiny, similar in size to a large Lebanese cucumber with an almost warty skin. They need to be treated properly before eating otherwise they are a bitter nightmare. To temper the bitterness, cut them open, scrape out the seeds and slice, then either soak them in salted water or coat in turmeric and salt for at least an hour before you cook.

## Buffalo curd

මීකිරි | *mee-kiri*
எருமைத்தயிர் | *erumai thayir*
This curd is made from buffalo milk in much the same manner as a yoghurt. The milk is cooked down, then poured into shallow unglazed clay pots (called kirri hatti) similar to Spanish cazuelas. When it has cooled a little, a natural culture is added and the curd is left to set. The high fat content of buffalo milk gives it a thick, rich result with a slightly sour and tangy flavour. Originally a speciality of the south, curd is now found all over the island, in markets and often

in roadside stalls that advertise their goods by stacking large walls of the clay pots. You can buy large pots to take home, or small ones to eat then and there, with a good splash of kithul or honey.

## Cashews
කජු | *kaju*
முந்திரிப்பருப்பு | *munthiri parruppu, kasukottai*
The cashew tree is native to Brazil and was introduced to Sri Lanka by the Portuguese. The trees flourished all over the island, many clustered in a place called Kajugama (cashew village), and the nuts have become embedded in Lankan cuisine. It is said that Lankan cashews 'fall from the heavens': they are larger than most, juicy and plump, and easy to buy fresh. They are mostly used in sweet preparations but are also made into a curry.

## Cassava
මඤ්ඤොක්කා | *mayi-yokka*
மரவள்ளி | *maravazhi kizhangu*
This starchy root native to South America was brought to Sri Lanka by the Dutch. It appears in curries, and can be steamed or used to make one of my favourite street food snacks, tapioca chips – fried and crunchy, like a potato chip, but denser, and usually served with chilli powder.

## Chillies
මිරිස් | *miris*
மிளகாய்கள் | *mizhakai*
Sri Lankan food is notoriously hot, and you will find some form of chilli in almost everything, used dried as a spice or fresh in both cooked and raw dishes. Depending on the type you use, the flavour of chilli can be almost as distinctive as its heat. The concept of prescribing exact amounts of chillies is troubling for me. There are so many factors: the type of chilli, where you live, what season it is and of course your own tolerance for heat.

Quantities are expected in a recipe book so I have provided them, but please do with them what you will. To keep things simple in the recipes I specify either long chillies (red or green) or bird's eye (also red or green). Generally, the long ones tend to be less hot than the small fiery ones.

## Chow chow preserve
චව් චව් ජෑම් | *chow chow jam*
பாகுப்படுத்திய சவ் சவ் | *paahupaduthiya chow chow*
This is a sweet candied preserve made from that curious gourd we know in Australia as choko. Native to Mexico, this sprawling fruit appeared in Sri Lanka courtesy of the Portuguese or Spanish. In Australia, choko has a bad reputation as it's usually poorly cooked and therefore tasteless and tough. In Sri Lanka it's used in a much more delicious manner, including the stems and leaves, often lightly cooked or made into a curry. This sweet preserve is an essential ingredient in Christmas cake (see page 256).

## Coconut | පොල් | *pol* | தேங்காய் | *thengai*
Coconuts are essential in Sri Lankan cuisine, with elements from the whole tree used in some way. Many rural homes have their own trees to cover their household needs, and bunches of coconuts, young and old, are a common sight piled up outside kitchens and houses, both in villages and cities.

**DRINKING** | බොන පොල් | *thambili* | இளநீர் | *illaneer* | Not to be confused with the water released from a mature coconut, drinking coconuts are always young and specifically in Sri Lanka are from the King coconut palm. The liquid has a cooling effect on the body and is good for dehydration, digestion and fatigue. The flavour is mild with a savoury note, and the thin layer of flesh inside is sweet and jelly like.

**GRATED** | ගාප පොල් | *gana pol* | துருவிய தேங்காய் | *thuruviya thengai* | Fresh grated coconut comes from the flesh of a mature coconut and is used to make sambols and sweets and added to curries as a thickener. Scraping coconuts for your own home cooking sounds admirable but you will need the right tools, a good supply of coconuts and more than a little patience. Luckily in this modern world it's not difficult to find frozen

grated coconut. Most brands are Thai but if you can find a Sri Lankan version you will notice a difference as they do use different nuts.

Grated coconut in this book always means freshly grated (either fresh or frozen). If you can't find it at all, you can make do with desiccated coconut. Add 30 ml (1 fl oz) of water or any milk for each 100 g (3½ oz) of desiccated coconut, mix with your hands and let it sit for at least 5 minutes before using. It isn't nearly as good, but it will do.

**MILK** | පොල් කිරි | *pol kiri* | தேங்காய்ப்பால் | *thenkai paal* | In Sri Lanka coconut milk is made by adding water to grated coconut, squeezing and mixing it through with your hands and then straining. The resulting liquid is the milk. This step is repeated up to three times and used for different preparations, as the milk becomes more diluted with each pressing. They don't talk so much of actual coconut cream (the solid fat that rises to the top when the milk is left to sit); rather, they refer to each step as the first, second or third press.

That said, I assume most people will buy coconut milk rather than making their own. Supermarkets carry a large range of both coconut milk and cream, which can vary enormously in thickness and flavour. In all these recipes, I specify using a combination of coconut cream and water. This is not traditional in any way but is what we do at LFS (because we use a very delightful Sri Lankan organic coconut cream that is never quite the same from batch to batch), and it is the best way to ensure consistency when there is so much variation between coconut milk brands (even more if you make it yourself). All the recipes in this book have been tested using this method and with Kara coconut cream as it is a consistent, stable and easily sourced product.

If you wish to use coconut milk instead, convert the recipes to this ratio: 250 ml (8½ fl oz) coconut milk = 100 ml (3½ fl oz) coconut cream + 150 ml (5 fl oz) water. If you want a richer curry, add more milk or cream; if you want a thinner version, add more water.

**OIL** | පොල් තෙල් | *pol thel* | தேங்காய் எண்ணெய் | *thenkai ennai* | Coconut oil is one of the most commonly used fats in Sri Lankan cooking. It has a very particular smell and strong taste, and can very quickly become rancid. It's never been my favourite fat to use but these days there is more of a range to choose from. At LFS we use a cold-pressed organic oil which still has that distinctive smell, but with a more delicate flavour. Substitute with any vegetable or neutral oil.

**TODDY & ARRACK** | රා සහ අරක්කු | *ra saha arakku* கள்ளும் சாராயமும் | *kazhum sarayamum* | Toddy is made by gathering the sap from the flower of a coconut palm. The fresh liquid is slightly sweet and a little tangy with background notes of coconut. Left to ferment for a day, it becomes slightly alcoholic, a palm wine that is sour and acidic, an easy go-to booze for village life. Once fermented it can be distilled in the same way as whisky (which can also be used as a substitute) to become a hard liquor, called arrack. This is very different from the Middle Eastern drink of the same name, which has a strong aniseed flavour. Lankan arrack sits between a whisky and a rum. As with most products, quality varies from brand to brand; find a good one and you have a strong drink with subtle hints of sweet coconut but with a punch. It's often served on the rocks or with ginger beer, and is very good for making cocktails.

**VINEGAR** | පොල් විනාකිරි | *pol vina-kiri* | தென்னை வினிகர் | *thennai vinegar* | Coconut vinegar is the sap of the flower of the coconut palm (toddy) after it has been left to naturally ferment for up to a year. It is usually a little cloudy in appearance and the flavour can vary, depending on the brand. The one we use is very vinegary with a strong fermented taste and needs to be used judiciously. Cider vinegar works as a substitute.

_Fresh Grow_

## Curry leaves

කරපිංචා | kara-pin-cha

கறிவேப்பிலை | curryveppillai

Another essential ingredient in Sri Lankan cooking, curry leaves are native to Sri Lanka, India and the close surrounding areas. The plant is part of the citrus family. The flavour is broadly similar to bay leaves, although curry leaves are more savoury and have a zestier note inherited from their citrus family. They are becoming much easier to source these days, and are often stocked in supermarkets. You can also buy dried leaves but I find these usually don't have much flavour. The fresh leaves freeze well and, if you are interested, the plants are lovely and hardy, and flourish in the Australian climate. When I mention curry leaves in a recipe, I always mean fresh.

## Eggplant

බටු | wambatu

கத்தரிக்காய் | katharikai

Native to southeast Asia, this excellent vegetable is widely used in curries and pickles. Several varieties are used in Sri Lankan cooking, including large dark purple ones, long skinny ones with streaky skin similar to Japanese eggplants, and smaller round white ones. For ease, the recipes in this book use the large purple type.

## Ghee

එළගිතෙල් | elangi-thel

நெய் | nei

Ghee is not actually one of the main cooking fats used in Sri Lanka, although it does appear on occasion, often in Burgher recipes or for some celebratory dishes. I use it because I love the flavour and the extra richness it brings to a dish. Ghee is a form of clarified butter, a process whereby the fat in butter is separated from the milk solids, but it is cooked to the point where the milk solids begin to caramelise. We make our own at LFS and cook it until the milk solids are on the verge of burning. This results in a beautiful darker fat with a sweet caramel aroma. You can buy ghee or very easily make your own. To substitute, use a mix of half butter and half vegetable or other neutral oil.

## Ginger

ඉගුරු | in-guru

இஞ்சி | inji

Ginger is a rhizome native to Asia that is used both medicinally and in cooking, both fresh and as a ground spice. When it's in season you can usually find beautiful young ginger with thin skin and a pale interior. As it ages, the skin becomes drier and the flesh a deeper yellow. I find the measurement of ginger troubling as many recipe books just provide a metric or imperial length, with no mention of how thick the piece should be (let alone how strong the flavour should taste). This is where scales come into play. Ginger is one of the key ingredients in most Lankan curries. The main thing to note is that Sri Lankan ginger is spicier with more of a kick than we are used to in Australia. It gives an added pungency to their ginger beer and also features in their excellent ginger biscuits. Ginger preserve – small pieces of ginger sitting in a thick sugar syrup – is used specifically for Sri Lankan Christmas cake (see page 256) and is best bought from a Sri Lankan grocer, unless you wish to make your own (if you do, please make extra and send me some).

## Goraka (garcinia)

ගොරකා | gora-ka

கொரக்காய்புளி | gorokkapuzhi

This is the fruit of a tree related to mangosteen, native to India and commonly called kokum. It is a small orange fruit with lots of seeds that is sundried until black and sticky. This powerful souring agent is often added to curries as an alternative to lime or tamarind to achieve the balance of flavour so sought after in Lankan cooking. It is also said to tenderise meat and help fish hold its shape. It is not something I have used a lot in my cooking as I love the flavour of tamarind.

## Gotu kola (pennywort)

ගොටු කොළ | gotu kola

வல்லாரை | vallarai

This plant is native to Asia but can also be found growing wild in Australia. It is similar to clover in appearance with a dark green leaf that is usually quite tough. It has a strong bitter flavour and is medicinally useful for numerous ailments, including diabetes and heart disease, and is said to be an antidepressant. The leaves are used in sambols, cut or pounded, or made into a paste, and are also found in the breakfast dish kola kanda (Sri Lanka's congee; see page 118). Substitute with bitter wild leaves.

## Jackfruit

කොස් | *kos*

பலாப்பழம் | *palapa pazham*

Native to southeast Asia, the jack tree is related to the fig and bears jackfruit, a large and heavy pale-green bulbous fruit with spiky skin. When ripe the fruit is highly perfumed with hints of pineapple, banana and a slightly fermented note. The edible part comes in the form of small pods nestled inside, which can take a little work to reach. You have to use a bit of muscle to battle the thick outer skin and then the inedible feathery flesh that surrounds each pod. Once cut open, a latex-like secretion is released, making your hands very sticky and potentially staining your knife. In Sri Lanka this fruit is used from when it's young and unripe right through to fully ripe, with each stage having a different name. When it is very young (polos) and the seeds are not fully formed, it is boiled or very finely shredded and used in a mallung (see pages 188–9). A little later, still unripe but now with seeds (kos), it is cut and cooked in a curry, breaking apart in much the same way as tender braised meat. When fully ripe (varaka), it is a beautiful yellow or orange colour with a crunchy firm-jelly like texture and eaten as you would any other fruit. It is also deep-fried at this stage to make jackfruit chips. The seeds are delicious too, boiled as a snack, curried, toasted or turned into a dessert. Depending on where you live, jackfruit can be hard to source and are usually only sold when fully ripe.

## Jaggery & kithul

හකුරු සහ කිතුල් | *ha-kuru saha kithul*

சர்க்கரையும் கித்துளும், பனை வெல்லம் | *sarkari kiththul*

Most Asian countries have their own unrefined sweetener made from palm, corn or date sap, ranging in sweetness and colour, and usually referred to as palm sugar. Sri Lankan jaggery is made from the sap of the flower of either the palmyrah or kithul palm (the latter believed to produce a more superior product) and is generally quite dark, with a flavour that is sweet but not sugary – more like molasses with a hint of savoury smokiness. Jaggery is made by boiling the sap to produce a dark, sticky syrup; while still pourable, it's known as kithul, kithul treacle or kithul pani (pani is also the name for honey). After it has reduced further, it is poured into halved coconut shells and left to set; at this point it becomes jaggery. If the sap is left to ferment, it turns into kithul ra, which is alcoholic in the same manner as toddy. Jaggery is quite hard, a little crumbly, and doesn't melt as easily as a sugar, so it's best to use a cleaver or heavy knife to chop it into smaller pieces or coarsely grate it. Grating is a little more time-consuming but, especially for sweet preparations, it will melt and blend more easily. It is an unrefined product and therefore better for you but it is still a sugar. It can be used anywhere you want some sweetness. If you can't find jaggery you can always substitute with any other type of palm sugar.

## Lemongrass

සේර | *sera*

எலுமிச்சைப் புல் | *ellumichchai pull*

This plant is native to India and widely used throughout Asia. The long stalk has a slightly bulbous base, and this is where all the flavour is – citrusy, zesty and quite sharp. Lemongrass is very fibrous, so it is often bruised and added to infuse a subtle flavour into curries, or chopped as you would ginger or garlic. When I mention lemongrass, I always mean use the bottom white part (keep the stems and use them for stocks, broths and sugar syrups).

## Limes

දෙහි | *dehi*

தேசிக்காய் | *thesikai*

Citrus fruits are common to most of the world, their history a tangle of interbreeding. Limes are an excellent example of such hybrids and are an important ingredient in Lankan cooking, lending their sourness to curries and sambols. The limes found in Sri Lanka have the same flavour as limes everywhere, but they are usually smaller in size, sometimes with a more yellow hue to their green skin. Lime juice is added as a seasoning at the end of many Sri Lankan recipes, so if you are going to be cooking from this book, I would definitely have some spare limes on hand.

## Maldive fish

උම්බලකඩ | *um-bala-kada*

மாசிக்கருவாடு | *masi karuvaddu*

Along with curry leaves, this is the ingredient that makes Sri Lankan food distinctly Sri Lankan. As the name suggests, it comes from the nearby Maldivian islands, usually bonito or skipjack tuna, that is dried and smoked until it becomes very hard, almost like wood. It is usually sold in chips or flakes and can be found in Sri Lankan and some Indian grocers. The flavour is strong but not nearly as stinky as some other Asian dried shrimp pastes or fish sauces. (I grew up thinking it was called 'mouldy fish' which was always a little disconcerting.) It is either pounded until fine and mixed into sambols or the flakes are added to curries and vegetable dishes. It works as a thickener, an added source of protein and as a way to balance flavour, much like you would with fish sauce. Use it subtly to add a salty and smoky umami note, or more liberally as a flavour in its own right. You can substitute with Katsuobushi or dried anchovies (at a stretch).

## Mangoes

අඹ | *am-ba*

மாம்பழங்கள் | *maampazhangal*

When you think of tropical islands, coconuts and mangoes usually come to mind first, no? Sri Lanka has many excellent varieties of mangoes. Ripe mangoes are enjoyed as fresh fruit, and unripe (or green) mangoes are treated more like a vegetable – cooked into curries, made into pickles and eaten with salt and chilli as a snack.

## Moru (white) chillies

මීකිරි මිරිස් | *mee-kiri miris*

மோர்மிளகாய்கள் | *mormizhakai*

These little beauties are regular long red or green chillies that are salted and soaked in curd or buttermilk until slightly fermented, then dried out in the sun. They are briefly deep-fried until crisp, much like a pappadum, and served as an accompaniment. More often than not they are salty and sour in flavour but sometimes they can be extremely hot. The cooked chillies can also be ground and used as an all-purpose seasoning that is excellent on everything, particularly pizza.

## Murunga (drumstick)

මුරුංගා | *mu-run-ga*

முருங்கைக்காய் | *muringakai*

The fruit of the moringa tree, native to India, are long slender pods which are used as a vegetable all over southeast Asia. In Sri Lanka, they are made into a curry. The pods are scraped of skin, cut and cooked whole, although the outer layer is not actually eaten. You break it open with your fingers to reach the flesh inside; it's a little stringy with soft beans and a flavour reminiscent of asparagus. The outer pod may be scraped with your teeth to extract all the flavour. The leaves can be used in mallungs (somewhat like Sri Lankan salads) and traditionally are added as a herb in crab curry.

## Mustard

අබ | *aba*

கடுகு | *kadugu*

Most cuisines have their own version of a mustard and Sri Lanka is no exception. Their version includes ginger and sometimes turmeric, and can be used to make a mustardy curry. Substitute a 1:1 ratio of wholegrain and hot English mustard.

## Okra

බණ්ඩක්කා | *ban-da-kka*

வெண்டைக்காய் | *vendaikai*

I have put this ingredient here as it is quite common on the island and often used to make curries and vegetable dishes. Despite the best efforts of many people, I am yet to taste a dish with okra that I like so there are no recipes for it here. However, if you are fond of it, please do go hunting for a curry recipe with okra, or substitute it for the snake beans in the recipe on page 200.

## Onions

ළුනු | *lunu*

வெங்காயம் | *vengayam*

Names and varieties of onions vary depending on where you are. In Sri Lanka I love the tiny red ones, which are generally known as Thai onions in Australia. The only downside to these, especially if you have a restaurant that uses kilos and kilos every day, is that they are very fiddly to peel. For ease, in the recipes I have just specified whether to use red or brown onions or the smaller French or banana eschalots which can be used interchangeably. If you can get the tiny red ones, use them instead of eschalot.

## Pandan
පන්දාන් | *rampe*
இரம்பை இலை | *rampa illai*
Native to southeast Asia, the
long aromatic leaves are a dark
to light green, and the flavour
is subtly sweet with hints of
vanilla. In Sri Lanka dried
pandan is usually added to curry
powders, and the fresh leaves
are cut into pieces and cooked
with rice or in curries. It is there
to infuse flavour, not to eat. Feel
free to fish them out before you
serve (or not).

## Pineapple
අන්නාසි | *an-nasi*
அன்னாசி | *annasi*
Sri Lanka grows very fine
pineapples, often quite small but
generally super sweet with no
hint of that sour acidic note that
can turn your tongue furry. It
is often served fresh with black
pepper or chilli powder, but
can also be cooked, made into
chutneys or even curries.

## Pumpkin preserve
පුහුල් දෝසි | *puhul dosi*
பாகிலிட்ட வெண் பூசணி |
*paahilidda poosani*
This preserve is predominantly
used for Sri Lankan Christmas
cake and love cake (see pages
256 and 254) and is best sourced
from a Sri Lankan grocer. It's
made from winter melon, which
is also called white pumpkin
in Sri Lanka even though
it's a melon. The fruit is cut
into pieces and candied, then
covered in crystallised sugar. It
is very sweet and can be eaten
on its own as a lolly.

## Rice
බත | *bath*
அரிசி | *arisi*
Rice is such an important
ingredient that I've devoted a
whole chapter to it (see page
113). If you can, do try and find
some native Sri Lankan grains,
either samba or red rice, which
are healthful and delicious.
Substitute sushi rice or Japanese
short-grain brown rice.

## Rice flour
හාල් පිටි | *hal piti*
அரிசி மா | *arisima*
Rice flour is only used in a
couple of recipes in this book;
however, various versions are
available. There is a Thai brand
of flour that is very fine, which
is not to be confused with the
glutinous version usually found
next to it at Asian grocers. The
other types you can find will
range along a spectrum of fine
to coarse. At LFS we use three
different grades to make our
hoppers so we grind our own,
using either a Sri Lankan samba
or an Australian organic rice.
For the purposes of the hopper
recipe in the book you will need
to go hunting for a fine version
and a medium coarse version,
health food shops are usually a
good place to find this.

## Rose essence & syrup
රෝස එසන්ස් සහ සිරප් | *rosa essans
saha syrup*
ரோஸ் சாறு, ரோஸ் பாகு |
*rose charity, rose paahu*
Let's be clear, rose essence is
not the same as rosewater. Rose
essence is much stronger and
thicker and is used in desserts,
often in combination with
almond essence. Rose syrup is
thick, lurid pink and incredibly
sweet, and used to make faluda
(see page 260). There are a
variety of brands, but the best
ones have just the right balance
between rose and sweet. It can
be used like you would a cordial.

## Tamarind
සියඹලා | *siya-mbala*
பழப்புளி, புளியம்பழம் |
*pazhappuzhi*
Tamarind trees are not native
to Sri Lanka but are now grown
all over the island. They have
a beautiful canopy and are
wonderful to sleep under. Part
of the legume family, the fruit
grows in long brown pods
containing a soft tangy pulp
and large seeds. It can be eaten
as a sweet and sour delicacy,
sugared or made into lollies,
but it is more commonly
partially dried (though still
sticky) and used in savoury
preparations. You can buy it in
blocks, rehydrate it and press
out the many seeds, leaving a
thick liquid, or buy it as a paste
or concentrate. The tamarind
concentrate used in these
recipes is an Indian brand
called Tamicon, which is
thick, sticky, almost black and
super concentrated, but it
may be hard to source. Thai
versions are easier to find but
they are more watery and less
concentrated so you may need
to add a little more, but be aware
that this might affect the texture
of some recipes. Again, adapt
and use your personal taste
as a guide.

**Other fruits** | ඵලතුරු | *pala-thu-ru* | மற்றைய பழங்கள் | *mattaiya pazhangal*

There are many tropical fruits in Sri Lanka that don't appear in the book because they are usually something you eat rather than include in a recipe. They are such a big part of daily eating that I wanted to include a list of some of the more distinct ones:

**AMBARELLA** | ඇඹරිල්ල | *amba-ralla* | அம்பிரலங்காய் | *ambarellankai* | Crunchy, sour, pineapple/mango flavour, often used to make acharu or cooked into a curry; also made into a sweet, sticky preserve.

**BREADFRUIT** | දෙල් | *del* | ஈரப்பலாக்காய் | *eerapallakai* | From the same family as jackfruit and quite similar; can be eaten cooked as a curry or sweet when ripe.

**CASHEW APPLE** | කජු පුහුලම් | *kaju puhu-lam* | முந்திரிப்பழம் | *munthiri pazham* | This is the fruit from the cashew tree; the nut grows from the bottom of it. The apples are yellow, pink or orange with a crunchy, watery texture, reminiscent of a nashi.

**CUSTARD APPLE** | අනෝදා | *anoda* | அன்னமுன்னா | *seethapazham* | Soft grainy flesh, almost custard-like, with a sweet and slightly sour flavour and many small, smooth seeds. Needs to be eaten at just the right moment when the fruit is ripe, soft and yielding; otherwise it can be unpleasantly grainy.

**DRAGON FRUIT** | ඩ්‍රැගන්ෆ්රුට් | *dragon fruit* | டிராகன் பழம், கமலம்பழம் | *dragon pazham, kamalam pazham* | Striking to look at, the outside is bright pink with little green protruding wings; the inside is either white or a deep pink speckled with small black spots. At its best the flavour is sweet, a bit like kiwi with hints of crunchy pear, but unfortunately the flavour often doesn't live up to its beauty and just tastes watery.

**LONGAN** | ලොන්ගාන් | *mora* | லோங்கன் பழம் | *longan* | The fruit has a similar texture to rambutan, also with a large seed, but with smoother skin.

**PAPAYA** | පැපොල් | *pa-pol* | பப்பாப்பழம் | *pappapazham* | A Sri Lankan papaya might just be my favourite way to start the day (hopefully followed by hoppers).

**MANGOSTEEN** | මැංගුස් | *man-gus* | மங்குஸ்தீன் | *mangosteen* | Rich, unctuous white flesh, segmented fruit with large seeds, hiding beneath a thick, hard dark-purple shell.

**RAMBUTAN** | රඹුටන් | *rambu-tan* | இரம்புட்டான் | *rambuttan* | Looks like a fuzzy red ball, with sweet jelly-like fruit and a big stone.

**WOOD APPLE** | දිවුල් | *di-vul* | விளாம்பழம் | *vizhampazham* | Very distinct round brown fruit with a hard shell and soft flesh. It has a sickly sweet fermented smell and sweet and sour flavour. Definitely an acquired taste.

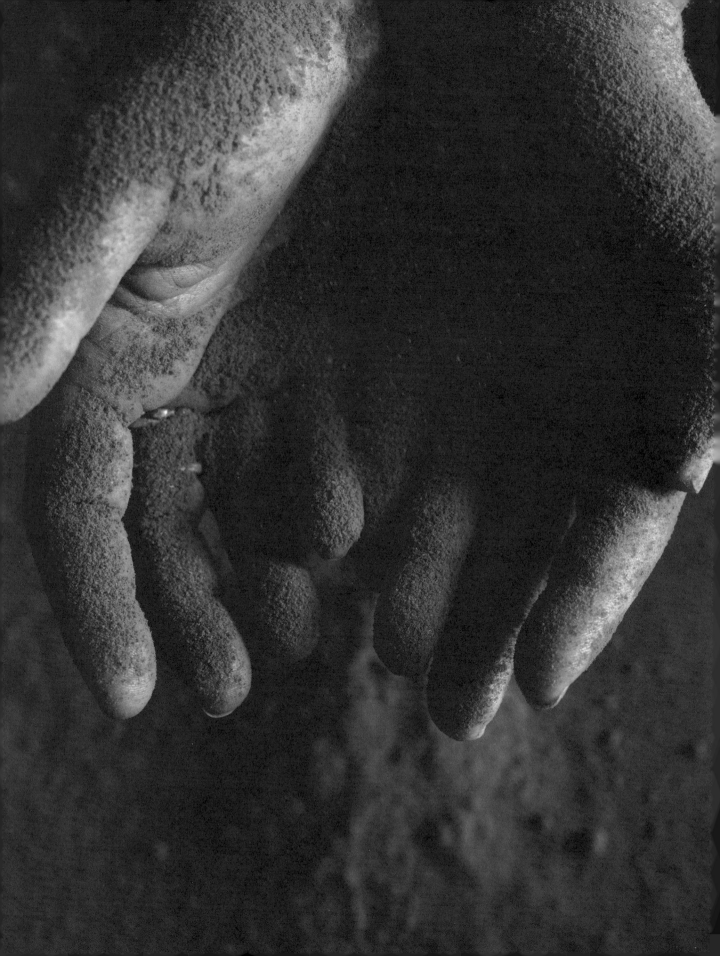

කුළුබඩු සහ තුනපහ

# SPICES & CURRY POWDERS

மசாலாக்களும் கறிப்பொடிகளும்

*If I were a
cinnamon peeler*

*I would ride your bed
And leave the yellow
bark dust*

*On your pillow*

Michael Ondaatje,
'The Cinnamon Peeler'

Follow the trail of spices and you find stories of civilisations built and lost, wealth and wars, conquerors and invaders. The irresistible lure of spices throughout the ages cannot be underestimated.

Every spice has its own unique aroma, its essence used as the base of perfumes and, less glamorously, historically helpful in disguising rank odours from pestilence and decay. Spices also help preserve food, particularly in times before refrigeration and in hot and humid climes. Their medicinal properties provide cures, preventions and general healthfulness. And, most importantly, they taste amazing.

Learning how to dry fruits, buds, barks, berries, seeds, stigma and leaves and turn them into spices was a great catalyst for world trade. It enabled these usually fragile ingredients to be transported and stored. The drying process heightened their flavours and intensified their scents, locking them away ready to be released when needed. Some spices are innocuous in their dried form, their true nature only appearing when coaxed out with grinding or heat; others have a smell so strong they can be detected oceans away. Their flavours can vary, depending on the way you treat them and when you add them. However, most taste exactly as they smell, which might seem obvious but isn't actually true of everything.

All of this can be seen to great effect in Sri Lanka, an island rich in native spices of the finest quality, with a history of spice trade and battles for its control. The island's food culture also places much importance on the healing nature of food by balancing the properties of spices particular to each dish. I consider this one of the most important chapters in the book as Sri Lankan food is such an intricately spiced cuisine, yet the layers of flavour are beautifully balanced, with nothing competing or overpowering. Understanding the spices used in Sri Lankan cooking is an integral part of understanding the food of the country.

When I began properly cooking Sri Lankan food and really trying to understand it, rather than just following recipes or asking my mum what to do, I started by researching curry powders. I read countless books, looked at combinations and ratios and tested variations. Curry powders were my way in.

Traditionally each Sri Lankan house would mix their own curry powder, perhaps grinding it with a little salted water or grated coconut to make a paste. A basic curry powder can be a blend of just

five spices: coriander seed, cumin seed, fennel seed, cinnamon and curry leaves.

Sri Lankan curry powders all start with a base of coriander. It's an amalgamating spice, earthy and mild, that brings all the other spices together. Turmeric and fennel seeds are also good base notes, but they have a stronger flavour and are used in smaller quantities. Cumin has a strong, savoury flavour and sits comfortably between the base note spices and the sweet ones. The sweet spices, cinnamon, clove and cardamom, add depth as well as flavour, particularly in meat dishes. They provide a warmth without being hot. Heat can come from mustard seeds, pepper and chillies, although sometimes they are omitted from curry powders, then added later during cooking. Each brings its own style of heat and I love the balance you can achieve by using all three together. As well as spices and curry leaves, other ingredients that you find in curry powders are pandan, ginger, salt, rice or grated coconut, the latter two often toasted and there as a thickener.

Curry powders can become very complicated and vary wildly depending on the type of curry powder you want. But at its simplest they are the foundation on which you build a dish, adding more spices to suit the curry you are making. Sometimes it's the subtle hints you are after, other times you are looking for something more robust. Sri Lankan cooking also uses 'fragrant powders': a mix of spices that are used at the end to season dishes before serving. Essentially though, curry powders and fragrant powders are both simply spice mixes.

Categorising Sri Lankan curry powders can get a little murky as there are as many as there are households, and not nearly enough specific names. If you go to a Sri Lankan grocer you will usually find four versions: untoasted, toasted, black and Jaffna. The untoasted and toasted tend to have similar ingredients, but the toasted one has a greater intensity and is used for more robust curries. The black powder is so called because the spices are toasted until very dark, almost burnt, and often contains more of the sweet spices. Jaffna curry powder is made with raw spices and is usually red and extremely hot.

The four powder recipes in this chapter will make everything in this book, but you can even just make the toasted (brown) one and use that as a base for all your curries, adjusting with extra spices where necessary. And feel free to experiment. The idea is that once you feel comfortable creating your own flavours, you use the powder as a base and add more spices relevant to the curry you want to produce.

# A few quick notes

◆ The difference it makes to use freshly ground spices in curry powders should not be underestimated. Once ground, spices deteriorate quite quickly, so it's always better to buy whole and grind as you need. (Turmeric is the exception – it's very hard to grind it yourself and much easier to buy as a powder.)

◆ Spices are best stored in airtight containers away from direct sunlight.

◆ Spices toast better whole rather than ground; if you do need to toast ground spices, you will need to do this super gently (as per the black curry powder, where the toasted chilli powder is integral to the flavour and colour of the mix).

◆ In a perfect world, when making curry powders, each spice should be toasted separately to release optimal flavour as they all cook at different times. This can become a little too time-consuming so in my recipes I have grouped certain ones together; the difference in flavour is minimal.

◆ If you are making a small batch of curry powder to use quickly, fresh curry leaves and pandan leaves can be used and give a lovely flavour. If left too long, however, their moisture can seep into the curry powder and turn it soggy.

◆ I haven't added salt to any of the curry powder recipes. If you wish to, do so in the ratio of 18% salt flakes to the total weight of your mix. Adding a little will also help in the grinding of the spices, particularly if you are using a mortar and pestle. This just means less seasoning when you are cooking.

◆ Cool spices before grinding. If you are using powdered spices, always add them at the end, after grinding, unless specified.

◆ The amount of curry powder you make is entirely dependent on your needs. Small batches are easier to handle and better for freshness, larger batches are better for convenience.

◆ Small batches work best in a mortar and pestle or if you are using a traditional Sri Lankan grinding stone, miris gala: a flat piece of stone with a large fat stone cylinder. You use a hand on each end to roll it back and forth to grind. (I once tried to bring one back to Australia but as I could barely even lift the base I had to concede defeat. Not all was lost – I did manage to smuggle the pestle bit back in my hand luggage.) Using an electrical spice grinder is perfectly acceptable, as is a good blender – this is usually more effective when you are doing larger amounts.

◆ You can jazz up slightly tired curry powders with extra fresh spices if you must.

# Spices

**Cardamom (green & black)** | කරදමුංගු | *karanda mun-gu* | ஏலக்காய் | *eellakai*

There are two types of cardamom; the green is native to Sri Lanka and therefore the most widely used. It has a camphor-like eucalyptus taste with an afternote of sweetness. Cardamom is the perfect foil for garlic and works to balance and cleanse sharp flavours; it's also exceptionally good in sweet preparations. You can buy it in pod form or as seeds (which are much more expensive – just try and extract the seeds from a pod and you'll see why). When I grind cardamom, I prefer the seeds as you get a stronger, purer flavour, but the downside is that they lose their pungency a lot faster than the pods. When using the pods, it's best to gently bruise them before adding them whole in curries and rice dishes. Fish them out at the end if you're worried about someone accidently biting down on one (which can be a flavour shock), but I prefer to leave it to chance.

**Chilli (powder & dried)** | මිරිස් කුඩු සහ වියලි මිරිස් | *miris saha vi-yali miris* | மிளகாய்த்தூள் மற்றும் காய்ந்த மிளகாய் | *mizhakai thool, kaayntha mizhakai*

The heat from chilli is integral to Sri Lankan food. The powder is used in the base of curries, curry powders and sambols, while whole dried chillies are employed in various ways: as they are (sometimes fried or roasted over fire), broken in pieces or ground into flakes. There are countless varieties of chillies and this obviously goes for the dried versions as well. All you really need to know is that chilli powder gives a heavier rounded flavour and chilli flakes or pieces give a sharper, more lively heat (but even so it can vary wildly depending on the batch). All these recipes assume you are using a hot chilli powder. If spicy food isn't for you, try buying a sweet chilli powder instead. Go with your taste preference and tolerance for heat and adjust your amounts accordingly.

**Cinnamon** | කුරුඳු | *kuru-ndu* | கறுவா, இலவங்கப்பட்டை | *karuwa, illanga pattai*

Cinnamon native to Sri Lanka is widely regarded as the finest in the world, and is one of the more important spices in Lankan cooking. It appears in most curry preparations, curry powders, vegetable dishes and desserts, adding depth and a gentle sweetness. There is plenty of romantic rhetoric on the scent of it drifting around the 'cinnamon isle'. (It's actually the source of a wonderful story of folk lore my mum tells involving Sinbad, sailors fighting for their lives, the discovery of the island and the word serendipity, all because of that alluring smell.) Scent aside, cinnamon is also a beautiful spice to look at, especially when you see the metre-long lengths tied up in bundles, all made by hand. Cinnamon is the outer layers of bark from the cinnamon tree; the larger pieces are wrapped around smaller ones and dried so it looks like one piece made up of paper-thin concentric swirls. If you are using quills, as I have specified, break them into pieces with your hand or use a mortar and pestle to lightly crush them. This will make it easier to weigh correctly and is better for toasting evenly.

### Cloves | කරාබු නැටි | *kara-bu nati* | கராம்பு | *karambu*

The clove tree is not native to Sri Lanka, although it has lived there for a very long time. The spice is the dried form of the unopened flower bud. It has an extremely strong flavour that can easily become numbing; it's warm and woody yet astringent, and can very easily overpower so use it sparingly. Try heating just one clove in a pan and you'll quickly realise just how pungent they are. Cloves are added when cooking rice to infuse the fragrance, they add a warm depth of flavour to meat and can also be used with seafood (though, again, use a light touch), but is generally considered too strong for vegetable preparations. They find their way into some curry powders and are actually very good in desserts. Cloves also have many medicinal benefits, often made into an oil.

### Coriander seeds | කොත්තමල්ලි | *koth-tha-malli* | கொத்தமல்லி விதைகள் | *kothamalli*

Native to southern Europe and the Middle East, this spice was cultivated quite early on in Sri Lanka. The seeds tend to be ground and used in most curry powders. The leaves are not used as widely in Lankan food as in other southeast Asian cuisines but you do sometimes find them in sambols. We use them a lot in the restaurant as coriander leaves add a calming note to heavily spiced foods, and also because I love the taste. Both the seeds and leaves have a mild, earthy flavour with hints of citrus. The seeds do not have the brightness of the leaves, but they also don't have the slight soapiness that can make some people averse to coriander, and they have a warming quality that brings flavours together. Toasted, the seeds have such a pleasant, mild flavour you could almost eat them on their own as a snack. Coriander seeds are good for digestion and a traditional tea brewed from the seeds is regarded as a cure for colds, sore throats and muscle pain.

### Cumin seeds | සුදුරු | *su-duru* | சீரகம் | *seeraham*

Cumin is native to the Middle East but is now also grown in Sri Lanka. It isn't used as much as some other spices and is mostly ground into curry powders to help blend and balance flavours. It does have a strong, slightly bitter flavour and is best used in moderation but I love that it is so savoury. Pungent, warm and earthy, it is said to be a carminative and is also used as a stimulant.

### Fennel seeds | මාදුරු | *ma-duru* | பெருஞ்சீரகம் | *perumseeraham*

Fennel is a prolific plant native to the Mediterranean, and all of it can be used, although only the seeds have found their way into Sri Lankan cuisine. Like cumin, the seeds have a helpful blending quality and are often used in curry powders, adding a sweet aniseed flavour that amplifies and gains a hint of nuttiness when toasted. Medicinally, it is an excellent digestive and according to Ayurveda it is a spice that cools the body, which makes sense when you consider that curry powders are combined to create balance in flavour and health. There must be harmony between heating and cooling.

**Fenugreek seeds** | උඑඁාඤ | *ulu-hal* | வெந்தயம் | *venthayam*
Fenugreek is a legume and a member of the pea family native to
western Asia and southern Europe, but also grown in India. In
Sri Lanka the seeds are usually soaked in water before being added
to dishes. Fenugreek is used to thicken dishes and add a bitterness to
balance the richness of all the coconut milk used in Sri Lankan
cooking. It is also a powerful digestive, which goes hand in hand
with bitter flavours.

**Long black pepper** | දිග කලු ගම්මිරිස් | *diga kala gum-miris* |
பிப்பிலி | *pippili*
This is an uncommon one, but we use it at LFS and it has a significant
history with Ayurveda and therefore Indian cookery. There is a version
native to Indonesia, which is slightly different from the Indian one,
although both are close relatives of the common pepper vine. These
little beauties become very hard when dried, are difficult to grind and
look a little like small, elongated pinecones. There is a definite heat to
them, but it is floral and a little bit perfumed with a flavour similar
to Sichuan pepper that carries the heat and makes it a little tingly.

**Mustard seeds** | අබ | *aba* | கடுகு | *kadugu*
When raw these seeds are flavourless and odourless, becoming
pungent and spicy when cooked or pounded. The flavour varies
greatly depending on how they are used. In Sri Lankan cuisine you'll
find them in mustards, pickles, mustard oil (both for eating and
medicinal purposes) and in curry bases. The practice of tempering
is often applied to these seeds, but care must be taken as the flavour
becomes very bitter and unpleasant if overcooked. I tend to favour
black mustard seeds but changing them for brown seeds won't have
a huge effect.

**Nigella seeds** | නයිජෙලා | *nai-jela* | கருஞ்சீரகம் | *karunjeeraham*
Native to western Asia and southern Europe, these little black seeds
(often referred to as black cumin) are grown and used extensively
in India. They are less common in Sri Lankan cookery, but they do
appear a little, particularly in breads, vadai (fried snacks) and potato
dishes. They are sharp, peppery, slightly nutty and strong with an
excellent savoury flavour and good digestive qualities.

**Nutmeg & mace** | සාදික්කා සහ වසාවාසි | *sadikka saha vasa-vasi* |
சாதிக்காய் மற்றும் சாதிப்பத்திரி, சாதிக்காயின் வெளிப்புறத்
தோல் | *jaathikai, jaathipathiri*
The tree on which this fruit grows is originally Indonesian although
it has been adopted by many tropical countries. Nutmeg is the actual
fruit which, when raw, is sour and unpleasant. When dried it becomes
a very hard oval shape with a latticed covering, which is the mace.
Mace is generally used for medicinal purposes and has a much
more delicate flavour than nutmeg, which is mainly used in sweet
preparations in Sri Lankan cooking. My nan always used nutmeg
with eggs as she said it helped temper their hints of sulphur.

### Paprika | රතු මිරිස් | *rathu miris* | குடைமிளகாய்த்தூள் | *kudaimizhakai thool*

Paprika is a spice made in the same way as chilli powder but from sweet rather than hot capsicums or chillies. Originally North American, it was adopted by the Portuguese, which is how it found its way to Sri Lanka. There are hot and smoked varieties, but sweet paprika works best in Lankan cuisine, bringing colour and flavour without the excessive heat. It's a good way to start people on their chilli journey, much like using training wheels. If you use both chilli and sweet paprika, you can adjust the ratios to suit your heat preference without messing with the flavour too much.

### Pepper (white & black) | ගම්මිරිස | *gum-miris* | மிளகு | *mizhagu*

Native to the south coast of India but widely grown in Sri Lanka, pepper is used as a seasoning and in curry powders. Prior to the introduction of chillies, it was the main source of heat in the food and as a result it's still used liberally. Pepper is a great enabler – when used in combination with other spices, it allows the body to more readily absorb their medicinal properties. The heat from black pepper is deep, earthy and pungent. White pepper (which is simply black pepper treated differently) offers a zippier version of the warmth of black pepper and is less common; however, you will find it throughout this book because I love its flavour.

### Saffron | සැෆ්රෝන් | *kaha* | குங்குமப்பூ | *kunkumapoo*

Originally native to southeast Asia, saffron does grow in Sri Lanka and is used sparingly in the food, mainly because it is so expensive. You'll generally find it in rice dishes, such as yellow rice and biryani, and in recipes with a Muslim influence.

### Star anise | අසමෝදගම් | *tharu* | நட்சத்திர சோம்பு | *nakshathra soombu*

The plant from which this fruit comes is grown in India and appears in dishes from the south of the country. It is far less common in Sri Lanka, but my mum uses it in her Lankan cooking and it is one of my favourites for both sweet and savoury food. It is almost a blend of fennel seeds, cloves and cinnamon – a sweet aniseed flavour with warmth, woodiness and pungency.

### Turmeric | කහ | *kaha* | மஞ்சள் | *manjal*

Native to southeast Asia, turmeric is a rhizome related to ginger and is used extensively in Sri Lankan cooking. Fresh turmeric is sharp, bitter, lively, a little earthy and very brightly coloured. In Sri Lanka it is more commonly used dried and ground, which intensifies the flavour, though it can veer towards a dustier, earthier savour. However, it doesn't lose its very intense colour, which stains everything it touches. Many cookbooks claim it's there more for colour than flavour but I disagree; the flavour (and fragrance) can be underlying but it is very distinct, especially when overused. Turmeric is well known for its health properties, especially when used with black pepper – a magic combination that can cure all.

# Curry powders

Pictured overleaf →

## White curry powder
Makes approximately 220 g (8 oz)

**This simple yet aromatic mix is a good introduction to the world of curries. The spices are untoasted, which makes it quite mild. It is used for white or yellow curries, vegetable curries or anywhere you want spice but no heat. You can also use this fragrant mix to season dishes right at the end, like a tomato salad or perhaps a deep-fried morsel.**

| | |
|---|---|
| 6 g (⅕ oz) curry leaves | |
| 70 g (2½ oz) coriander seeds | |
| 60 g (2 oz) fennel seeds | |
| 30 g (1 oz) nigella seeds | |
| 30 g (1 oz) cumin seeds | |
| 25 g (1 oz) turmeric powder | |

Place the curry leaves in a frying pan over a medium–high heat and cook gently for about 2 minutes. Reduce the heat a little and cook for another 1–2 minutes until they are dry and toasted, but not browned.

Allow the leaves to cool completely, then combine them with the remaining spices and grind to a fine powder. Store in an airtight container.

## Brown curry powder
Makes approximately 200 g (7 oz)

**If you had to pick one all-purpose curry powder to serve all your needs, this is the one. It has a little heat to it and is perfect for any recipe that calls for a toasted, Sri Lankan or Ceylon curry powder. Use it as your base and add extra spices to build different flavours.**

| | |
|---|---|
| 45 g (1½ oz) coriander seeds | |
| 30 g (1 oz) fennel seeds | |
| 30 g (1 oz) white peppercorns | |
| 30 g (1 oz) mustard seeds | |
| 20 g (¾ oz) cumin seeds | |
| 12 g (½ oz) curry leaves | |

| | |
|---|---|
| 1 g (1/32 oz) pandan leaf, cut into 5 mm pieces | |
| 15 g (½ oz) cinnamon quill, roughly crushed | |
| 8 g (¼ oz) cardamom seeds | |
| 11 g (⅓ oz) turmeric powder | |
| 11 g (⅓ oz) chilli powder | |

Place a wide shallow frying pan over a medium–high heat, add the coriander and fennel seeds and toast gently, tossing regularly for even cooking. After about 2 minutes the spices will start popping and releasing their aromas. Reduce the heat and keep toasting for another 4–5 minutes until the spices start to darken and the aroma becomes stronger and sweeter. Tip them into a bowl.

Add the peppercorns, mustard and cumin seeds, curry leaves and pandan to the pan and toast over a medium–high heat for 2 minutes or until they start to pop. Reduce the heat and toast for another 2–3 minutes until the pepper smell is pronounced, the mustard seeds are not only popping but grey in colour, the cumin darkens, and the fresh leaves are dry. Tip them into the bowl with the coriander and fennel seeds.

Next, toast the cinnamon and cardamom seeds over a medium–low heat for 4–5 minutes, then add to the bowl with the other spices and allow to cool completely.

Grind to a fine powder and then mix through the turmeric and chilli powder. Store in an airtight container.

# Red curry powder

Makes approximately 150 g (5½ oz)

**Filled with sweet spices and chilli, this curry powder is used to make fiery red curries. Use it in any recipe that calls for a Jaffna curry powder. I know there are a lot of ingredients in this one, but the spices are all untoasted so it's just a matter of measuring and grinding. It has a good chilli kick to it, but if you want a rich redness in your curry without the heat, reduce the amount of chilli powder and flakes (or leave them out completely) and increase the paprika accordingly.**

5 g (⅕ oz) curry leaves

24 g (⅞ oz) sweet paprika

20 g (¾ oz) chilli powder

20 g (¾ oz) coriander seeds

15 g (½ oz) white peppercorns

13 g (½ oz) chilli flakes

12 g (½ oz) cumin seeds

10 g (⅓ oz) cardamom seeds

8 g (¼ oz) fennel seeds

8 g (¼ oz) cinnamon quill, roughly crushed

7 g (¼ oz) turmeric powder

5 g (⅕ oz) fenugreek seeds

3 g (⅒ oz) cloves

3 g (⅒ oz) star anise

Place the curry leaves in a frying pan over a medium–high heat and cook gently for about 2 minutes. Reduce the heat a little and cook for another 1–2 minutes until they are dry and toasted, but not browned.

Allow the leaves to cool completely, then combine them with the remaining spices and grind to a fine powder. Store in an airtight container.

# Black curry powder

Makes approximately 130 g (4½ oz)

**This complex curry powder has a special place in my heart. It has all the types of heat from the pepper, mustard and chilli, it's bursting with sweet spices and is toasted to the point of being almost burnt, adding a bitter edge to balance out the flavours. A word of advice before you start: when you toast the chilli powder and flakes, things can get a little intense, so open a window. Make sure you stick to the specified toasting times, especially with the chilli powder and flakes; you need to take everything right to the edge of darkness, but not too far or you will end up with a bitter mess.**

16 g (½ oz) coriander seeds

16 g (½ oz) cumin seeds

16 g (½ oz) nigella seeds

8 g (¼ oz) fennel seeds

16 g (½ oz) black peppercorns

20 g (¾ oz) mustard seeds

8 g (¼ oz) curry leaves

1 g (¹⁄₃₂ oz) pandan leaf, cut into 5 mm pieces

5 g (⅕ oz) cardamom seeds

5 g (⅕ oz) cloves

3 g (⅒ oz) cinnamon quill, roughly crushed

16 g (½ oz) chilli powder

16 g (½ oz) chilli flakes

1 g (¹⁄₃₂ oz) freshly grated nutmeg

Place a wide shallow frying pan over a medium–high heat, add the coriander, cumin, nigella and fennel seeds and toast gently, tossing regularly for even cooking. After about 2 minutes the spices will start popping and releasing their aromas. Reduce the heat and keep toasting for another 6–7 minutes until the spices start to darken and the aroma becomes stronger and sweeter. Tip them into a bowl.

Add the peppercorns, mustard seeds, curry leaves and pandan to the pan and toast over a medium–high heat for 2 minutes. Reduce the heat and toast for another 4–5 minutes until the pepper smell is pronounced, the mustard seeds are popping and grey in colour and the fresh leaves are dark and dry. Tip them into the bowl with the seed mix.

Next, toast the cardamom seeds, cloves and cinnamon over a medium–low heat for 4–5 minutes, then add to the bowl with the other spices.

Reduce the heat to low, add the chilli powder to the pan and stir constantly with a wooden spoon to keep the powder moving as it will turn very quickly. Toast for 4–5 minutes until the powder is dark with a strong chilli aroma. Add to the bowl of spices.

Toast the chilli flakes in the same way, though they will take a little longer, 8–9 minutes. They are ready when they release an acrid aroma and the flakes are so dark they are almost black. Add to the bowl of spices and allow to cool completely.

Grind the spices to a fine powder then mix through the nutmeg. Store in an airtight container.

← Red curry powder

Black curry powder →

← Brown curry powder

White curry powder ↑

# Spice mixes

## Fragrant spice mix

Makes approximately 190 g (6½ oz)

**This spice mix has a hint of chilli but not overpoweringly, so it's balanced enough to use with quite a heavy hand, either as a coating or as a curry powder. Use it to crust a piece of fish before pan-frying or rub it over meat before grilling or roasting. Alternatively, you can use it quite liberally as the base of a potato or fish curry. The spices do need to be ground separately as the beauty of this mix is the differing textures.**

70 g (2½ oz) coriander seeds

35 g (1¼ oz) fennel seeds

22 g (⅞ oz) cumin seeds

22 g (⅞ oz) tops removed, fried moru (white) chillies

15 g (½ oz) black peppercorns

10 g (⅓ oz) salt flakes

20 g (¾ oz) chilli powder

Place a wide shallow frying pan over a medium–high heat, add the coriander seeds and toast gently, tossing regularly for even cooking. After about 2 minutes, reduce the heat and keep toasting for another 4–5 minutes until the seeds start to darken and the aroma becomes stronger. Tip them into a bowl.

Add the fennel seeds and toast in the same way for a total of 3–4 minutes. Tip into a separate bowl. Repeat with the cumin seeds and tip into a third bowl. Leave all the seeds to cool completely.

Now to the grinding.

Grind the coriander seeds until they are broken down but still quite coarse.

Grind the fennel seeds and moru chillies until they are semi-coarse.

Grind the cumin seeds, peppercorns and salt to a fine powder.

Combine all the ground spices with the chilli powder, and store in an airtight container.

## Pepper spice mix

Makes approximately 140 g (5 oz)

**This simple little mix makes a great seasoning for finished dishes (and is also very good on hot chips). It's a lovely way to taste different types of pepper and see the contrasting yet complementary way they work together. Use it whenever you would normally add salt and pepper for a little extra flavour. It has a hint of heat, similar to what you would expect from a good grinding of pepper.**

25 g (1 oz) black peppercorns

20 g (¾ oz) white peppercorns

15 g (½ oz) long black pepper

15 g (½ oz) coriander seeds

10 g (⅓ oz) fennel seeds

5 g (⅕ oz) cinnamon quill, roughly crushed

30 g (1 oz) salt flakes

Place a wide shallow frying pan over a medium–high heat, add all three types of pepper and the coriander and fennel seeds and toast gently, tossing regularly for even cooking. After about 2 minutes, reduce the heat and keep toasting for another 3–4 minutes until the spices release a lovely strong aroma.

Add the cinnamon and toast for another minute, then tip the spice mix into a bowl and allow to cool completely.

Add the salt to the spices and grind to a slightly coarse texture. Store in an airtight container.

## Seeni sambol spice mix

Makes approximately 23 g (⅞ oz)

**As the name suggests, this spice mix is specifically for making seeni sambol (see page 228) but it works well as a fragrant seasoning for meats before grilling. It has a good bite but is not too hot. None of the ingredients need toasting so it's very quick to put together.**

7 g (¼ oz) chilli powder

7 g (¼ oz) salt flakes

3 g (¹⁄₁₀ oz) cinnamon quill, roughly crushed

3 g (¹⁄₁₀ oz) cardamom seeds

3 g (¹⁄₁₀ oz) black peppercorns

1 g (¹⁄₃₂ oz) whole clove (go a little under rather than over with this measure if needed)

Combine all the ingredients and grind to a fine powder. Store in an airtight container.

## Sweet spice mix
Makes approximately 15 g (½ oz)

**This all-purpose mix can be used in the base of any sweet recipe that requires a little spiciness, particularly custards or poached fruit. It has quite a gentle flavour as the spices are untoasted, but the pepper does give a little heat. The salt is good for balancing out overly sweet flavours.**

4 g (⅛ oz) salt flakes

2 g (¹⁄₁₆ oz) white peppercorns

2 g (¹⁄₁₆ oz) star anise

2 g (¹⁄₁₆ oz) cinnamon quill, roughly crushed

2 g (¹⁄₁₆ oz) freshly grated nutmeg

2 g (¹⁄₁₆ oz) cardamom seeds

1 g (¹⁄₃₂ oz) whole clove (go a little under rather than over with this measure if needed)

Combine all the spices and grind to a fine powder. Store in an airtight container.

කුමන ආහාර කුමන වේලාවටද

# WHAT TO EAT WHEN
# (& HOW TO EAT IT)
எதை எப்போது உண்பது

*It is traditional to eat a Sri Lankan meal with one's fingers, as most Sri Lankans do ... to partake in a gourmet's dream come true, a taste of paradise.*

Felicia Wakwella Sørensen,
*The Exotic Tastes of Paradise*

For the uninitiated arriving in Sri Lanka, the concept of what you eat and when you eat it can be a little confusing. If you are a westerner, you could be unlucky enough to be fed continental breakfasts and bad attempts at western food for lunch and dinner, and you would leave the island having not enjoyed the delights of its cuisine. But if you insist on local food, you may be confounded by the fact you are being fed variations of rice and dhal for breakfast, lunch and dinner. The other concept to get your head around is sweet and savoury flavours being a little more fluid: you're just as likely to be served the spiciest of sambols with a slightly sweet rice for breakfast as you are a sweet fruit chutney alongside a spicy curry for dinner.

Obviously what you eat on holidays, as you hunt for traditional fare, is not necessarily what you would eat on a day-to-day basis if you were a local – a quick coffee before you run out the door, a salad for lunch, and dinner at a new restaurant your mate recommended. Another factor is whether you have staff on hand to cook for you, which is much more common in Sri Lanka than it is in western cultures, where it is generally seen as the purview of the wealthy.

The other thing to consider is that Sri Lanka is a country with more public holidays than almost anywhere else in the world, as Buddhist, Hindu, Muslim and Christian days are all marked. This opens up a whole new world of special foods associated with specific festivals, and rituals are shared throughout all communities. My mum loved this growing up as it meant more days off school and it felt like there was always something to celebrate and treats to eat. I think this reflects Sri Lanka at its finest, as a country that respects and understands all the different cultures that make up its population and shares all the traditions that go with it. Many dishes once reserved for special occasions are now available at other times, in the same way we can buy hot cross buns at Australian supermarkets months before Easter.

While there are guides on putting together the dishes in this book to create certain meals on pages 266–80, this should hopefully serve as an introduction to a day of food in Sri Lanka.

## Breakfast

A Sri Lankan breakfast is a thing of beauty. My favourite (of course) are the hoppers (see page 108), both egg and plain, which can be served simply with a sambol or two or with a generous array of curries and sambols. String hoppers (see page 106) may also appear, usually served with a kiri hodi (see page 146), sometimes with boiled eggs, at least one sambol and perhaps extra curries.

Pol roti (see page 96) are regularly on offer, and kiri bath (see page 120) is another popular choice – a subtle coconut milk and rice dish served with either hot sambols or sweeter accompaniments. There is a Tamil dish along similar lines called pittu, steamed with layers of fresh grated coconut and flour or rice flour in a cylindrical mould. When pressed out, this firm, slightly crumbly cake-like affair is served with sweet or savoury accompaniments, perhaps with sambols and curries or just a sauce or gravy.

For a quicker option you might try a bowl of kola kanda (see page 118) or perhaps a Sri Lankan omelette, a thin well-cooked egg dish with red onion, green chilli and curry leaves, maybe served with some kade paan (see page 89). Or perhaps you would like some curd and kithul (see page 251) for a simpler start? Or fruit? There will always be fruit.

If you're visiting Sri Lanka I would recommend going to a fancy hotel for a buffet breakfast (something I would normally avoid). This is a good way to sample all of these things, and usually there will be a hopper station with someone cooking them to order for you.

## Lunch

Generally you will be out of luck if you want hoppers at lunch, although some of the smaller restaurants on the outskirts of cities may have them. Rice and curry for lunch is the standard: this can range from a simple meal to an elaborate spread, which may leave you wanting a nap. It could also be a rice and curry packet (see page 116), a plate of fried rice or the slightly fancier lamprais (see page 127). So much rice ...

If you are on the go, street stalls offer stuffed godhamaba roti (see page 99) cutlets, rolls and other savoury pastries, or pop into a bakery for the same, along with a tempting array of cakes and sweet things. Lunch through to early evening is also prime vadai eating time (see page 68).

## Dinner

Again, a rice and curry meal is standard, although it's likely to be a larger array of dishes: rice (always), some sambols (usually a coconut version, perhaps one of the more salad-like ones and a pickle thing as well), a mallung (see pages 188–9), another vegetable dish or curry, perhaps even two, dhal, a meat or seafood curry or maybe even some sort of fried fish. Whatever is served, there will always be a balance of flavours, textures and spice levels, generally with more emphasis on vegetable dishes than those containing seafood or meat.

You may find hoppers and/or string hoppers making another appearance, served in much the same way as you find for breakfast but with more accompaniments. This a popular option for parties, as is a late-night lamprais meal.

Street or roadside restaurants come into their own in the evening and do a brisk trade into the early hours of the morning. Their menus feature paratha, fried rice and roti of all types, particularly the classic late-night dish of kottu roti (see page 100) in all its glorious incarnations.

After dinner you may be served sweets, curd and kithul, a more traditional dessert dish like wattalappam (see page 252), or the infamous chocolate biscuit pudding cake made with the very English Marie biscuits, layered with chocolate buttercream. Or fruit again – my personal favourite after a generous curry meal.

## How to eat it

The next question is: how to eat all of this glorious fare? Traditionally food is eaten with the fingers, both at home and out and about, although using a spoon and fork is perfectly acceptable. I must say, I firmly believe that eating with your fingers does make the food taste better (except in the case of soup).

Sri Lankan dishes are designed with this in mind: whole spices are easily discovered with the fingers and discarded, bones can be chewed around, and everything is cut into bite-sized pieces or cooked to the point where you can delicately deal with it. You will also find that the food is rarely served at a temperature too hot to handle. In fact, a lot of dishes are prepared and then left to cool to room temperature (which is usually hot and humid year-round) so there is little chance you will burn your paws.

No matter what you are eating, there is definitely a technique for eating gracefully without ending up with curry and gravy halfway up your arm.

- To start, wash your hands. There will always be a tap nearby or finger bowls to use before and afterwards for cleanliness.

- While it is more acceptable to eat with the right hand, this rule is observed more in India than it is in Sri Lanka; but whichever you choose make sure you only use one hand, never both. This leaves one hand free and clean to gather more food from the communal serving dishes, which will always have a spoon.

- When serving yourself, start with a mound of rice in the middle of your plate, then take a small sample of each dish and arrange it around the rice, either at the edge or just on top. Don't pile everything on top of each other. I usually start with a modest serving, as when there are so many dishes to choose from you can easily end up with more food than you expected. Also, be warned that you will likely be encouraged to have more than one helping.

- To eat, use just the tips of your fingers; food is never meant to go above the second knuckle and ideally mostly remains on the inside of the hand rather than the outside. If you start getting food above this or on the palms or side of your hand, things are going to get messy.

- The idea is that you start with a small portion of rice, then add in or drag towards it a little bit of a curry or dhal. It's best to begin with only a few things, and use your first three fingers and thumb to kind of mash it together into a small ball. Then, gently lift the ball to your mouth and use your thumb in a flicking motion to get the food off the fingertips into your mouth. Using this technique means your fingers barely touch your mouth.

- Continue in this manner, delicately gathering various combinations of all the dishes and experiencing the delightful mix of flavours.

- As you become more confident with the 'gather, mash, ball, flick' action you will find it easier to deal with runnier or less sticky dishes. The main thing is to use the rice as the anchor.

It can be a little tricky at first and may even seem daunting, but it is well worth making the effort to learn. Just try to be as neat as possible, resist waving your dirty hand around, and avoid overt finger licking.

පාරේ තොටේ ආහාර, සුළු කෑම වර්ග,
මිරිස් තුනපහ දමා බදින ලද දේවල්

# Street Food, Short Eats & Devilled Things

தெரு உணவு, சிற்றுண்டி மற்றும் மிகுந்த
மசாலா இட்டு சமைக்கப்பட்டவை

One of the joys of travelling or living in most Asian countries is the tradition of street food. The knowledge that there is always a snack close to hand is something I find both comforting and very sensible, and Sri Lanka certainly doesn't disappoint with its own particular mix of snacks and substantial bites.

Street food can be as simple as fresh fruit but also goes far beyond this, offering sweet and savoury snacks that reflect the eating culture of the country. The term 'short eats' originally referred to something you ate before dinner, like a canape, but these days it's a more general term for snacks eaten throughout the day. The definition of 'devilled dishes' is broader still, covering small bites as well as more substantial meals.

Devilled dishes are usually dry and hot, cooked without the coconut milk so often found in Sri Lankan food. A thel dala is also a name given to these types of dishes, although thel dala dishes are a little more specific and often their origins are South Indian. Many devilled dishes are cooked in a wok and the parallels with Chinese food are easily detected. The famous Sichuan dish of kang po chicken, hot and laden with chillies, is not a far cry from some versions of devilled chicken you would find on the island. Hot butter cuttlefish (see page 84), a modern Sri Lankan classic, falls into a slightly saucier subset of the devilled category and again echoes Chinese-style cooking.

When travelling in Sri Lanka, you will find that specific types of food stalls tend to congregate in one area, so there will be a glut of vendors selling one particular item that you may never see again on your travels. The only sensible solution is to take every opportunity to try all the things in case you can't find them again.

Many street snacks are deep-fried which, although delicious, can be a little on the heavy side. I suspect this can be traced back to the poverty of the country and the need for cheap, filling food that's easy to eat on the go.

Vadai or vada (see page 68) are an excellent example of this. Indian in origin, these fried hand-sized snacks come in a variety of guises. Usually lentil based, they are sometimes vegetarian, sometimes not; some are rolled out flat and almost biscuit like. A popular Sri Lankan version called isso vadai is a lentil-mix disc with a few prawns pressed onto one side. They are usually made in the morning and carted around until the vendor has sold out. If you are catching a train in Sri Lanka it's almost impossible to miss out on these snacks, as sellers jump aboard yelling 'vadai, vadai, vadai' and enjoy a brisk trade before jumping out at the next stop to repeat the process.

And then there are the more snacky things like tapioca chips (my favourite): slightly dense rounds or shards of cassava, deep-fried and seasoned with salt and chilli. Or devilled cashews or peanuts. And what my nan called murukku (see page 62): various mixes of crunchy fried bits, hot with chilli and fragrant with curry leaves – again, Indian in origin. You can buy all of these by weight from street vans or stalls.

Sometimes street foods are as simple as boiled corn, bought roadside, or seasonal bunches of rambutan or longans hanging from stalls, perfect for snacking on as you drive. You will find many versions of acharu (see page 230), which can be as basic as sliced fruit with a little bag of chilli salt to dip it into, a beautifully balanced snack common to many southeast Asian countries. Other versions of acharu are more complicated, using pickling or salting methods, such as the very excellent green olive acharu. All of these are ideally suited to hot, humid weather: the sugar is good for energy, the salt replaces what you sweat out, and the chilli adds to the sweating, which is your body's way of cooling down.

The best way to wash these snacks down is with thambali, the liquid from young King coconuts. Sellers pile up bunches of the hard-to-miss orange coconuts and crack them open for you to drink on the spot; aside from being gloriously refreshing, the liquid is also a great way to replace electrolytes in the body.

There is also a range of bakery-style snacks, such as cutlets, patties, buns, stuffed roti and rolls, found in street stalls, roadside restaurants and bakeries. Cutlets (see page 66) are crumbed and deep-fried spicy balls of goodness; patties (see page 72) have similar fillings to cutlets but are wrapped in flaky pastry. There are soft, white, slightly sweet yeasted buns that are stuffed with spicy fillings before being baked, and delicious grilled stuffed roti. Chinese rolls or pan rolls (see page 74) are a slightly more complex version with a thin pancake rolled around the filling, then crumbed and deep-fried. A similar concept to a spring roll, these are closer in size and flavour to other spawned versions, like the Australian chiko roll or the American Chinese egg roll. And all because the Portuguese introduced the breads, which led to the other European influences of pastries and crumbed delights.

Lunch or curry packets are a neat, easy way to eat a rice and curry meal on the go. Hoppers can also fall into the category of street foods, as they are often made at roadside stalls, where you can eat them with a curry or just a sambol. Alternatively, you can buy a pile to take home and have them with a home-cooked curry.

As you can see, there is a huge variety of street food styles to eat your way through. Because I had to draw a line somewhere, the recipes in this chapter focus more on the snack versions rather than the more substantial or roadside ones.

# Devilled cashews

**SERVES 6–8**

| | |
|---|---|
| 400 g (14 oz) whole raw cashews | |
| 40 g (1½ oz) ghee | |
| 10 g (⅓ oz) mustard seeds | |
| 6 g (⅕ oz) curry leaves | |
| 8 g (¼ oz) salt flakes | |
| 5 g (⅕ oz) chilli flakes | |
| 10 g (⅓ oz) chilli powder | |

**Who doesn't love a hot salty nut? This addictive little snack is simple to make and perfect as a nibble with drinks, on a road trip, or anytime really. Make a larger batch if you like as they keep well for weeks.**

Preheat the oven to 150°C (300°F).

Spread out the cashews on a baking tray and toast for 12–15 minutes until they are uniformly pale golden, giving them a jiggle every 5 minutes or so to ensure they are cooking evenly. Set aside to cool (you can do this step in advance).

Place the ghee in a large frying pan over a high heat. Once it's melted, add in the mustard seeds and cook, shaking the pan regularly until the seeds just start to pop. Add the curry leaves and fry for 30 seconds, stirring so they don't burn, then add the cooled cashews and stir to coat in the ghee. Sprinkle in some of the salt.

Fry the cashews, stirring occasionally, for 2–3 minutes to give them a little colour – a bit of dark char is more than acceptable. Add the chilli flakes, give them a quick stir through and then swiftly remove the pan from the heat.

Stir through the chilli powder and remaining salt. Taste and add more chilli and/or salt if you like.

Set aside until just cool enough to easily eat with your fingers. Otherwise, cool completely and store in an airtight container to enjoy later. The nuts should have a pleasant, almost sweet flavour and be on the verge of being too salty and too hot. This will help you drink more beer.

# Murukku

FILLS 2 X 1 LITRE
(36 FL OZ) JARS

Murukku is a Tamil word meaning twisted and actually refers to only one part of this mix, which also goes by the names bhuja, Bombay mix or the more traditional Indian name chevda. It can include any number of ingredients, but it is usually a mix of dried legumes that are soaked, fried and spiced, sometimes raisins, sometime cashews and often a fried noodle made with flour, either rice, urad dhal (black gram) or chickpea (that's the murukku bit). My version is based on my nan's, although it has strayed slightly over the years. It makes a fine snack with drinks or on car trips.

Ideally the fried noodles are made with a murukku gun (available online or from Sri Lankan grocers). If you don't have one, use a ricer.

180 g (6½ oz) dried chana dhal

180 g (6½ oz) dried white peas

180 g (6½ oz) small dried chickpeas

10 g (⅓ oz) fennel seeds

10 g (⅓ oz) salt flakes, plus extra for seasoning

250 g (9 oz) chickpea (besan) flour

10 g (⅓ oz) chilli powder, plus extra for seasoning

vegetable oil, for deep-frying

**SEASONING MIX**

60 g (2 oz) ghee

30 g (1 oz) coriander seeds

25 g (1 oz) fennel seeds

25 g (1 oz) curry leaves

Soak the dried chana dhal, white peas and chickpeas in separate bowls of cold water overnight. Use about three times as much water as legumes.

The next day, drain and let them sit in separate colanders to release all the excess water and pat dry with paper towel as best you can.

Meanwhile, gently toast the fennel seeds in a frying pan over a medium heat for 4–5 minutes until they start to colour. Tip into a mortar, then add the salt and pound until very fine.

Sift the chickpea flour into a mixing bowl, adding in the fennel mix and chilli powder. Slowly pour in approximately 125 ml (4 fl oz) cold water and mix with a spatula to form a thick, firm, quite sticky paste. It will only just come together.

Pour vegetable oil into a large heavy-based saucepan to a depth of 4–6 cm (1½–2½ in) (the oil should come no more than two-thirds of the way up the pan). Place over a high heat and heat to 160°C (320°F). If you don't have a thermometer you can check by dropping a little of the chickpea paste into the oil; if it falls to the bottom of the pan and springs straight back up again, the oil is ready. As you go along with the frying in this recipe, do your best to keep the oil at the same temperature – this just means you may need to adjust the heat as you go.

Spoon some of the chickpea paste into a murukku gun fitted with holes about 2 mm (1/12 in) in diameter (or use a ricer) and press the mixture straight into the oil. You will need to do this in about two batches so you don't overcrowd the pan. Once the noodles are frying, use a pair of tongs to move them around to cook them evenly. Cook for 4–5 minutes until they just start to colour and the bubbles in the oil have almost subsided, then remove onto a wire rack to cool using your tongs and a slotted spoon for any stray bits. Let the noodles cool a little and then try one. They should be nice and crunchy. If not, you may not have cooked them for long enough so pop them back in the oil for a second fry. If they are already dark your oil is probably too hot.

Repeat until all the mix is cooked (this can get a little messy as the chickpea flour paste is quite sticky, especially as you negotiate refilling the murukku gun). Transfer the cooled noodles to a large mixing bowl and use your hands to break them into bite-sized pieces.

Each of the legumes needs to be fried until completely dried out and slightly coloured, and you will need to do this in separate batches as they cook at different rates. If you overcook them they become bitter and extremely hard (I'm talking potentially tooth breaking here); undercook them and your final mix will be soggy. You should be able to fry each of the legumes in one go. Start by slowly adding in about half of each batch into the oil – it will fizz up, but as it subsides add in the rest. As they cook, use a slotted spoon to stir them around occasionally for even cooking.

Start with the chana dhal; this will take about 12–14 minutes to cook. Remove them using a slotted spoon or wire strainer. Next cook the white peas, also 12–14 minutes of cooking, and then the chickpeas. The chickpeas take much longer, about 16–18 minutes, and they will also colour more than the others. They will sit at the bottom of the pan and pop up about halfway through. They also have a habit of spitting sometimes so be careful.

When you remove each batch of legumes from the oil, tip it onto a tray lined with paper towel and, while still hot, season liberally with salt and a little chilli powder. Leave to cool and dry out, then add to the fried noodles.

To prepare the seasoning mix, melt the ghee in a medium saucepan over a medium heat, add the seeds and cook gently for 1–2 minutes until they start to release their aromas. Add the curry leaves and cook for another 3–4 minutes until the leaves are crisp and the seeds have started to colour.

Pour the mix over the fried ingredients in the bowl and give it a very good stir. Taste and add more chilli and salt if required. You're after a nice hot, salty flavour with the occasional pop of whole spices and crunch from the noodles and legumes. This mix can be eaten straight away or cooled and stored for later.

---

**NOTES** The murukku will last for months stored in airtight containers or jars, but make sure you mix it well before serving as the seasoning tends to settle at the bottom.

Don't feel tied to the dried legumes specified in the recipe; by all means experiment with different varieties, and you could also add fried or toasted nuts – cashews and peanuts are both good options.

---

**Pictured overleaf** →

← **Murukku**  ↑ **Crab cutlets**

# Crab cutlets

MAKES 36

In Indian and Sri Lankan cooking, the term cutlet refers to a spicy ball of filling, which is then crumbed and deep-fried. There are endless versions using meat, seafood and vegetables. In Sri Lanka they are usually made with fish or meat and tend to be large-ish, but I prefer slightly smaller balls which are excellent at parties and gatherings, served hot or at room temperature. They can easily be made ahead and stored in the fridge or freezer until needed.

This recipe is almost exactly as my nan taught me, although she made fish cutlets using tinned mackerel (equally as good) rather than crabmeat.

150 g (5½ oz) plain (all-purpose) flour

2 eggs

80 ml (2½ fl oz) full-cream (whole) milk

200 g (7 oz) fine dried breadcrumbs

vegetable oil, for deep-frying

lime cheeks, to serve (optional)

## CRAB FILLING

500 g (1 lb 2 oz) desiree potatoes, peeled and cut into 1 cm (½ in) dice

30 g (1 oz) ghee

90 g (3 oz) eschalot, peeled and finely sliced

10 g (⅓ oz) finely chopped garlic

3 green bird's eye chillies, finely chopped

4 g (⅛ oz) curry leaves, finely sliced

4 g (⅛ oz) White curry powder (see page 42)

300 g (10½ oz) cooked crabmeat (see note)

salt flakes and freshly ground white pepper

3 g (1/10 oz) chopped dill

Preheat the oven to 160°C (320°F).

To make the crab filling, place the potato in a medium saucepan and cover with lightly seasoned cold water. Bring to a simmer over a medium heat and cook for 14–18 minutes until the potato is tender. Drain, then spread out on a baking tray and place in the oven for 6–7 minutes to dry out.

Use a ricer or a potato masher to finely mash the potato, then set aside.

Meanwhile, melt the ghee in a small saucepan over a medium heat. Add the eschalot, garlic, chilli and curry leaf and cook, stirring occasionally, for 4–5 minutes until the eschalot has softened. Stir in the curry powder and cook for another minute or so until you feel the powder sticking to the base of the pan.

Add the curry mix and crabmeat to the mashed potato and gently stir to combine. Taste for seasoning and adjust if needed. Once the mixture is reasonably cool, stir through the dill. The mixture should be thick and a little sticky; if it feels a bit soft and difficult to roll, put it in the fridge for a while to firm up before you move onto the next step.

Measure out the mix with clean hands – you need about 1 tablespoon (20 g/¾ oz) per ball. Roll each portion into a ball and set aside on a tray.

Now set up a crumbing station: tip the flour in a bowl; whisk together the eggs and milk in a second bowl; and place the breadcrumbs in a third bowl. Have a clean tray or plate handy to put the crumbed balls on.

Gently roll each ball in flour, shaking off the excess, then coat in the egg mixture, allowing the excess to drip off. Finally, roll the balls in the breadcrumbs. Place on the clean tray or plate.

At this stage, the balls can be kept in the fridge for a few days or frozen to fry later. If you are going to cook them straight away, give them at least half an hour in the fridge to firm up before you start frying.

This will also give you time to clean up all your crumbing mess.

Pour vegetable oil into a large heavy-based saucepan to a depth of 4–6 cm (1½–2½ in) (the oil should come no more than two-thirds of the way up the pan). Place over a high heat and heat to

170°C (340°F). If you don't have a thermometer you can check by dropping a few breadcrumbs into the oil; if they sizzle immediately, the oil is ready.

Working in small batches, fry the cutlets for 3–4 minutes until they are a dark golden-brown colour, gently swishing them around so they cook evenly. Lift them out with a slotted spoon and drain on a wire rack. Give the oil a moment to heat up again before you fry the next batch.

The cutlets are now ready to serve, although they are just as good left to sit at room temperature and eaten a few hours later. (They're also excellent eaten straight from the fridge if you happen to have leftovers.) If eaten straight away they'll be nice and crunchy on the outside with a soft, delicate, lightly spiced interior. Serve with lime wedges if you like, but this isn't entirely necessary.

NOTE I have found that most commercial varieties of cooked crabmeat aren't great, and would encourage you to cook it yourself. Spread 350 g (12½ oz) raw crabmeat over a baking tray and gently roast in a preheated 160°C (320°F) oven for 5–6 minutes until just cooked. Obviously, if you do find a product you are happy with, use that. Alternatively, follow my nan's lead and substitute with tinned mackerel.

# Vadai

EACH MAKES 20

Pictured overleaf →

I have tried making many versions of vadai, often without much success as I think I may have a vadai curse; however, what follows are two different recipes that do work. One is based on the idea of an ulundu vadai (vegetarian, usually made with ground lentils and formed into a doughnut shape) but is strictly non-traditional as the batter is lightened with ricotta. The other version is more traditional: a flat vadai made with flour, soaked urad dhal and spices. By their very nature, most vadai do tend to be a little dense and heavy.

## Vadai 1

vegetable oil, for deep-frying

salt flakes

lime wedges, to serve

### VADAI MIXTURE

10 g (⅓ oz) chopped garlic

8 g (¼ oz) chopped ginger

salt flakes and freshly ground white pepper

125 g (4½ oz) firm fresh ricotta, drained

100 g (3½ oz) grated coconut

100 g (3½ oz) fine rice flour or chickpea (besan) flour, sifted

80 g (2¾ oz) finely diced eschalot

5 g (⅕ oz) curry leaves, finely julienned

3 g (1/10 oz) green bird's eye chilli, finely sliced into rounds

5 g (⅕ oz) White curry powder (see page 42)

4 g (⅛ oz) baking powder

2 g (1/16 oz) chilli powder

2 g (1/16 oz) turmeric powder

To make the vadai mixture, use a mortar and pestle to pound the garlic, ginger and 3 g (1/10 oz) salt to a fine paste. Transfer to a large mixing bowl, add the remaining ingredients and give it a good stir to break up the ricotta and make sure everything is well combined. Taste to check the seasoning and adjust if necessary. Add just enough water to bring the mix together, approximately 20 ml (¾ fl oz) – it should be a little sticky but not wet. Cover and rest in the fridge for 30 minutes.

Remove the mixture from the fridge and use a tablespoon to make 20 even balls, each about 20 g (¾ oz). Use your little finger to make a small hole in the middle to make a plump doughnut shape. Set aside on a tray.

Pour vegetable oil into a large heavy-based saucepan to a depth of 4–6 cm (1½–2½ in) (the oil should come no more than two-thirds of the way up the pan). Place over a high heat and heat to 170°C (340°F). If you don't have a thermometer you can check by dropping a vadai into the oil; if it drops to the bottom, then quickly springs back up to the top, the oil is ready.

Working in small batches, fry the vadai for 4–5 minutes until they are evenly golden, turning occasionally and gently swishing them around so they don't stick to the bottom of the pan or each other. Lift them out with a slotted spoon and drain on a wire rack. Season with salt flakes. Give the oil a moment to heat up again before you fry the next batch.

Serve warm with lime wedges and perhaps a green pol sambol or raita (see page 216). When you eat one it should be fluffy but a little gooey on the inside. The flavour should be aromatic, with a hint of coconut and very mild heat from the chilli.

# Vadai 2

vegetable oil, for deep-frying

**VADAI MIXTURE**

220 g (8 oz) whole dried skinless urad dhal (black gram)

325 g (11½ oz) plain (all-purpose) flour

4 g (⅛ oz) fennel seeds

8 g (¼ oz) garlic, roughly chopped

6 g (⅕ oz) salt flakes

4 g (⅛ oz) chilli flakes

80 g (2¾ oz) finely diced eschalot

2 g (1/16 oz) curry leaves, finely julienned

freshly ground black pepper

For the vadai mixture, start by soaking the urad dhal in a large bowl of cold water for 4 hours. Drain.

Place half the flour in a steamer between two pieces of muslin (cheesecloth), forming it into a low mound rather than spreading it out in a thin layer. Steam gently for 30–40 minutes until firm. This process is said to help make the flour less sticky.

Use a drum sieve or fine strainer to sift the steamed flour into a mixing bowl, using your hands to scrape it through, then sift in the remaining flour.

Gently toast the fennel seeds in a frying pan over a medium heat for 4–5 minutes until they start to colour. Meanwhile, using a mortar and pestle, pound the garlic and salt to form a paste. Add the fennel seeds and chilli flakes and briefly pound to break the seeds a little.

To the flour, add the drained dhal, the spice mix, eschalot and curry leaves and mix together. Season with pepper and add in just enough water to form a dry dough, approximately 110 ml (4 fl oz).

Form the dough into 20 even balls, each about 45 g (1½ oz). Use a rolling pin, or even easier a tortilla press, to flatten the balls into rounds about 3 mm (⅛ in) thick.

Pour vegetable oil into a high-sided frying pan to a depth of 2–3 cm (¾–1¼ in). Place over a high heat and heat to 170°C (340°F). If you don't have a thermometer you can check by laying a vadai in the pan; it should rapidly sizzle and very soon float to the top.

One by one, fry the vadai for 2–3 minutes, turning occasionally with tongs until they are evenly golden in colour. Lift out, place onto a rack to drain and season with salt.

These vadai will be crisp like a chip but slightly denser, with a nice bite of fennel and a moderate hint of chilli. They are best eaten swiftly or at least on the same day you make them.

↑ Vadai    Fish patties →

# Fish patties

MAKES 20

This short eat does very little to hide its origin. One glance shows that it's basically the Lankan version of an empanada, much like the Malaysian curry puff: flaky pastry encasing a dry, often spicy filling. In Sri Lanka this fish version is very popular, but meat and vegetable fillings are just as common. Any oily fish works well in this recipe, and if you don't have the time for cooking the fish yourself, a sustainable tinned version will work instead.

1 egg

20 ml (¾ fl oz) full-cream (whole) milk

vegetable oil, for deep-frying

salt flakes

**PASTRY**

400 g (14 oz) plain (all-purpose) flour

4 g (⅛ oz) baking powder

3 g (¹⁄₁₀ oz) cooking salt

80 g (2¾ oz) unsalted butter, chilled and diced

100 ml (3½ fl oz) coconut cream

2 egg yolks

For the pastry, you can either use a food processor or make it by hand; the method will be the same. Combine the flour, baking powder and salt in a bowl, then mix through the butter until it resembles fine breadcrumbs.

Lightly whisk together the coconut cream, egg yolks and 40 ml (1¼ fl oz) water, then slowly add to the dry ingredients and mix or pulse until just combined.

Turn out the dough onto a floured bench and gently knead until it just comes together in a ball. Flatten the dough into a disc (this will make it easier to roll later), then wrap in plastic wrap and rest in the fridge for at least a few hours, or preferably overnight. Pastry can also be frozen for storage.

When it comes to rolling out the dough a pasta machine is very useful, but of course you can do it by hand. This pastry has quite a lot of fat in it so it will be relatively easy to work with and should only need dusting with a little extra flour to prevent sticking.

Working in batches, roll out the dough to an even 3 mm (⅛ in) thickness, then cut it into discs using a 10 cm (4 in) round pastry cutter. Re-roll your scraps as you go to get the 20 rounds needed. Place your pastry rounds on a tray between layers of baking paper and keep them cool in the fridge. When you are ready to wrap your patties, take out small batches of pastry rounds as you go. You will probably have pastry left over; this can be rolled into a ball, stored in the fridge and re-used.

To make the filling, preheat the oven to 160°C (320°F) and line a baking tray with baking paper. Rub the bonito fillet with a little olive oil, season generously with salt and pepper and place on the prepared tray. Bake until the fish is cooked through – this will take 8–15 minutes, depending on the thickness of your fillet. To check, insert a metal skewer in the middle, hold it for a few seconds and then rest it against your lip; if it's warm, the fish is cooked through enough. Remove and cool on the tray, then break it into large flakes and set aside. Leave the oven on.

Place the potato in a medium saucepan and cover with lightly seasoned cold water. Bring to a simmer over a medium heat and cook for 14–18 minutes until the potato is cooked through. Drain, then spread out on a baking tray and place in the oven for 5 minutes to dry out. Remove from the oven and set aside.

Melt the ghee in a medium saucepan over a medium heat, add the fennel and cumin seeds and fry for a minute or so. Add the curry leaves and stir for moment, then add the onion, garlic, ginger

## FISH FILLING

125 g (4½ oz) bonito fillet, skinless and boneless, at room temperature

olive oil, to coat

salt flakes and freshly ground white pepper

200 g (7 oz) desiree potatoes, peeled and cut into 1 cm (½ in) dice

15 g (½ oz) ghee

3 g (1/10 oz) fennel seeds

1.5 g (1/20 oz) cumin seeds

4 g (1/8 oz) curry leaves

150 g (5½ oz) diced red onion

12 g (½ oz) finely chopped garlic

12 g (½ oz) finely chopped ginger

1–2 long green chilli, finely chopped

8 g (¼ oz) Brown curry powder (see page 42)

3 g (1/10 oz) ground Maldive fish flakes

1 g (1/64 oz) grated nutmeg

juice of up to 1 lime

and chilli. Season with a little salt and pepper and cook, stirring occasionally, for 6–8 minutes until the onion has softened.

Mix in the curry powder and Maldive fish flakes and cook, stirring, for 1 minute. Add the potato and fry for a minute or so, gently crushing the potato to make a slightly sticky amalgamated mixture. Remove the pan from the heat and carefully stir through the flaked bonito and nutmeg. Season to taste with salt, pepper and lime juice, then set aside to cool completely.

Once the mixture has cooled, take about 1 tablespoon (25 g/ ¾ oz) of the filling, form it into a log shape and set aside on a tray. Repeat until all the mix is divided and ready.

Whisk the egg and milk together to make an egg wash.

To make your patties, place a round of pastry on the bench in front of you, take one of the bits of filling and put it along the middle of the pastry. Lightly brush a little egg wash around the edge of half the pastry round.

Gently fold the pastry over the filling to form a semi-circle, and lightly press down to flatten a little. Seal the edges and crimp with a fork, then transfer to a clean tray and place in the fridge. Repeat with the remaining pastry and filling, adding each patty to the tray in the fridge as you go. You can stack them in two layers, but make sure you separate them with a piece of baking paper.

At this stage, the patties can be kept in the fridge for a few days or frozen to fry later.

Pour vegetable oil into a large heavy-based saucepan to a depth of 4–6 cm (1½–2½ in) (the oil should come no more than two-thirds of the way up the pan). Place over a high heat and heat to 170°C (340°F). If you don't have a thermometer you can check by dipping the edge of a patty into the oil; if it sizzles immediately, the oil is ready.

Working in small batches, fry the patties for 4 minutes or until they are a dark golden-brown colour, turning them halfway through and gently swishing them around so they cook evenly. Lift them out with a slotted spoon and drain on a wire rack. Season well with salt flakes. Give the oil a moment to heat up again before you fry the next batch.

The patties are now ready to serve, although they are just as good eaten a few hours later. Serve on their own or with a chilli or tomato sauce.

**NOTE** You can also use any other dry filling to make meat or vegetarian variations; perhaps start with either of the pan roll fillings (see page 76).

← **Pictured page 71**

# Pan rolls

MAKES 40

These rolls were a particular speciality of my nan's and are probably my favourite short eat of all. The beef version is almost exactly as she showed me, without the Deb mashed potato mix she liked to use. Preparing them can be a little fiddly, but this is exactly the kind of thing that's nice to make when you have plenty of time and a few hands to help. This recipe makes a lot, but they freeze very well or you can halve the recipe.

Overleaf there are instructions for two different fillings for you to choose from: beef and potato. The beef recipe can be adapted to use any other type of meat, or a combination, such as pork and beef. Both fillings can be made a day or two ahead and stored in the fridge. Each recipe makes enough to fill 40 pancakes.

Making the pancakes is the only part of the recipe that needs to be done just before you roll. You can cook all the pancakes at once, stack and wrap them in a tea towel (dish towel) to keep warm, then move on to the rolling. Or, if you have a helper in the kitchen, have one person making the pancakes and another wrapping and rolling. I suppose this is the trickiest element; the pancakes should actually be more like crepes, thin enough to be delicate and pliable enough to wrap, yet strong enough to hold the filling. For this reason the recipe makes a few more than you'll need, as you will probably tear a few along the way.

The beauty of pan rolls is in the layers of texture: the crunchy fried outer layer gives way to the soft pancake, which encloses the highly spiced filling. Serve them on their own or with a good chilli or tomato sauce.

## PANCAKES

600 g (1 lb 5 oz) plain (all-purpose) flour

12 g (½ oz) cooking salt

960 ml (32½ fl oz) full-cream (whole) milk

8 eggs

vegetable oil, for pan-frying (optional)

**Before making your pancakes, prepare your filling of choice (overleaf) →**

To make the pancakes, sift the flour into a mixing bowl and add the salt. Whisk together the milk, eggs and 100 ml (3½ fl oz) water in a jug. Gradually whisk the milk mixture into the flour, taking care to avoid any lumps forming. Once you have a nice smooth batter, vigorously whisk for another minute or so, then let it rest at room temperature for half an hour. (Alternatively, place all the ingredients in a blender and blitz until smooth.)

Now it's time to test your pancake-making skills. If you are using a non-stick pan you will not need any oil; if not, use a bit of paper towel dipped in oil to season your pan between pancakes.

Heat a 20 cm (8 in) non-stick frying pan or crepe pan over a medium heat, pour in approximately 45 ml (1½ fl oz) of batter and swirl it around to evenly cover the base, forming a nice, thin pancake. Cook for 1–2 minutes until just about cooked through – the top should not be sticky to touch but you also don't want the pancake to have any colour. Slide the pancake out of the pan and onto a tray with the more cooked side on the bottom. As you cook the pancakes, make sure to stack them up the same way. This stage is the trickiest to monitor. If you cook the pancakes too much they

## FOR CRUMBING & FRYING

100 g (3½ oz) plain (all-purpose) flour

5 eggs

100 ml (3½ fl oz) full-cream (whole) milk

450 g (1 lb) coarse breadcrumbs (I like panko crumbs)

vegetable oil, for deep-frying

salt flakes

will crack and not hold together when rolled; if you don't cook them enough they will stick together in the stack and be hard to separate. This will become fairly easy to get the hang of once you are actually doing it and the recipe does allow for some mistakes.

Once all your pancakes are cooked you can start the filling and rolling (see pages 78–9 for step-by-step images).

Place one pancake flat in front of you, again with the more cooked side down. Use a spoon to shape about 50 g (1¾ oz) of the filling into a log shape and place it in the middle of the bottom third of the pancake. The beef filling is easiest to manage when the mix is slightly chilled, the potato filling when the mix is at room temperature. Fold up the bottom so it covers the filling, fold in the two sides, then snugly but not super tightly roll it up to form a log (like a large spring roll). The pancake should be soft and sticky enough to hold itself together once rolled.

Set aside, seam side down, and repeat with the remaining pancakes and filling to make 40 rolls.

Wipe down the bench and set up a crumbing station.

Tip the flour in a bowl; whisk together the eggs and milk in a second bowl; and place the breadcrumbs in a third bowl. Have a clean tray or platter handy to put the crumbed rolls on.

Gently dust each roll in flour, shaking off the excess, then coat in the egg mixture, allowing the excess to drip off. Finally, coat the rolls in the breadcrumbs. Place on the clean tray or platter. At this stage, the rolls can be kept in the fridge for a few days or frozen to fry later.

Have a little clean, then get ready for frying.

Pour vegetable oil into a large heavy-based saucepan to a depth of 4–6 cm (1½–2½ in) (the oil should come no more than two-thirds of the way up the pan). Place over a high heat and heat to 170°C (340°F). If you don't have a thermometer you can check by dropping a few breadcrumbs into the oil; if they sizzle immediately, the oil is ready.

Working in small batches, fry the rolls for 5–6 minutes until they are a dark golden-brown colour, gently swishing them around so they cook evenly. Lift them out with a slotted spoon and drain on a wire rack. Season well with salt flakes. Give the oil a moment to heat up again before you fry the next batch.

Pan rolls are ready to be eaten when hot and go nicely with some chilli or tomato sauce. They can also be left for a few hours and served at room temperature. Alternatively they can be re-heated in an oven for serving later.

NOTES If you are having trouble with your pancake batter you may need to make it slightly thicker or thinner. If you do add more flour or water, let the batter rest again before cooking with it.

If you find you are getting too many tears in your pancakes, cut some of the less perfect ones into quarters and place a piece in the middle of each whole pancake to reinforce it before rolling.

STREET FOOD, SHORT EATS & DEVILLED THINGS

# Potato filling

2 kg (4 lb 6 oz) desiree potatoes, peeled and cut into 1 cm (½ in) dice

200 g (7 oz) ghee

40 g (1½ oz) moru (white) chillies, roughly crushed or chopped

30 g (1 oz) brown mustard seeds

20 g (¾ oz) fennel seeds

10 g (⅓ oz) curry leaves

20 g (¾ oz) turmeric powder

8 g (¼ oz) cinnamon powder

salt flakes and freshly ground white pepper

For the potato filling, place the potato in a medium saucepan and cover with lightly seasoned cold water. Bring to a simmer over a medium heat and cook for 12–14 minutes until the potato is tender but not overcooked. The potato needs to hold its shape, otherwise the filling will be more like mashed potato. Drain well.

Melt the ghee in a wide-based saucepan over a medium heat, add the moru chilli, mustard and fennel seeds and cook, stirring, for 4–5 minutes until the mustard seeds begin to pop and the fennel seeds start to darken. Add the curry leaves and fry for a moment, then add the potato and stir to combine. Stir in the remaining spices and season well with salt and pepper. Cook for another 5 minutes, stirring to break up the potato a little (not too much) and make sure the mix doesn't catch on the bottom of the pan. Remove from the heat.

Your potato should be a little mushed up but still with at least half the dice holding its shape. The mixture should be dry and bright yellow with a pleasant mustard kick and hit of chilli heat. Set aside to cool to room temperature.

# Beef filling

70 g (2½ oz) coconut oil

1.7 kg (3 lb 12 oz) coarsely minced (ground) beef

340 g (12 oz) brown onion, finely diced

35 g (1¼ oz) finely chopped garlic

35 g (1¼ oz) finely chopped ginger

35 g (1¼ oz) chilli powder

30 g (1 oz) Brown curry powder (see page 42)

75 g (2¾ oz) tomato paste (concentrated puree)

salt flakes and freshly ground black pepper

12 green bird's eye chillies, finely chopped

340 g (12 oz) celery, finely diced

To make the beef filling, begin by browning off the meat. Heat half the coconut oil in a frying pan over a high heat and add the beef in batches, cooking and stirring until well browned and breaking up any large clumps. Cook each batch for about 15 minutes to ensure the mix is dry and liquid free. Transfer each batch to a colander over a bowl to drain while you fry off the rest. (Any oily liquid that pools in the bowl can be kept for other cooking.)

Melt the remaining coconut oil in a wide-based saucepan over a medium heat, add the onion, garlic and ginger and cook, stirring occasionally, for 4–5 minutes until the onion has softened. Add the chilli and curry powders and the tomato paste and cook, stirring, for another minute or so until the curry powder starts to catch on the bottom of the pan. Add the beef and season well with salt and pepper, then stir thoroughly to combine.

Add the chilli and cook for another 2 minutes, then stir in the celery. Remove from the heat and have a taste – there should be a substantial hit of chilli heat, with the gentler spices from the curry powder and a little crunch of celery. The mixture should be dry and almost a bit sticky. Set aside to cool to room temperature, then place into the fridge to chill a little.

↑ Pan rolls

# Devilled school prawns

SERVES 2

30 g (1 oz) ghee

1 g (1/32 oz) curry leaves

100 g (3½ oz) eschalot, finely sliced

4 g (1/8 oz) chopped garlic

1 long red chilli, finely chopped

6 g (1/5 oz) Red curry powder
(see page 43)

2 g (1/16 oz) chilli powder

salt flakes and freshly ground
black pepper

lime wedges, to serve

### FRIED PRAWNS

200 g (7 oz) chickpea (besan)
flour, sifted

6 g (1/5 oz) freshly ground
black pepper

4 g (1/8 oz) cooking salt

300 g (10½ oz) fresh school
prawns (shrimp)

vegetable oil, for deep-frying

4 g (1/8 oz) curry leaves

**I have taken the idea of a dry, hot 'devilled' dish and applied it to the excellent school prawns we have available in Australia, which you can eat shell, head, tail and all. The prawns are deep-fried until crisp, then tossed through a garlicky escalot mixture with a powerful chilli kick. This dish is perfect for a snack or starter, or scale it up and serve as part of a main meal.**

For the fried prawns, combine the chickpea flour, pepper and salt in a mixing bowl. Add the prawns and toss to lightly coat in the seasoned flour; if it's not sticking at all, add a small splash of water.

Pour vegetable oil into a large heavy-based saucepan to a depth of 4–6 cm (1½–2½ in) (the oil should come no more than two-thirds of the way up the pan). Place over a high heat and heat to 180°C (350°F). If you don't have a thermometer you can check by dropping a prawn into the oil; if it bounces straight up to the top, the oil is ready.

Working in small batches, gently lower the prawns into the oil. Use a slotted spoon to jiggle them around and try to keep them separate. Cook for 3–4 minutes until they start to turn golden brown, adding the curry leaves for the final 1–2 minutes of cooking. Lift them out and drain on a wire rack. Give the oil a moment to heat up again before you fry the next batch.

Melt the ghee in a wok or large frying pan over a high heat, add the curry leaves and cook, stirring, for a minute or so until the leaves are fried. Add the eschalot and cook, stirring rapidly, for 4–5 minutes. Stir in the garlic and red chilli and cook for a moment, then add the cooked prawns and toss to coat. Sprinkle in the curry and chilli powder. Toss again for about a minute, then season to taste with salt and pepper.

Serve immediately with lime wedges to squeeze over as you go.

NOTE If you want to try this recipe with larger prawns, I suggest using peeled and deveined prawns with the tail still on.

# Devilled chicken livers

SERVES 4–6

Liver dishes are fairly common in Sri Lanka, either devilled or cooked in curries. While I classify this as a devilled dish, it is decidedly non-traditional in terms of technique, although the ingredients are mostly true to Lankan cuisine. The flavour is fragrant, hot and highly spiced, with the herbs offering a fresh respite. The liver will have a nice crust with a soft and creamy inside. This recipe appeared as a special on the Lankan Filling Station menu early on and we love it so much we keep bringing it back.

200 g (7 oz) whole chicken livers (see note)

50 g (1¾ oz) Fragrant spice mix (see page 46)

20 g (¾ oz) picked coriander (cilantro) leaves

10 g (⅓ oz) picked flat-leaf parsley leaves

10 g (⅓ oz) picked mint leaves

40 g (1½ oz) ghee

4 g (⅛ oz) curry leaves

½ medium red onion, quartered and sliced across the grain into 2 mm (1/12 in) slices

1 long green chilli, cut into thin rounds

salt flakes and freshly ground black pepper

lime wedges, to serve

Separate the two lobes of each chicken liver, then use a sharp knife to remove any sinew and blood clots. Cut the smaller lobe into its two natural pieces, and cut the larger lobe into three to five pieces – you just want them all to be a similar size. Place the liver in a bowl with the spice mix and give it a good mix to coat. Set aside.

Roughly chop all the herbs together so they remain slightly coarse. Set aside.

Melt the ghee in a wok or wide-based frying pan over a high heat, then quickly and carefully lift the liver pieces out of the spice mix, leaving the excess spice in the bowl, and drop them into the ghee. Fry each side for 1–2 minutes, just long enough to form a crust, taking care as they may spit. Return the liver to the bowl of spices and reduce the heat a little.

Add the curry leaves, onion and chilli to the wok, season with a little salt and pepper and stir-fry for 1–2 minutes until the onion starts to caramelise. Turn the heat back up to high, tip the livers and all the spice mix into the wok and cook, stirring and tossing, for another minute or so. Remove from the heat and taste for seasoning, then mix through the chopped herbs. Serve immediately with lime wedges to squeeze over as you eat.

NOTE If possible, source good hand-picked or whole livers for this dish as you want to be able to clean and cut them into distinct pieces without dealing with mushy squished bits.

**Pictured overleaf →**

**Devilled chicken livers →**

# Hot butter cuttlefish

**SERVES 4**

This dish is a modern Sri Lankan classic that I suspect has origins in Chinese cooking. Some say it first appeared on the menu at the Colombo Swimming Club, and I can attest that their version is particularly fine; however, you can now find variations all over the island. The cuttlefish is either dipped in flour or batter before frying to protect the flesh and keep it lovely and soft. The batter in this recipe is not traditional, but when cooked it maintains a wonderful crispness. If preferred, you could substitute a simple tempura batter or even just dust the cuttlefish in cornflour before frying.

vegetable oil, for deep-frying

160 g (5½ oz) cleaned cuttlefish, cut into triangular pieces about 6 cm (2½ in) at their longest edge

fine rice flour, for dusting

**BATTER**

45 g (1½ oz) fine rice flour (preferably Thai brand)

45 g (1½ oz) tapioca flour

8 g (¼ oz) xantham gum

10 g (⅓ oz) turmeric powder

**HOT BUTTER & BITS**

splash of vegetable oil

1 long red chilli, finely chopped

4 g (⅛ oz) chilli flakes

7 g (¼ oz) caster (superfine) sugar

40 g (1½ oz) butter

10 g (⅓ oz) finely chopped garlic

½ medium red onion, cut into 3 wedges

3 spring onions (scallions), cut into 6 cm (2½ in) lengths, including most of the green part

1 small banana chilli, cut diagonally into 3 cm (1¼ in) rounds, seeds removed

5 small dried chillies

freshly ground black pepper

To make the batter, place the flours, xantham gum and turmeric in a blender. With the motor on high, slowly pour in 410 ml (14 fl oz) water and mix to form a light, fluffy batter. You can use it immediately or keep it in the fridge for a day or so. If you're using it straight away, transfer about half the batter to a small mixing bowl. (Store the other half in the fridge and use it within a week.)

Pour vegetable oil into a large heavy-based saucepan to a depth of 4–6 cm (1½–2½ in) (the oil should come no more than two-thirds of the way up the pan). Place over a high heat and heat to 180°C (350°F). If you don't have a thermometer you can check by dropping a little batter into the oil; if it sits on the top and immediately starts to sizzle, the oil is ready.

Very lightly dust the cuttlefish pieces in rice flour, then use a spoon to dip them into the batter. It's quite thick so take your time and make sure every piece is coated in a nice layer of batter.

Working in batches so you don't overcrowd the pan, use the spoon to carefully drop the battered cuttlefish into the hot oil. Use a slotted spoon to gently jiggle them around so they don't stick to the bottom of the pan or each other. Cook for 2–3 minutes until the batter is super crispy. Lift them out and drain on a wire rack. Give the oil a moment to heat up again before you fry the next batch.

For the sauce, heat the vegetable oil in a wok or large frying pan over a low heat, add the red chilli and chilli flakes and cook gently for 1–2 minutes until the fresh chilli starts to soften. Add the sugar and give it a moment to caramelise, then get ready to start cooking swiftly.

Add the butter and garlic, increase the heat to high and cook, stirring, for a minute or so until the garlic starts to fry. Add the onion, spring onion and banana chilli and cook, stirring and tossing, for another minute, then add the dried chillies and a good grinding of black pepper. Cook for another minute, then add the fried cuttlefish and toss for a minute or so to coat and combine.

Serve immediately. The dish should be hot, rich and buttery with a faint hint of sweetness and a substantial kick of chilli.

පාන්, රොටි සහ ආප්ප

# Breads,
# Roti
# &
# Hoppers

பாண், ரொட்டி மற்றும் அப்ப வகை

T raditional cooking in Sri Lanka didn't involve the use of ovens, and it wasn't until the Portuguese arrived with their pao (bread)-eating ways that paan (bread) became a thing – although there is some suggestion that the use of refined flour and bakeries may have come from the Middle East and Muslim communities. Regardless, baking was adopted into Lankan culture and people started consuming an everyday bread called kade paan, (literally meaning shop bread). Found in most village shops, this high loaf is soft, white and fluffy with a hint of sweetness to it.

These days bakeries serve all manner of baked goods, including buns with a similar dough to the kade paan encasing spicy fillings, such as malu (fish) or mas (meat) paan, both of which have endless variations (my favourite is a seeni sambol one). There are also sweet offerings, many of which have a Dutch influence. While all of this is delicious, the introduction of refined white flours significantly reduced the use of traditional grains, leading to health problems and the slow creep of homogenisation in food.

The other recipes in this chapter are roti and hoppers, which are either completely unleavened or use the process of fermentation, both for rising and flavour. These have a longer, and healthier, history in Sri Lanka with clear origins in southern India. Some of the dishes are found mainly in Tamil communities, while others have spread and become part of the whole country's tradition.

There are two main types of roti. Godhamba roti (meaning flour roti; see page 99) is a slightly soft, sometimes flaky flatbread made in a similar way to an Indian chapati or paratha. The main difference is that once the dough is made and rolled into balls, it has a long rest in a pool of vegetable or coconut oil, in much the same way the Malaysians do for their flakier roti canai or parata. This suggests that roti could well be a confluence of influences, from both India and Muslim/Malay communities. Godhamba roti are used either with a spicy filling, forming a wrapped snack served during the day, or they are grilled flat to accompany a curry meal.

Roti are also excellently employed in a more modern dish called kottu (meaning chopped in Tamil) or kothu roti (see page 100). Originally intended as a cheap and filling dinner dish using leftovers, it has since become wildly popular with an almost cult-like status. Godhamba roti are cut into strips and cooked on a flat plate with vegetables, curry or curry sauce, often egg, maybe some

BREADS, ROTI & HOPPERS

cheese. In some versions, string hoppers are used instead of the roti. Part of the allure of this dish is the way it's cooked by the street vendors: the maker stands over the flat plate, with a metal pastry scraper in each hand. As the ingredients cook, the scrapers cut, mash and toss everything together, making a distinct and noisy taka-taka sound, a siren call to hungry humans, particularly late at night post revelry. It can also be cooked in a wok, highlighting the blatant similarities to Chinese fried rice – both are a mishmash of ingredients fried together to create a dish greater than the sum of its parts.

The other roti are the pol roti (see page 96), made with a mix of grated coconut, water and flour, traditionally kurukkan (finger millet) flour but now usually wheat flour. Extra ingredients can be added, such as onion, chilli and curry leaves. These slightly charred flatbreads are usually eaten for breakfast or dinner with curries and sambols. They are uniquely Sri Lankan and I love them.

There is also a Tamil dish in this section called thosai (see page 95), confusingly similar in name, method and ingredients to dosai, both of which are south Indian fermented pancakes. Thosai are a smaller, softer version.

Although there is no recipe for them here, pappadums also deserve a special mention. They originated in northern India but thankfully managed to find their way to the island. Pappadums are delicious in any form, but the Sri Lankan version (which I have never found in Australia) is a little denser and often served in shards rather than the usual round shape.

And then there are the hoppers.

There are two types: appa/appam (hoppers; see page 108) and idiyappa/idiyappam (string hoppers; see page 106), both originally from south India, but they are now so entrenched they have become emblematic of Sri Lankan cuisine. Made with rice flour, usually white but often red, both are generally eaten for breakfast or dinner rather than lunch.

For years I thought of idiyappam as the *other* hopper, as they didn't inspire the utter devotion I have for appa, but over the years my appreciation has grown. A stiff dough made with fine rice flour and hot water is pushed through a hand-held extruder with very fine holes onto a string hopper frame. Traditionally made from cane, the frame is a small circular mat that is slightly convex, with a flat edge running around the base. The thin vermicelli-like noodles form a delicate, almost flat nest, each on its own tray. The trays are stacked up in batches and steamed; the string hoppers are piled on a large plate and usually served with a kiri hodi (see page 147). As you will have gathered, they are extremely time-consuming to make. We serve them at the restaurant, but we buy them in from someone who has a fancy mechanical hopper maker.

Appa (hoppers) are also made with a base of rice flour but the dough is slightly fermented. The traditional recipe called for rice grains flattened with a grinding stone, water and coconut milk, a little salt, some sugar and toddy as a leavening agent. The rice is used to make a dough, usually a day ahead to give it time to ferment, and then the dough is turned into a batter. The ingredients are simple yet there are countless variations, but the magic is in the fermentation. You can use rice soaked and blended to make a batter or you can use rice flour, usually a combination of grades for texture and structure. Instead of toddy, most recipes today use yeast, although a slice of bread or even some crumbs can be substituted, or you can even use some of yesterday's batter to make tomorrow's dough. There are also recipes that use more coconut milk to make a milk hopper, which is usually served as a sweet option. Some recipes can be made in a few hours; at Lankan Filling Station ours take more than two days.

Despite the few ingredients, hoppers are fiddly to make and are hard to perfect. Once you have managed to wrangle your batter, the next step is perfecting the cooking technique. First you need a thachchi, a lidded hopper pan, traditionally made out of aluminium but now available in non-stick varieties. They come in all shapes and sizes, but the 'standard' is about the size of half a rockmelon. The actual cooking can be a bit tricky too, but once mastered your reward is a delicate bowl-shaped pancake with crisp latticed edges and a spongy soft centre. A thing of beauty.

When you eat them, it's mostly about the hopper, without too many accompaniments, and you can usually choose between a plain version and an egg version (see note on page 109). You might start with an egg hopper and a sambol; you tear the edges, scooping and dipping it into the sambol and the runny yolk. Then move on to the plain hoppers, perhaps with a curry or two or just more sambol.

Some people prefer the crispy edges, some the doughy middle; others remain firmly in the string hopper camp, and some people go the roti. Regardless of your preference, this chapter will have you covered.

# Malu paan

**MAKES 25 BUNS**

1 quantity fish patty filling
(see page 72)

1 egg

10 ml (¼ fl oz) full-cream
(whole) milk

80 g (2¾ oz) butter, melted

### DOUGH

40 ml (1½ fl oz) slightly warm
water (no more than 27°C/80°F)

6 g (⅕ oz) dried yeast

185 ml (6 fl oz) full-cream
(whole) milk

145 ml (5 fl oz) pouring
(single/light) cream

470 g (1 lb 1 oz) plain (all-purpose)
flour

40 g (1½ oz) caster (superfine) sugar

7 g (¼ oz) cooking salt

**NOTES** Fish buns are delicious
eaten warm – soft, light and fluffy
with a spicy fish surprise in the
middle. They can be stored in the
fridge for 4–5 days, though I would
suggest gently heating them before
serving. They can also be frozen for
a few months.

There are endless options for
what you can stuff the bread with;
just make sure it's a dry mixture –
anything too wet won't work.
As a starting point, try either of
the pan roll fillings (see page 76)
or seeni sambol (see page 228).
Another good one is the goat curry
on page 177; all you need to do is
shred the meat a little.

The dough for these buns is fairly easy to make and handle, but
even at its simplest, bread making is filled with mystery and takes
practice. This recipe makes bite-sized buns but you can easily
make them a little bigger if you like; you will just need to adjust
the cooking time. The shape of these buns can be triangular,
round or torpedo shaped and usually depends on the type of
filling that goes inside, but I say go with whatever shape you like.
The filling can also be adapted to suit your taste.

To make the dough, pour the water into a small bowl, mix in the yeast
and leave for a few minutes until bubbles appear and it starts to froth.

Warm the milk and cream together in a small saucepan to 27°C
(80°F); if you don't have a thermometer, it should be just warm
enough that you can comfortably place your little finger in the liquid
and leave it there for a moment.

Place the flour, sugar and salt in the bowl of a stand mixer fitted
with a dough hook. On a slow speed, slowly pour in all the wet
ingredients. Once fully combined, turn the mixer to medium and
mix for 3–4 minutes until the dough is smooth and comes away from
the side of the bowl. You can also do this step by hand, though it
may take a little longer. Place the dough in a greased mixing bowl,
cover and leave in a slightly warm spot for 45 minutes or until it has
doubled in size.

Knock back the dough by giving it a few folds, then turn it out
onto a clean bench. Use a pastry cutter or knife to cut the dough
into 35 g (1¼ oz) portions and roll each into a ball. (I would suggest
having a little internet moment to see the best way to do this.) Place
the balls on a greased baking tray, then cover with a clean tea towel
(dish towel) and allow to prove for about 15 minutes until they
bounce back when you gently poke them with your finger. By this
stage they will be looking nice and fluffy.

Line a few baking trays with baking paper. Use a tablespoon to
measure the filling into 20 g (¾ oz) balls and set aside.

To fill, place a dough ball on the bench and flatten it into a round
about 5 mm thick. Place a ball of filling in the centre and use your
fingers to pick up and pinch the dough over the filling, with the
top meeting the bottom, then squeeze together the edges to form
a small torpedo shape. Don't be scared to stretch the dough a little,
it is very forgiving. Make sure the dough seam is nicely sealed.
Place the bun, seam side down, on one of the prepared trays. Repeat
with the remaining dough and filling, making sure you leave room
for spreading between the buns as they rise.

By the time you have made all of your buns they should have
proved enough to be ready for baking. To check, lightly press on
the dough – if it springs back, they're ready; if not give them
another 10 minutes or so.

Meanwhile, preheat the oven to 180°C (350°F).

Whisk together the egg and milk and gently brush over the tops
of the buns. Bake for 15 minutes, turning the trays halfway through,
then remove from the oven. Immediately brush the tops with melted
butter, then brush twice more as the buns cool down.

# Thosai

**MAKES 14**

Thosai are soft, slightly fermented and super-savoury pancakes that are eaten simply with a sambar (a south Indian saucy lentil dish) and or sambol for breakfast or dinner. There are various ways to make them; the more traditional methods involve soaking urad dhal (black gram) and rice grains in water for hours, before grinding to make a paste, combining to make a batter and then fermenting. This can be a little fraught, not to mention time-consuming, so here I offer an easier version based on a recipe from Chandra Dissanayake's book *Ceylon Cookery*. Thosai are traditionally made on a flat pan called a tava pan, but a large non-stick frying pan works just as well.

9 g (⅓ oz) dried yeast

5 g (⅕ oz) caster (superfine) sugar

175 ml (6 fl oz) coconut water, at room temperature

110 g (4 oz) undu flour (see note)

110 g (4 oz) plain (all-purpose) flour

50 ml (1¾ fl oz) coconut cream

ghee, for pan-frying (optional)

**TEMPER**

30 g (1 oz) ghee

5 g (⅕ oz) curry leaves

180 g (6½ oz) diced brown onion

3 small dried chillies, sliced into thin rounds

4 g (⅛ oz) salt flakes

3 g (1/10 oz) mustard seeds

3 g (1/10 oz) cumin seeds

2 g (1/16 oz) fenugreek seeds

½ g (1/64 oz) turmeric powder

Mix together the yeast, sugar and coconut water in a bowl and leave for 5 minutes so it starts to bubble and froth up.

Combine the flours in a mixing bowl and slowly stir in the coconut water mix until it all comes together. Cover with a tea towel (dish towel) and leave for about an hour, after which time it will become a little puffy.

Mix together the coconut cream and 300 ml (10 fl oz) water, then slowly whisk into dough until you have a thickish pancake batter. It will probably be a little lumpy, but there's no need to worry about that as we will fix it later. Rest at room temperature for 30 minutes.

Meanwhile, prepare the temper. Melt the ghee in a small frying pan over a medium heat, add the curry leaves and cook, stirring, for a minute until the leaves are fried. Add the onion and cook, stirring, for 2 minutes. Stir in the dried chilli, salt and all the seeds and cook for 4–5 minutes, stirring occasionally until the onion has softened. Add the turmeric and cook for another minute.

Allow this mix to cool, then add it to the batter and whisk together – this should fix any remaining lumps. The batter can be used immediately, but I prefer to let it sit out for a few hours to get a more fermented flavour. You can even rest it overnight in the fridge to use the next day, you will just need to add a little extra water and give it a moment to come up to temperature.

Place a tava pan over a medium heat and rub with a small amount of ghee (if you are using a non-stick frying pan you won't need the ghee). Ladle about 80 ml (2½ fl oz) of batter into the middle of the pan, then use the bottom of the ladle to spread it out evenly in a circular motion to a thickish pancake. Cook for 1 minute until small bubbles appear, then flip and cook the other aside for 1–2 minutes. Remove and serve hot from the pan, then repeat with the remaining batter.

**NOTES** Undu flour is urud dhal (skinned black gram) flour, and you will need to buy this from a Sri Lankan grocer. If you can't find it, you could probably use another type of lentil flour, though I have not tried this myself.

If it's not feasible to serve individual thosai straight from the pan, you can keep them warm in a low oven, then serve them all at once.

# Pol roti

MAKES 10

These roti are more like a flatbread, although they do puff up a little when freshly made and have a nice fluffy lightness to them. They are really simple to make, with hints of coconut and a pleasant savouriness from the onion and curry leaves. These can be enjoyed in many different ways: as a side to a curry meal, for breakfast with a runny dhal, boiled eggs and pol sambol, or treated like toast and spread with butter and Vegemite or even jam for an intriguing blend of sweet and savoury.

200 g (7 oz) grated coconut

325 g (11½ oz) self-raising flour

8 g (¼ oz) baking powder

65 g (2¼ oz) eschalot, finely sliced

4 g (⅛ oz) curry leaves, finely sliced

15 g (½ oz) melted ghee

good pinch of salt flakes

Place all the ingredients in a bowl and mix well. I find using your hand in an almost kneading action is best. Slowly add approximately 50 ml (1¾ fl oz) water and continue mixing with your hand until the mixture just comes together to form a slightly sticky dough. You may not need all the water so keep an eye on the texture as you mix; alternatively, you may need a little more water to achieve the right consistency.

Cover the bowl with a tea towel (dish towel) and leave to rest at room temperature for 30 minutes.

On a lightly floured bench, roll the dough into 10 balls (about 65 g/2¼ oz each), then flatten each ball into a round about 5 mm (¼ in) thick. You can use a rolling pin if you like, although flattening the dough with your hands is also very effective. If you happen to have a tortilla press, this is the most effective tool.

You can cook the roti straight on a barbecue flat plate or use a frying pan. Whatever you choose, the roti will take 4–5 minutes to cook in total – you want to start it hot to get a little char, at which stage it will puff up a little, before cooking the other side over a slightly lower heat.

Serve immediately or cook them all together and rest on a wire rack before serving.

NOTE The uncooked roti freeze well, though the texture will be a little less fluffy. Roll them out between sheets of baking paper and make a stack, then store in an airtight container in the freezer for a few months. You can cook them straight from frozen.

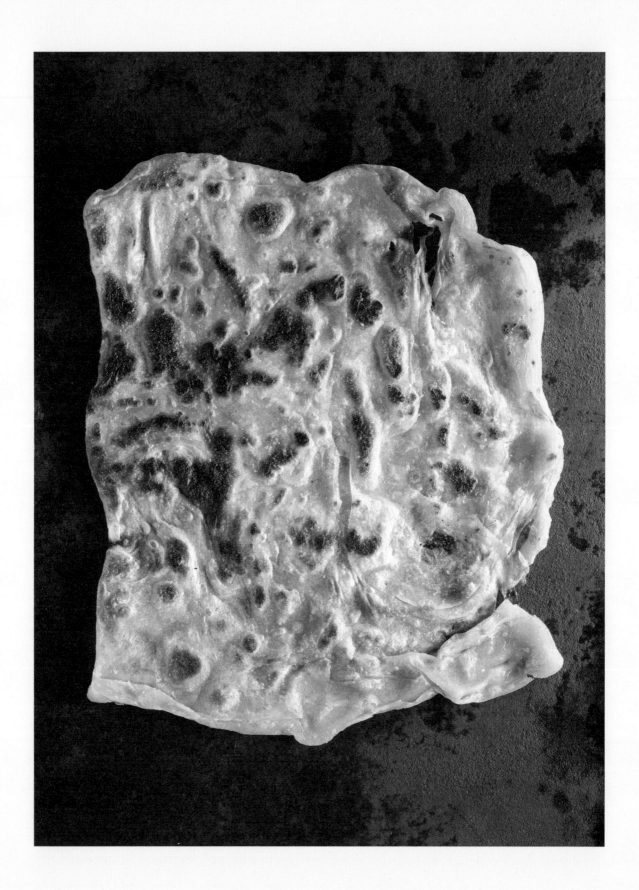

# Godhamba roti

MAKES 8

300 g (10½ oz) plain (all-purpose) flour

8 g (¼ oz) cooking salt

approximately 140 ml (4½ fl oz) coconut oil, melted and cooled

**NOTES** The cooked roti will keep in the fridge for a good few days, and also freeze very well. Make sure you freeze them flat for best results.

If you are cooking the roti ahead of time, gently rewarm them in a low oven before serving. You could also brush them with some ghee and cook on both sides in a pan for a slightly crisper finish.

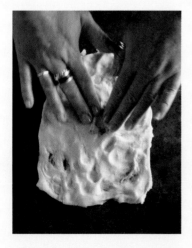

**The dough for this type of roti is simple; the challenge lies in the technique of rolling and shaping the breads. You can make them flatter or more layered, depending how many times you pull and fold the dough – this is entirely a matter of preference (and perhaps dexterity). Because you only cook them briefly, the roti will be soft and a little flaky. Serve as a side to curry or use to make a pretty special toasted sandwich or wrap.**

**A lot of fat is used to coat the roti, and this will become the dominant flavour. I use coconut oil but be careful here as it must be a good-quality one. You can use other fats, such as vegetable oil and ghee, or a combination for a more subtle approach.**

Combine the flour and salt in a mixing bowl, then slowly mix in 100–140 ml (3½–4½ fl oz) water, kneading, until it just comes together to form a dough; the exact quantity of water will depend on your flour so add it gradually and keep an eye on the consistency. Turn it out onto a bench and knead for 2–3 minutes until you have a smooth, non-sticky dough.

Divide the dough into eight even pieces and roll each one into a ball. Pour the coconut oil into a container that will fit the balls snugly, then add the dough balls. You want them to be almost completely submerged in the fat. Roll the balls around so they are well coated in oil, then cover with a tea towel (dish towel) or lid and leave at room temperature for at least half an hour. You can, however, happily leave the balls sitting in oil at room temperature overnight, to roll and cook the next day.

When you are ready to cook, start by making sure you have a clean bench. Remove one ball of dough from the oil, place it on the bench in front of you and use your fingertips to flatten it into a rectangle. With your fingers, gradually push out the dough evenly on all sides, maintaining a rectangular shape. At this stage it becomes a matter of gentle teasing, pushing and pulling the dough until it becomes a large paper-thin piece that you can see through (like strudel dough). Don't worry if you tear some small holes.

Fold the top edge into the middle, and repeat with the bottom edge, then fold in the two sides to form a neat rectangle (approximately 20 cm x 15 cm/8 in x 6 in). Transfer to a baking tray and repeat with the remaining dough balls. Add layers of baking paper if you need to stack them.

By the time you have finished shaping all the dough, the roti will have had time to rest and shrink a little. You can just flatten them out again, or repeat the pushing out and folding technique once more to give a flakier texture.

Heat a barbecue flat plate or a large frying pan over a medium heat (no need for extra oil). Cook the roti for 1 minute or until patches of colour start to appear, then flip and repeat on the other side. Don't cook them for too long as they should be soft rather than crisp.

Eat hot or warm.

# Kottu roti

SERVES 2

Aside from being completely delicious, kottu roti is a great way to use up leftover roti and curry or even just leftover gravy from a curry. The technique for cooking this is similar to making that other catch-all dish, fried rice. The recipe below is a simple vegetarian version with the addition of grated cheese. It's hot, eggy and a little smoky with a faint whiff of char. Excellent food for hungover people.

| |
|---|
| 125 ml (4 fl oz) vegetable oil |
| 4 eggs |
| 2 g (1/16 oz) chilli powder |
| 2 g (1/16 oz) curry leaves |
| 120 g (4½ oz) finely sliced red onion |
| 14 g (½ oz) finely chopped garlic |
| 10 g (⅓ oz) finely chopped ginger |
| 3 green bird's eye chillies, finely sliced into rounds |
| 140 g (5 oz) cabbage, shredded into a medium shred |
| salt flakes and freshly ground black pepper |
| 4 Godhamba roti (see page 99), cut into 3 cm x 2 cm (1¼ in x ¾ in) strips (approximately) |
| 2 large spring onions (scallions), white and green part julienned |
| 50 g (1¾ oz) grated cheddar |
| 250 ml (8½ fl oz) Kiri hodi (see page 142), gently heated |

Heat the vegetable oil in a wok over a high heat.

Meanwhile, whisk together the eggs and chilli powder. When the oil is hot to the point of just smoking, pour the egg into the wok and let it sit for 30 seconds until it fluffs up a little, then use a wok spoon to stir it around for a few moments until it is just set. Carefully tip the egg and most of the oil into a bowl and set aside.

Put the wok back on the heat, immediately add the curry leaves and stir-fry for 1 minute until the leaves are fried. Add the red onion, garlic, ginger and chilli and cook, tossing, for 1–2 minutes until the onion has softened. Add the cabbage and cook for 1–2 minutes until just tender with a little char. Season with a little salt and pepper.

Add the roti and toss to combine, then let it sit for a moment before returning the egg to the wok (leaving most of the oil behind).

Now it's a matter of cooking, tossing and using your wok spoon to break up the roti, almost mashing it, for about 2 minutes until all the ingredients are thoroughly combined. Add the spring onion, cheese and one-third of the kiri hodi and toss for another 2 minutes.

Remove from the heat, taste and adjust the seasoning if necessary. Serve immediately with the remaining kiri hodi to pour over at your whim.

NOTES This version is made in a wok, but you could also use a barbecue flat plate if you prefer. Search for videos on the internet to see the technique.

Like fried rice, this dish has endless flavour variations; if you can accept cheese then anything is possible.

# Hoppers &
# plaster of Paris

My love of hoppers is a well-established fact. Long before I opened the restaurant, every trip to Sri Lanka inevitably turned into a mini hopper pilgrimage. I watched them being made, I questioned their makers and occasionally someone would let me onto their pans to attempt a hopper swirl. They were the food I would seek out first and my only request any time anyone asked me what I wanted to eat.

Despite this borderline obsession, I had only really tried to make them from scratch once, with my nan in Perth. We used a coarse rice flour from the supermarket and they were so dense and soggy I didn't even record the recipe. I let it go until Lankan Filling Station (or The Hopper Shop, as it was known then) was about to become a reality. On reflection, it might have been a good idea to nail a good recipe before committing to the restaurant …

The first test in the path to creating the LFS hopper was with an instant hopper mix; they actually weren't too bad, which was encouraging. I then tested version after version, trying to find the perfect mix and types of rice flour and the perfect ratio of sweet to fermented flavour. The recipe I finally settled on is the one we still use today: three grades of rice flour mixed with a little sugar, salt, yeast and water into a dough, which is left in the fridge for about twelve hours. Coconut cream and water are added to make a batter, which then goes back in the fridge for another twelve hours or so until it is fluffy and fermented enough to use. Fermenting slowly in the fridge gives us more consistency, although at least once a week the batter still has a tendency to overflow and explode a bit.

Once I had conquered the recipe, we (which at that stage included my mate Nick and my cousin Odette, who both helped me set up the business, and Muu, who was always on hand) set up a market stall, our first foray into actually cooking and selling hoppers to real people. It was a nice easy entry; the hoppers came out well and we probably only made about 50 over a few hours.

However, this was closely followed by one of the worst kitchen experiences of my life.

We still didn't have a restaurant site but I decided it was time to introduce LFS to Sydney with two Sunday night pop-ups at a friend's bakery in Chippendale. The menu was sorted, I had three ladies out the front ready to serve, and there were four of us in the kitchen. I felt we were well prepared to feed a room that could barely fit 18, and perhaps throw in a few takeaways as well.

Half an hour before opening, with a queue of about 40 people out the front, Muu started to test the batter. The hoppers weren't coming out very well and a lot were sticking. Then two of our six hopper burners decided not to work, closely followed by a third. (Meanwhile, more and more people were joining the queue.) Things started getting very tense in the kitchen as we all stared at Muu, unable to help as he struggled with the hoppers. There was a sense of doom in the air when it was time to open the doors. We were full in about two minutes, with a waitlist on the go, and a flurry of takeaway orders for 10 and 20 hoppers at a time.

It was like a bad dream. We were managing about one good hopper from every three and even they were slow going. The last batch of people to arrive didn't even get one hopper. Muu disappeared as soon as we finished cooking and I found him later in his restaurant around the corner, sitting in the dark, drinking a bottle of wine. I think all he managed to say was that

he didn't think he could be a chef anymore. He didn't speak again until the next morning, and to this day still shudders at the memory and claims it was the night I tried to kill him.

We had already committed to the following Sunday so we had to pull ourselves together. We got some better burners (ones that actually worked) and some non-stick pans (up until then I'd been using traditional aluminium ones that need to be seasoned correctly with perfect batter to work). I looked at the batter recipe again, which for some reason I'd tried to tweak, and went back to the original. We made it through, much more successfully, but the fear of that night will always stay with me.

After that there were a few more pop-ups, one in Singapore (which Muu only agreed to help me with if I didn't make him cook hoppers), and several months of cooking at a market. By this stage I was cooking hoppers with speed and confidence, but I still felt an underlying unease about my recipe and its credibility.

We finally found a site for LFS and I arranged another trip to Sri Lanka to hunt for suppliers and bits and pieces for the restaurant. I was also determined, yet again, to eat as many hoppers as I could, following up every recommendation I had. It was while on this trip, as I asked incessant questions about hoppers, that I first heard the rumour of certain roadside stalls using a little plaster of Paris in their batter to help the edges stay crisp for longer. I was convinced it was an urban myth; however, my research (talking to everyone I came across) uncovered many people who had heard of this phenomenon. Perhaps there was some truth to it?

I had two particularly special hopper moments on this trip. One was at a roadside stall near Sigiriya, a little hut with one table that opened at 3 pm. There was just one hopper maker, Ratna, who cooked hoppers over a traditional fire hearth until sold out. She reserved a little of her batter each day to ferment the following day's mix, resulting in a more savoury hopper than many. All she served were plain and egg hoppers with lunu miris (see page 222), which is really all you need.

The other one was at Cafe On The 5th in Colombo. The hopper section was staffed by a delightfully smiley chef in proper whites and a chef's toque, and he'd been the head hopper maker there for 17 years. His were the most delicate I had ever eaten. I stood there, trying to make friends as he cooked, and he was clearly amused when I told him I was opening a hopper shop in Australia. Then, with some deft wrist-flicking action, he made me a hopper flower. The pancake had petals. I was utterly entranced.

After again spending my time eating too many hoppers, all made differently with varying texture and flavours, I finally realised that, like so many things, there is more than one way to make a hopper. My recipe was how I wanted it to be, it was most definitely a hopper, and therefore everything would be OK.

But just before we opened the restaurant, a supply problem developed with the people who were grinding my flour, so I had to slightly alter the recipe. Again, tweaking proved a little problematic and the first three months at LFS were riddled with batter issues. The restaurant was packed from the beginning and the two-day fermenting time made everything just that little bit harder. My first main hopper chef was Finnish and in many ways completely overqualified for the role – but had no experience with hoppers. Every night we would discuss and fiddle with the dough, trying to figure out what was going wrong. Eventually the supply issue righted itself and we were able to go back to my original recipe. Apart from the occasional rogue dough, our hopper batter now behaves itself. The experience has been fraught though; perhaps a little plaster of Paris would have made things a whole lot easier.

# String hoppers

Yes, the technique of pressing these hoppers correctly is fiddly and a little tricky to master, and yes, the whole process can be rather time-consuming, but I promise it's great fun to try. It might help to watch a few videos so you're clear on the method before your first attempt. You will be rewarded with gently flavoured noodles, just set and soft to the touch. The main flavours come from the accompaniments you choose to serve alongside. Start with kiri hodi (see page 142) and a sambol or two.

You'll need a bit of special equipment to make these: a string hopper press, about eight string hopper mats and a steamer. They do make special string hopper steamers, which are higher than usual, but a regular steamer will work just as well. You can buy everything you need from a Sri Lankan grocer or online.

450 g (1 lb) fine rice flour (use Thai brand; see note on page 32 and below)

5 g (⅕ oz) cooking salt

approximately 400 ml (13½ fl oz) boiled water, cooled just enough so you can work with it using your hands

**NOTE** You can make these using red rice flour if you have some, and there are even versions that use wheat flour.

Tip the rice flour into a large saucepan and cook, stirring regularly, over a low heat for 5 minutes or until nicely toasted.

Transfer the flour to bowl and add the salt. Slowly start pouring in the water, mixing constantly with a spoon, until the dough just comes together. At this stage, swap the spoon for clean hands and knead for 2–3 minutes until it becomes soft and pliable. The texture should be soft, not sticky and a little less firm than playdough.

Have your string hopper mats ready, face up in front of you. Push enough of the dough into the string hopper press to fill it. These usually require both hands to press, although you can get some that use a trigger or a turning action.

The next step is to press out the dough onto the hopper mats to form thin long noodles. You need to start in the middle and continue in a circular motion to the outside of the mat, and then come back to the middle so you form two layers. They should look like lace, hopefully with a nice even consistency. Use a knife to cut the strands of noodles and repeat with your remaining hopper mats.

Have a steamer ready, water boiling over a medium heat.

Stack the hopper mats in the steamer to form a tower, making sure none of the noodles are touching each other. Cover and steam for 4–5 minutes until just cooked.

Remove the mats from the steamer, gently pull off the string hoppers and place them on a plate. Now they are cooked you can stack them so they are overlapping.

Continue with the remaining dough to make about 70 hoppers all up.

Once cooked, the string hoppers can sit at room temperature, covered with a tea towel (dish towel), for a few hours until you are ready to eat. You can also keep them in the fridge, then steam or microwave them in small overlapping layers to reheat. Serve at room temperature or just warm.

# Hoppers

**MAKES 16–18**

Make sure to read the hopper story on page 102 before you attempt this because, although they seem simple, they can be hard to master. But they truly are worth the effort. You will need hopper pans to make these, available from Sri Lankan or Indian grocers or online. The dough needs to rest overnight so start the recipe a day ahead.

| |
|---|
| 400 g (14 oz) medium coarse rice flour |
| 100 g (3½ oz) coarse rice flour |
| 11 g (⅓ oz) caster (superfine) sugar |
| 10 g (¼ oz) dried yeast |
| 7 g (¼ oz) cooking salt |
| 300 ml (10 fl oz) coconut cream |

Place the flours, sugar, yeast and salt in a bowl and mix well with your hands. Add 300 ml (10 fl oz) water and combine with your hands to form a dough – it will be a little crumbly and not very sticky. Turn it out onto your bench and knead briefly until it just comes together.

Return to the bowl, cover with a tea towel (dish towel) and leave to rest at room temperature for 2 hours.

Wrap the dough or place in a container with a lid and rest in the fridge overnight.

The next morning, place the dough in a large bowl and whisk in the coconut cream and another 300 ml (10 fl oz) water to form a batter. Leave at room temperature for 1–1½ hours until it becomes light and fluffy in texture. The fluffy texture is the key as this indicates fermentation. Once it hits this stage, the batter will last for another few hours or can even be placed in the fridge and used the next day. At some point though the batter will over-ferment and will no longer be any good. You will be able to tell when this happens as the batter will lose its lightness and become very thin.

To cook your hoppers, heat a hopper pan over a medium heat. Ladle 80 ml (2½ fl oz) of batter into the middle of the pan, then use your hands to swirl it around in a circular motion to the top edge. You will know the temperature is right when the batter makes only a very slight sizzle as it goes in and, when you swirl it, it sticks in a nice 1 mm layer around the edge of the pan. There should be enough batter to coat the edge and still have about a tablespoon of batter in the base. If you find you have too much batter tip a bit out. The hopper batter around the edge should be thin and delicate, and dotted with little lacy holes.

If the pan is too hot the batter may not stick to the edge as you swirl it, or you may find that it swirls but is very thick. If the pan is not quite hot enough the layer of batter around the edge will be too fine. You can remedy this by doing a double swirl.

Just accept that you will need to experiment the first few times to get the heat just right.

Once the pan is coated, turn the heat up slightly and cook without the lid until you start to see bubbles forming in the batter puddle on the base. At this point, put the lid on, turn the heat down a little and cook for 1 minute.

Remove the lid to release the steam and have a look; the extra batter in the bottom should be a little doughy and puffy. Put the lid back on and cook for another minute.

Remove the lid again. To make sure the doughy bit is cooked, test it with your finger: it should be soft and spongy, not wet and sticky.

**NOTES** If you want to make egg hoppers, use the same method but with a tiny bit less batter, as you don't need any extra pooling in the bottom. Crack an egg into a bowl and pour it into the batter as soon as you have swirled it. Season with salt and pepper or pepper spice mix (see page 46) and continue cooking as described above. The only difference is that you will need to cook with the lid on for an extra 1–2 minutes to set the egg. If you don't like runny egg yolks you can give the egg a little whisk before cooking.

You can also make a sweet hopper. Once you have removed the lid the first time, add 20 g (¾ oz) of grated jaggery and continue cooking as above. Just note that when you try and remove it from the pan the hot sugar might have caramelised and stuck to the bottom. Your trusty bamboo skewer should help here. Serve with whipped or runny coconut cream.

If it's not quite cooked, put the lid back on for a moment.

After the lid comes off for the final time, continue cooking the hopper for another minute or so until the outside edge begins to colour and come away from the pan. Hold the pan with a tea towel (dish towel) and give it a firm tap on the edge to release the hopper a little. Cook for a moment more, then turn out the hopper onto a wire rack. You should be able to remove it just by turning it, but if it's a little stuck use a bamboo skewer to help release any caught bits. Let it sit for a moment and then serve immediately. Repeat with the remaining batter.

Hoppers are best eaten fresh out of the pan, which requires a hopper maker and a hopper eater. Otherwise, leave them to rest on a rack in a warm spot and eat them all together at the end.

# How to eat a hopper

Place your hopper on a plate in front of you, sitting slightly to the edge.

Add a little sambol and perhaps some curry to your plate. Tear a hopper edge.

Use this torn hopper edge to dip into your yolk and have a taste. If eating a plain hopper, use the crispy edge to scoop up a little sambol and eat that.

From here it's a matter of tearing, scooping and dipping your hopper either into the egg or with curries or sambols. Use it in much the same way you would a roti or bread. You are still eating with your fingers, so the rules are the same (see page 53). Continue in this manner until you have finished and need another hopper. Repeat.

බත්

# Rice

சோறு

*Sooo tasty,*
*a real rice-puller*

Colloquial saying

Along with coconut, rice is a symbol of prosperity. It is said that this grain, cooked in coconut milk, was one of the first offerings made to Buddha, a significant combination still celebrated in the dish of kiri bath (see page 120). In Hindu and Muslim cultures, the sacred nature of rice is just as apparent in celebratory dishes such as biryani (see page 123). This delicate grain is such an important part of Asian food and culture, particularly in Sri Lanka, where its cultivation and consumption have shaped and mirrored the country's political landscape.

Most of Sri Lanka's early civilisations, when the country was ruled by Sinhalese kings, were based around rice cultivation. Anuradhapura, in the arid northern central area of the island, was the first capital, and its prosperity was due in no small part to the building of large earthen tanks linked by canals that enabled the irrigation of rice. The massive tank systems required hydraulic engineering, which is still thought to be the most advanced in the ancient world. These large reservoirs in formerly waterless parts of Sri Lanka changed the landscape, bringing irrigation, wildlife and vegetation, along with advances in art and culture. As the fortunes of kings rose and fell, the capital moved to nearby Polonnaruwa and then to Sigiriya. This whole area is now called the cultural triangle and remains a living temple and place of pilgrimage. A branch of the bodhi tree that Buddha sat under was planted and still grows there today; beautiful stupas, shrines and frescos abound, and remains of these ancient cities are still visible. The area is hot and dry yet filled with wildlife because of the water drawn to the area, all for the sake of rice.

With European settlement and the arrival of bread, rice cultivation took a back seat. The British in particular focused more on the cultivation of rubber, tea and coconuts. Sri Lanka went from a country with hundreds of native grains, varietals that were nutritious, had ayurvedic value and worked with the climate of the regions, to a country that had to import rice. Homogenous hybrid varieties were grown instead, offering a high yield and good resistance to pests; convenience was chosen over the health of the people and the land. In the post-colonial politics of the country, the issue of rice and what it stood for became a symbol of nationalism.

But through it all, rice and curry remained the national dish, impervious to the changing politics. Plates are still piled high with rice, and a pot belly is referred to as a rice bundy (belly). The deliciousness of something is still measured against its ability to make you want to eat more rice.

These days the government and smaller companies are increasingly working to bring back traditional rice types and work them in an organic manner, as rice cultivation continues to follow the zeitgeist. On my last trip back to Sri Lanka, just prior to the opening of Lankan Filling Station, I was lucky enough to meet a man called Charitha, head of the charity organisation Rural Returns, who was doing just that: working with farmers in rural areas to help grow heirloom varietals, providing a product, jobs and a source of income in poorer areas. They are currently focusing on six varietals – three samba and three red rice – all of them delicious and always at least one on my restaurant menu.

Samba is a short-grain rice, also called village or paddy rice, with a very distinctive smell that is stronger in some varieties than others. At its strongest it can be almost unpleasantly pungent with a fermented stench, though luckily the taste doesn't reflect the smell; it actually has a deliciously mild and earthy flavour to it, with fluffy grains that are white to yellow in hue. The various red rices are also short grain and, when cooked, are drier than the samba, with firm grains that are even a little coarse in texture. They share the same aromatic earthiness, though the red types are less delicate, with a more savoury, nutty flavour.

Apart from simple steamed rice served in mounds with a curry meal there are many other rice dishes of note for various times of the day. Kiri bath is an excellent breakfast dish, made with rice, coconut milk and some spices, traditionally served at auspicious times and for celebrations. It is the first thing eaten for Sinhalese new year, the symbolic first food for children, fed by a bride to her groom at a wedding and eaten on poya days (when there is a full moon).

Another great breakfast dish is kola kanda (see page 118), Sri Lanka's congee, made with wild greens and herbs. Usually thin enough to almost drink, the rice is cooked down and the greens are added at the end as a puree; sometimes the mix has just two greens, others contain a blend of many more.

Lunch is generally rice and curry, streamlined down to a rice and curry packet on the go or a lamprais (see page 127), also essentially a rice and curry packet but much more specific and complicated. Traditionally it consists of rice cooked in ghee, spices and a meat broth, a curry made from three meats (pork, chicken and beef), an eggplant pahi or moju (see pages 202 and 130), seeni sambol (see page 228), blachan paste (see page 131) or prawn paste and frikadels (Dutch beef meatballs). Fried ash plantain curry and a whole fried egg are common additions.

There are other celebratory rice dishes cooked for special occasions, such as fragrant yellow rice (see page 122), usually made with basmati grains. It is served as a side to a curry meal, like simple steamed rice, but fancied with spices and turmeric or saffron to give it colour, and topped with an onion temper and cashews.

There are many versions of this dish throughout Asia, echoing the Indian influence with the type of rice, the Muslim influence with the use of saffron, and the Indonesian tradition of serving it with boiled eggs.

Sri Lanka also has its own version of biryani, or buryiani, a dish usually associated with India that may actually have its origin in Persia. Regional variations abound throughout India but also in other parts of the world, such as South Africa and all through Asia. In Sri Lanka it's often served as the first meal to break the fast after Ramadan or at other Muslim festivals.

The following pages contain all the key recipes, but what they don't have is a recipe for simple steamed rice. I have worked in various Asian restaurants, all of which have relied on rice cookers and all of which have descended into a panicked flurry when the cookers have died, inevitably halfway through a busy service, leaving the cooks unsure how to cook rice without these magical machines. I find the easiest method is a ratio of 1:1½ parts rice to water; bring it to the boil in a saucepan, cover with a lid and then cook super gently for 12 minutes. However, different grains (and even the same grain from a different batch) often require slightly different ratios and times. So the moral of the story is this: if you want to cook some rice to go with one of the curries in this book, choose your favourite grain, check the packet instructions and go with your preferred cooking method.

# Kola kanda

SERVES 4–6

This makes a particularly fine breakfast for a healthy start to the day. A form of rice porridge with medicinal greens mixed through, it has an earthy flavour and can be served as a thin, almost drinkable soup or with a little more texture. The mix of herbs depends on who is making it and where you are; they are either juiced or pureed and added at the end, rounding out the delicate flavour of the dish.

130 g (4½ oz) red rice

8 g (¼ oz) finely chopped ginger

8 g (¼ oz) salt flakes

80 g (2¾ oz) picked gotu kola (pennywort) leaves

60 g (2 oz) picked watercress

5 g (⅕ oz) curry leaves

150 g (5½ oz) grated coconut

Wash and drain the rice, then place in a medium heavy-based saucepan. Add the ginger, salt and approximately 2 litres (68 fl oz) water and bring to the boil, then reduce to a gentle simmer and cook for 40 minutes.

Meanwhile, make your green puree. Bring a saucepan of salted water to the boil and fill a bowl with water and ice to cool your green leaves.

Separately blanch each variety of greens in the boiling water for 30 seconds, then refresh in the iced water and drain, squeezing out as much liquid as possible.

Using a blender or mortar and pestle, blend or pound the greens to a paste, adding just enough water to loosen the mix and bring it all together in a smooth bright-green paste.

When the rice has been cooking for about 40 minutes, add the coconut and give it a little stir. Cook for another 20 minutes or until the rice has broken down and the mix has a gruel-like consistency.

Remove the pan from the heat and stir through the green paste. Let this sit for a few moments before serving. This is best eaten hot.

NOTE When you order this in Sri Lanka it's usually from a stall that cooks nothing but kola kanda, and it will be served with some small pieces of jaggery. The idea is that you hold a piece between your teeth as you sip, letting it gradually dissolve, or chew a little bit after every few mouthfuls.

Feel free to experiment with your own combination of herbs and bitter green leaves.

# Kiri bath

**SERVES 6–8**

300 g (10½ oz) red rice (see note)

1 star anise

3 cloves

salt flakes

325 ml (11 fl oz) coconut cream

Pani pol and Lunu miris (see pages 248 and 222), to serve

**Milk rice is a breakfast or celebratory dish laden with significance. In itself it is very simple: the rice is cooked in coconut milk until sticky, shaped, and left to cool and set. The creamy, mildly spiced rice is then cut into diamond shapes and served alongside a sambol, usually lunu miris. It can also be paired with jaggery and banana for a sweeter finish. At Lankan Filling Station we serve it with katta sambol (see page 222) and pani pol for a hot and sweet taste sensation.**

Wash and cook your rice using your preferred method, including 400 ml (13½ fl oz) water, the star anise, cloves and a little salt. (If you like, you can do this step the day before and continue the next day with cold rice; it will only add a few minutes to the cooking time.)

Fish out the whole spices as best you can and transfer the cooked rice to a medium saucepan. Add the coconut cream and 250 ml (8½ fl oz) water, then place over a medium–low heat and cook gently, stirring often, for 14–16 minutes until the rice has thickened, become sticky and all the liquid has been absorbed.

Turn out the rice onto a large shallow tray and use a spoon or spatula to smooth it into a rectangular slab about 5 cm (2 in) high. Allow to cool completely, then cut into large diamond shapes. The rice will be firm enough to hold its shape.

Serve at room temperature with a side of pani pol and lunu miris.

Invite your guests to put a rice diamond and a little of each sambol on their plate. To eat, use your fingertips to mash a little of the rice with a dab of either or both the sambols. Form into a little ball and use the finger flick method to eat.

**NOTE** This dish can be made with red or white rice but make sure it's a sticky, starchy short-grain variety – medium or long-grain rice will not work as well. If you can't find a Sri Lankan rice, Japanese sushi rice is a good substitute.

# Fragrant yellow rice

**SERVES 4–6**

This is a rice dish for special occasions. As the name suggests, the rice is tinted yellow with saffron, hinting at its Muslim origins. Turmeric can also be used. The rice is wonderfully aromatic, and the temper adds sweetness and texture. This rich, flavoursome dish is interesting enough to eat on its own, without any accompaniments. You will often find sultanas scattered on top of this dish. I have omitted them as I don't like sultanas with my savouries, but I know I am in the minority on this one. If you want them, add 20 g (¾ oz) sultanas (golden raisins) when you stir in the cashews to the temper.

400 g (14 oz) basmati rice

40 g (1½ oz) ghee

10 black peppercorns

8 cardamom pods, bruised

6 cloves

1 cinnamon quill

2 g (¹⁄₁₆ oz) curry leaves

170 g (6 oz) finely diced brown onion

5 g (⅕ oz) piece lemongrass, lightly bruised

12 g (½ oz) salt flakes, plus extra to serve

2 x 4 cm (1¼ in) pieces pandan leaf

150 ml (5 fl oz) coconut cream

¼ g (¹⁄₁₂₈ oz) saffron threads, soaked in 40 ml (1½ fl oz) warm water

5 eggs, at room temperature

**TEMPER**

50 g (1¾ oz) ghee

16 g (½ oz) mustard seeds

4 g (⅛ oz) curry leaves

270 g (9½ oz) finely diced brown onion

100 g (3½ oz) cashews, toasted (see note)

**NOTE** To toast cashews, preheat oven to 150°C (300°F), spread cashews on a baking tray and toast for 15 minutes until uniformly pale golden, giving them a jiggle every 5 minutes to ensure even cooking.

Wash the rice until the water runs clear, then leave to drain in a colander.

Melt the ghee in a saucepan over a medium heat, add the peppercorns, cardamom, cloves and cinnamon and cook, stirring, for 2–3 minutes until the spices become very aromatic. Add the curry leaves and cook, stirring, for a minute or so until the leaves are fried, then add the onion, lemongrass and salt. Cook, stirring occasionally, for 3–4 minutes until the onion has softened, then add in the rice and give it a good mix to coat.

Add the pandan, coconut cream, 600 ml (20½ fl oz) water and the saffron liquid and stir well. Allow the rice to come to the boil – this will take 4–5 minutes. Put the lid on, then reduce the heat to as low as you can and let the rice cook undisturbed for 10 minutes. Remove the pan from the heat and leave to steam, still covered, for another 10 minutes.

While the rice is cooking, boil the eggs and prepare the temper.

Bring a saucepan of water to a simmer, then gently lower the eggs into the water. Stir gently to create a little whirlpool a few times in the first couple of minutes (to help centre the yolks), then cook at a very low simmer for 10 minutes. Remove the eggs, cool in a bowl under running water and then peel. I find it helps to peel the eggs while they are submerged in water. Drain the peeled eggs on paper towel and, once dry, cut them in half lengthways.

For the temper, melt the ghee in a medium frying pan over a medium–high heat, add the mustard seeds and curry leaves and cook, stirring, for a minute until the seeds start to pop and the leaves are fried. Add the onion and cook, stirring occasionally, for 4 minutes or until it starts to catch on the bottom of the pan. Add the cashews and cook for another 2–4 minutes until the onion is nice and caramelised.

Take the lid off the pan of rice and fluff it up with a fork. Remove the cinnamon and lemongrass (I usually leave the remaining whole spices in as I like the danger).

Spread out the rice on a large platter, rather than piling it high. Scatter the tempered onion mixture over the rice, then arrange the eggs on top, cut side up. Lightly season the eggs with salt and serve immediately.

**Pictured pages 275 & 276** →

# Biryani

SERVES 6–8

Versions of this dish abound, from country to country and within Sri Lanka itself, but at its heart it's baked and layered rice cooked with spices and usually some sort of meat. In Sri Lanka it is served on special occasions and generally made with chicken. Here, for my not particularly traditional take, I've used lamb; you could also substitute goat. The ingredients list is reasonably long and there are quite a few steps, which might seem daunting, but the aromatic flavours and joy this special dish brings are well worth it. Just make sure you read the whole recipe before you begin, to get a sense of all the steps, ingredients and timings. Essentially you will be marinating and cooking the meat, cooking the rice, making a temper, constructing the dish and then baking.

### TO MARINATE THE LAMB

40 g (1½ oz) cashews, lightly toasted (see notes opposite)

30 g (1 oz) grated coconut

6 g (⅕ oz) salt flakes

1.2 kg (2 lb 10 oz) boneless lamb shoulder, cut into 3 cm (1¼ in) chunks (see note)

14 g (½ oz) Black curry powder (see page 43)

3 g (¹⁄₁₀ oz) turmeric powder

100 g (3½ oz) thick yoghurt

### TO COOK THE LAMB

50 g (1¾ oz) ghee

4 g (⅛ oz) curry leaves

3 cardamom pods, bruised

2 cloves

1 cinnamon quill

270 g (9½ oz) diced brown onion

11 g (⅓ oz) finely chopped garlic

9 g (⅓ oz) finely chopped ginger

salt flakes and freshly ground black pepper

1 x 400 g (14 oz) tin diced tomatoes

2 long green chillies, cut into thin rounds

For the marinated lamb, using a mortar and pestle, pound together the cashews, coconut and salt to form a smooth paste.

Place the lamb pieces in a bowl. Add in the cashew paste, curry powder and turmeric and massage into the meat, then stir through the yoghurt. Cover and marinate in the fridge for 2–3 hours, taking it out about 20 minutes before you start the next stage of cooking so it comes back to room temperature.

To cook the lamb, first place a large flameproof casserole dish with a lid over a medium heat. Add in half the ghee to melt and then the curry leaves to fry for a minute or so. Add the whole spices and cook for 2 minutes, then add the onion, garlic and ginger and cook, stirring occasionally, for 6–7 minutes or until the onion has softened. Season lightly with salt and pepper, then use a spoon to remove this base into a bowl and set aside.

Increase the heat to high, add in the remaining ghee and cook off your lamb pieces. Give them a good 10 minutes or so in the pan, stirring regularly, and season well. The yoghurt will start to stick but just keep stirring and scraping.

**Continues overleaf →**

## Biryani continued

**FRAGRANT RICE**

400 g (14 oz) basmati rice

40 g (1½ oz) ghee

4 cardamom pods, bruised

5 cloves

1 cinnamon quill

2 g (1/16 oz) curry leaves

170 g (6 oz) finely diced
brown onion

4 g (1/8 oz) salt flakes

2 x 4 cm (1½ in) pieces pandan leaf

100 ml (3½ fl oz) coconut cream

¼ g (1/128 oz) saffron threads,
soaked in 40 ml (1½ fl oz)
warm water

**TO ASSEMBLE**

1 quantity Temper (see page 122)

40 g (1½ oz) ghee

coriander (cilantro) leaves,
to garnish

Add the base back in with the lamb, along with the tomatoes, plus a splash of water to rinse out the tomato tin. Reduce the heat so the mix is sitting at a gentle simmer and cover with a lid. You want to cook the lamb, stirring occasionally, until it's well braised and just starting to fall apart, between 1½ and 2 hours. Once it's cooked, stir through the green chillies and set aside to cool, then remove from the casserole dish and clean.

While your lamb is cooking, prepare the rice and the temper.

Wash the rice until the water runs clear, then leave to drain in a colander.

Melt the ghee in a saucepan over a medium heat, add the cardamom, cloves and cinnamon and cook, stirring, for 2–3 minutes until the spices become very aromatic. Add the curry leaves and cook, stirring, for a minute or so, then add the onion and salt. Cook, stirring occasionally, for 3–4 minutes until the onion has softened, then pour in the rice and give it a good mix to coat.

Add the pandan, coconut cream, 500 ml (17 fl oz) water and the saffron liquid and stir well. Allow the rice to come to the boil – this will take 4–5 minutes. Put the lid on, then reduce the heat to as low as you can and let the rice cook undisturbed for 10 minutes. Remove the pan from the heat and leave to steam, still covered, for another 10 minutes.

Remove the lid and fluff up the rice. It should be dry, fluffy and still ever so slightly undercooked.

Make the temper as directed on page 122 and set aside, then preheat the oven to 220°C (430°F).

Place the clean casserole dish over a high heat, add the ghee and wait until it starts to smoke. Add in half the rice so it sits on an even layer at the base and then turn off the heat. Spoon in the lamb and sauce to sit over the rice, then finish with the remaining rice in another even layer. Cover with the lid and bake in the oven for 30 minutes.

Remove the biryani from the oven and take off the lid. Spread over the temper and return to the oven for an extra 5 minutes to dry out and heat the temper.

Remove from the oven, then use a fork to fluff up the top layer of rice so you can see the pieces of meat poking through. Garnish generously with coriander leaves and serve immediately. The biryani should be heavily fragrant with spice, the meat tender, the rice soft but not gluggy, and there should be a nice crunchy layer of rice at the bottom.

**NOTE** Biryani is traditionally served with some version of raita (see page 216) – often a more elaborate, salad-type version. You could also add a gotu kola and herb sambol (see page 220).

# Lamprais

MAKES 15 PACKETS

Lamprais are a Burgher specialty: a very specific mix of dishes, all cooked separately then constructed together, wrapped in banana leaves and heated. More often than not, lamprais are made in large batches, the packets frozen ready to be heated as an easy meal as required.

This is a very special dish. It's not difficult, but as you can see from the length of the recipe, it's time-consuming and labour-intensive. You can choose to tackle it in one go as long as you are prepared for an entire day of cooking, but it can also be broken down into elements and made over a few days (with the exception of the rice, which is best made on the day of construction). This is the way we go about it at Lankan Filling Station, as we find assembly easier if each element has been cooked and cooled. This is pretty much the recipe my nan taught me, with just a little tweak here and there.

LAMPRAIS ELEMENTS

Banana leaves

Ghee rice

Lamprais curry

Fish cutlets

Vambatu moju

Seeni sambol

Blachan paste

Continues overleaf →

# Banana leaves

Buy more banana leaves than you think you'll need. Ultimately you only need 15 perfect ones for this recipe but I always get spares as they are prone to tearing, and if they are small leaves then get double that. You will need enough to cut into 15 large rectangles (approximately 50 cm x 25 cm/20 in x 10 in). Alternatively, you can wrap your packets using a couple of smaller pieces overlapped but that can get a little fiddly. The other option is to use lotus leaves, available dried from Asian grocers, which need to be soaked in water before using. If you can't find either of these leaves, use large pieces of baking paper for each packet instead.

Make sure your leaves are clean, either by rinsing in cold water or wiping with a damp cloth. To make the leaves pliable enough to wrap you will need to heat them. At LFS we do this by placing them on our flat top for a moment on each side – they change colour and soften fairly quickly. At home, you can use an iron on a low setting to achieve the same result, or carefully wave them over a flame on your stovetop until they soften.

You can soften the leaves one by one as you wrap, or you can prepare them all just before you wrap. If you do this, pile them up and cover with a tea towel (dish towel) so they stay warm and pliable.

You will also need 15 large sheets of foil ready before you start assembling. They will need to be about 3 cm (1¼ in) larger on all sides than the pieces of banana leaf.

# Ghee rice

**If you can find it, samba rice is the best to use here, otherwise you can use basmati. Traditionally rice for this dish would be cooked in a meat broth, giving it a richer flavour, but I like this simpler version as there are so many other things going on in the lamprais.**

80 g (2¾ oz) ghee

2 cinnamon quills

5 cardamom pods, bruised

1.1 kg (2 lb 7 oz) samba rice

salt flakes

Melt half the ghee in a medium saucepan with a tight-fitting lid over a medium heat (or use a rice cooker), then add the spices and fry for a minute or so. Add the rice and stir well to coat in the ghee and cook, stirring, for another minute. Pour in 1.4 litres (47 fl oz) water and bring to the boil, then cover with a lid and reduce the heat to the lowest possible setting. Cook for 12 minutes, then remove the pan from the heat. Let the rice sit, covered, for at least 5 minutes.

Remove the lid and mix through the remaining ghee. Use a fork to fluff up the rice, remove any lumps and fish out the whole spices. Season to taste with salt and allow to cool to room temperature

# Lamprais curry

**The traditional way to start this curry is to boil all the meat in water first, which then becomes the broth to cook the rice in. Here I prepare it the way my nan did, currying each meat separately and mixing them together at the end. I find this works better as you can more accurately cook the meat to the right level of doneness and the result is a cleaner flavour, allowing you to taste each type of meat. This recipe isn't for a super-hot curry because, as I said earlier, there is a lot going on in these packets and a gentle touch works best.**

600 g (1 lb 5 oz) chicken thigh fillet, skin on, chilled

600 g (1 lb 5 oz) pork shoulder, chilled

600 g (1 lb 5 oz) beef chuck, chilled

50 g (1¾ oz) coconut oil

4 g (⅛ oz) curry leaves

360 g (12½ oz) diced brown onion

30 g (1 oz) finely chopped garlic

24 g (⅞ oz) finely chopped ginger

1 long red chilli, finely chopped

30 g (1 oz) tomato paste (concentrated puree)

16 g (½ oz) Brown curry powder (see page 42)

8 g (¼ oz) chilli powder

4 g (⅛ oz) caster (superfine) sugar

salt flakes and freshly ground black pepper

First, prepare all the meats. It is important that they are cut into fairly even 1.5 cm (½ in) dice as it will affect the mouthfeel of the curry. It's much easier to do this if the meat is cold as it won't be so floppy, and it also helps to have a good sharp knife. Place each type of meat in a separate bowl.

Melt the coconut oil in a medium saucepan over a medium heat, add the curry leaves and stir for a minute until the leaves are fried, then add the onion, garlic, ginger and chilli. Cook, stirring occasionally, for 4–5 minutes until the onion has softened.

Add the remaining ingredients, including a little seasoning, and stir to combine. Cook for another moment or so, then remove the curry base from the heat and divide evenly among the three bowls of diced meat.

The next step is to transfer each bowl of meat and curry base to a medium saucepan and cook over a medium heat until tender and cooked through. You won't need to add any fat. You can do this simultaneously or individually, depending on how many pans you have.

This is meant to be a dry curry so you will need to stir regularly, seasoning lightly as you go. The chicken will take 10–12 minutes, the pork 18–20 minutes, and the beef up to 25 minutes. Cover the pork and beef curries with a lid between stirs, and because the beef takes a little longer, you may need to add a few splashes of water to make sure it doesn't dry out too much.

Cook each meat until tender and remove from the heat as soon as they are done. Once they are all cooked, mix the curries together in one large saucepan and cook gently for another minute or two. Check your seasoning again; I like mine to be pepper heavy, and don't be scared to add a little more curry or chilli powder if you want to. The finished curry will be fairly dry and aromatic with a gentle kick of black pepper and a hint of sweetness. Set aside to cool.

## Fish cutlets

These cutlets are a substitute for the more traditional frikadels (Dutch meatballs). This is what my nan used to do and I much prefer them as they are lighter and more aromatic. Although fried, the cutlets become soft and unctuous in the lamprais.

Follow the recipe for the crab cutlets (see page 66), replacing the crabmeat with 280 g (10 oz) cooked mackerel fillet. If you can't get mackerel, bonito is a good substitute. At LFS we dry-roast the fish in the oven until it's cooked through, but if you don't want to fuss around with this extra step follow my nan's lead and use tinned mackerel. These days you can usually find good-quality sustainable tinned fish.

I would suggest making and crumbing the balls in advance (they last a good few days in the fridge and freeze very well) but they are best fried on the day you want to assemble your lamprais.

## Vambatu moju

**Meaning mustard eggplant, vambatu moju is one of my favourite eggplant dishes and I could eat it with just about anything. As a result, my lamprais have a little more of this element than usual. This recipe will leave you with leftovers after you've assembled the parcels, but I'm pretty sure you will be happy about that. You can eat the eggplant cold or at room temperature.**

60 g (2 oz) plain (all-purpose) flour

20 g (¾ oz) cooking salt

8 g (¼ oz) turmeric powder

2 medium eggplants (aubergines), skin on, cut into 2 cm x 1 cm (¾ in x ½ in) batons (chopped weight 1.5 kg/3 lb 5 oz)

vegetable oil, for deep-frying

4 g (⅛ oz) curry leaves

180 g (6½ oz) diced red onion

12 g (½ oz) finely chopped garlic

9 g (⅓ oz) finely chopped ginger

1 long red chilli, finely chopped

40 g (1½ oz) Sri Lankan mustard (see page 31)

26 g (1 oz) caster (superfine) sugar

125 ml (4 fl oz) cider vinegar

50 g (1¾ oz) tomato paste (concentrated puree)

11 g (⅓ oz) Maldive fish flakes

30 g (1 oz) coconut cream

salt flakes and freshly ground black pepper

Mix together the flour, salt and turmeric in a large dish, add the eggplant and turn to coat. Set aside for 30 minutes.

Pour vegetable oil into a large heavy-based saucepan to a depth of 4–6 cm (1½–2½ in) (the oil should come no more than two-thirds of the way up the pan). Place over a high heat and heat to 180°C (350°F). If you don't have a thermometer you can check by dipping a piece of eggplant into the oil; if it starts to sizzle immediately, the oil is ready. Add the eggplant in small batches and swish them around so they cook evenly. You need to fry each batch for longer than you think as you want them really dark, almost black, and nearly dried out; 8–9 minutes should do it. Lift them out and drain on a wire rack. Give the oil a moment to heat up again before you fry the next batch.

Combine the remaining ingredients, except the coconut cream and seasoning, in a medium saucepan and add just enough water to cover. Cover and simmer over a low heat for 8–10 minutes until the onion has softened and the mixture is cooked through. Add the eggplant and coconut cream and stir for another moment or so until the mix is quite dry yet unctuous. Season to taste and set aside to cool.

## Seeni sambol

The recipe on page 228 will make more than you need for the lamprais; however, it will last a long time and is delicious with many other things.

## Blachan paste

**Blachan, blacan or belacan paste all refer to a Malaysian fermented and dried shrimp paste of varying pungencies that has travelled throughout Asia, taking on different guises. Although simply called blachan paste by my nan, this recipe is really a super-strong and fishy sambol that I have only ever encountered in lamprais packets. If this is a flavour that appeals to you, I suggest you spread some on toast for breakfast, ready for dipping into soft-boiled eggs.**

| |
|---|
| 35 g (1¼ oz) dried shrimp |
| 50 g (1¾ oz) grated coconut |
| 90 g (3 oz) finely diced red onion |
| 1 red bird's eye chilli, finely chopped |
| 25 g (1 oz) blachan paste |
| 5 g (⅕ oz) finely chopped garlic |
| 5 g (⅕ oz) finely chopped ginger |
| juice of 1 lime |

Gently dry-roast the shrimp in a small frying pan over a low heat for 2–3 minutes, stirring regularly to ensure an even cook. Tip the shrimp into a bowl and set aside.

Add the coconut to the pan and dry-roast over a low heat for 3–4 minutes until it's an even mid-brown colour. You will need to stir the coconut constantly as it can catch and burn very easily. Add to the bowl with the shrimp and allow to cool slightly.

This next stage can be done with a mortar and pestle, small blender or spice grinder. You need to pound or blend all the ingredients, except the lime juice, to form a reasonably fine paste. Season with the lime juice – you are looking for a strong fishy flavour with a good balance of lime and heat. Store in the fridge until ready to use.

## Constructing your Lamprais

The best way to tackle this is to be well prepared. Have all your elements laid out with their own spoons and make sure you have plenty of clean bench space. At LFS we weigh each element to ensure every parcel is consistent, but you don't have to be that precise if you don't want to. Using the suggested weights here as a guide, you could measure out one of each ingredient using spoons or cups and keep them as a visual reference as you assemble the packets.

## QUANTITIES PER PACKET

| | |
|---|---|
| 1 banana leaf rectangle | |
| Ghee rice x 120 g (4½ oz) | |
| Lamprais curry x 85 g (3 oz) | |
| Fish cutlets x 2 | |
| Vambatu moju x 45 g (1½ oz) | |
| Seeni sambol x 40 g (1½ oz) | |
| Blachan paste x 10 g (⅓ oz) | |

**Please refer to the photos overleaf as a visual guide** →

Place a banana leaf rectangle on the bench in front of you with a longer side closest to you.

In the very middle, place a portion of rice. I find gently pressing the rice into a small bowl then tipping it onto the banana leaf helps contain it. If you do this, gently press down on the top of the rice to flatten slightly.

Place a portion of curry directly on top, in the middle of the rice without quite covering it all.

The rest of the elements should be placed around the rice, snuggled right into it. The easiest way to indicate where each one should go is to look at the rice round as we would a clock. Picture where the little hand would be on a clock for each time given and place the element there.

Place the two fish cutlets at 12.30 to 1 o'clock.

Vambatu moju goes top left, 11 o'clock.

Seeni sambol goes bottom right, 4.30.

And finally the blachan paste, bottom left, 7.30.

If you want to add the lime pickle (see note), place 12 g (½ oz), top middle left, 10 o'clock.

Once all the elements are in position, use both hands to pick up the bottom and top sides of the banana leaf and fold over so the two sides meet above the filling. Fold them over each other twice to seal and make sure they sit tightly across the top of the lamprais packet (lucky we have pictures, eh?).

Next fold in the two short sides, as you would when wrapping a present, then fold each triangle behind and under the packet to seal neatly.

Carefully lift this parcel onto a piece of foil and wrap, making sure the top side stays on top.

Now don't panic if this is all getting too confusing; all you really need to do is wrap everything together in your leaf and seal to form a nice even parcel. You can use skewers or toothpicks to help keep things in place, or simply use the foil to make sure it's all secure.

Repeat with the remaining ingredients to assemble all the parcels.

### Heating
The packets are now ready to go. They can be heated and eaten immediately, kept in the fridge for a few days and heated, or frozen for later. Heating instructions are as follows:

◆ Fresh at room temperature: place in a preheated 180°C (350°F) oven for 20–25 minutes

◆ Fresh from fridge or frozen and thawed overnight: place in a preheated 180°C (350°F) oven for 35–40 minutes

◆ Frozen: Place the curry packets on a tray in the oven as it heats to 180°C (350°F) for 45–50 minutes

Regardless of the way you heat them, they are very handy packets to have in the freezer at all times, ready for a complex curry meal with no effort and little washing up.

**NOTES** There are some accepted variations to lamprais, such as adding fried ash plantain or a whole fried egg, but if you start getting too wild and try a vegetarian version, you may well make something delicious, but it won't really be a real lamprais. At LFS we add some of our lime pickle (see page 224), which is a non-traditional touch, but I find this sharp citrus note adds another layer of flavour to this complex meal.

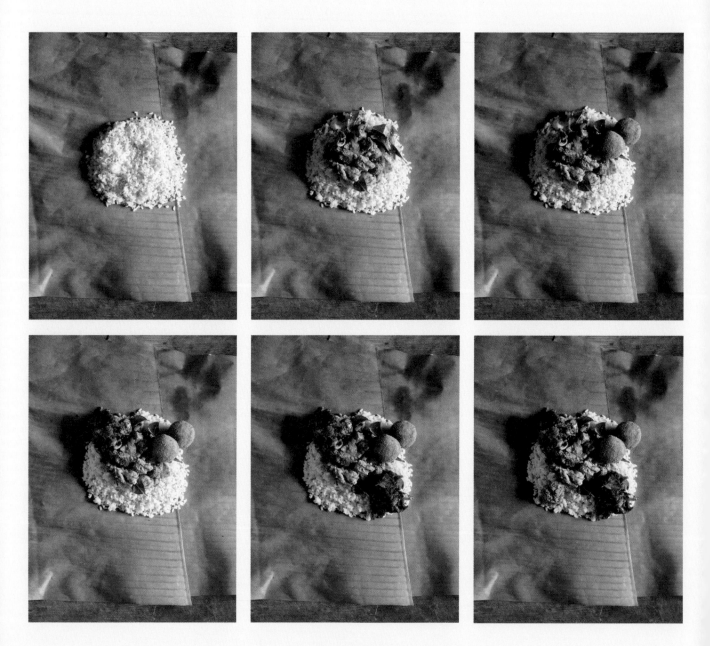

↑ Lamprais

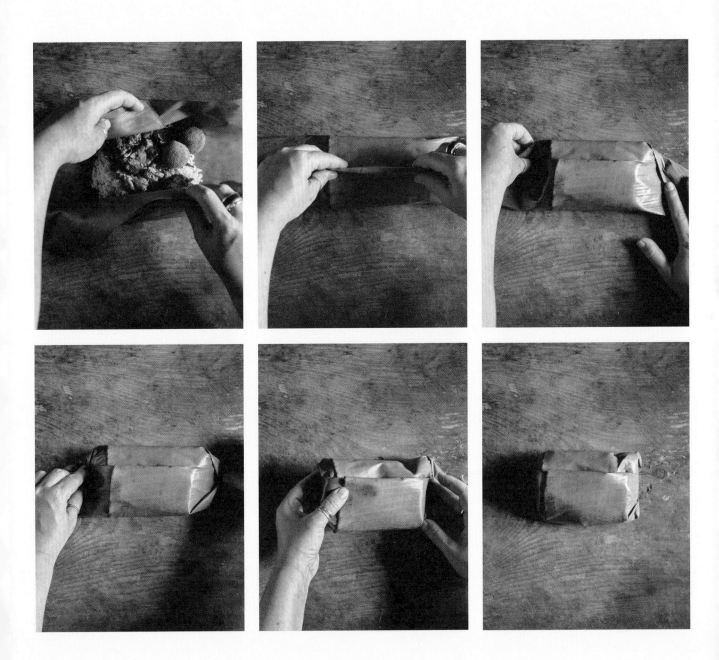

# Curries

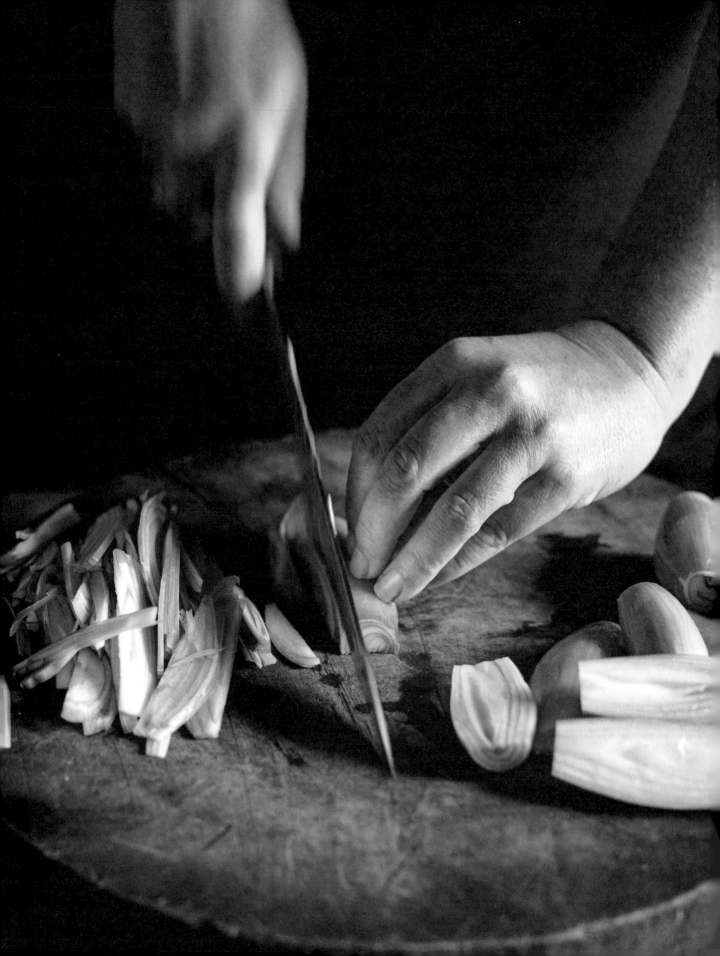

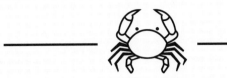

No matter where you are in Sri Lanka, the staple for everyday eating is rice and curry. It's the national dish. The generic term 'rice and curry' is perhaps too simple as it can cover anything from a modest plate of a rice, dhal, one curry and a sambol to a dazzling feast of intricate dishes, each serving its own purpose and all designed to complement each other. Even the term 'curry' can be tricky; for example, how many types of chicken curry do you know of in the world?

There is an almost endless array of curries available in Sri Lanka, with styles changing according to region and religion. Tamil curries are sometimes saucier, use more chilli powder and rely on tamarind as the main souring agent, while Sinhalese curries veer towards black pepper, giving a different kind of heat, and use the tartness of goraka (otherwise known as garcini, and an alternative souring agent to tamarind). Burgher curries are often richer and use ghee with a generous hand. To the untrained eater, discerning the difference between curries is almost impossible as they generally have more in common than not; though all tend to be classified by colour (white, yellow, red or black), which gives at least some indication of heat and flavour.

Sri Lankan curries tend to rely heavily on coconut, are often hotter than Indian curries and generally share the sweet, sour, savoury and hot balance characteristic of Thai food. The ingredients are cut into pieces to allow for ease of eating with fingers, and the spices are often left whole as fishing them out is easy to navigate when eating this way. The sauce from the curry (the gravy) is usually tasted by the person cooking it in a distinctly Sri Lankan way: dabbed onto the palm before being licked to test.

Most curries focus on one main ingredient, the idea being that it's the whole meal that provides the variety – often with a strong emphasis on vegetables, and just one or two meat or seafood dishes. The heat and sauciness of curries also varies within a meal, as does the colour. You are most unlikely to be offered just white or yellow curries, for example; there will always be a range.

Sri Lanka has an abundant supply of seafood and freshwater fish. Oily fish are very common, particularly tuna, bonito and mackerel (also known as seer fish), which are used in the very popular south coast Sinhalese curry called ambul thiya. Cooked with goraka, this dry, highly spiced curry is said to last for days at room temperature without spoiling. Squid is also common, curried or devilled, and curries often feature crustaceans such as prawns, lobsters and crab.

Crab curry is a particular favourite of mine and there are versions found all along the coast. In fact, the chilli heat in a crab curry in Jaffna was the first and only Sri Lankan curry to defeat me; it was one of the hottest things I have eaten in my life and I still feel the disappointment of being unable to finish it. A few years later, I attempted to cook my first crab curry with my nan. We went to the fish market together and she gave me invaluable advice on how to choose the best ones, then talked me through all the steps and ingredients in the recipe. But when it came time to actually make it, she woke very early and did the whole thing while I was fast asleep. This was the first time I realised how protective people could be of their recipes. Luckily for me, she thawed in that regard over time (see the recipe on page 170).

Meat curries are often made with the ubiquitous chicken, an easy choice in a country where religion has a real impact on what meats are used, but also pork, beef and goat (known as mutton in Sri Lanka). With their Christian background, the Burghers have no such restrictions and they make a mild three-meat curry for lamprais (see page 129) with all the animals: beef, chicken and pork.

That said, one of the best meat curries I have ever eaten in Sri Lanka was a dry black curry made with wild boar. I was invited for a meal at the Kandy home of a lovely couple I met while travelling, Ayra and Derrick. The curry was so delicious I never forgot it, and eventually wrote to Ayra to ask for her recipe. I still have her handwritten reply, and a decade later her recipe remains the inspiration for the black spiced curry we now serve at Lankan Filling Station.

But we need to talk about the profusion of vegetarian curries. During one trip, I was taken to what was essentially a cafe with a lunch buffet catering for workers, and was amazed by the vast quantity of vegetarian curries on offer. This is only to be expected on an island so rich in tropical produce, but it is also due to the high proportion of Buddhists and the vegetarianism that comes with it. Vegetarian curries range from simple and generally mild potato and pumpkin curries, sometimes with mustard, to a less obvious cucumber curry with an unexpected chilli kick, and the excellent murunga curry in a gentle sauce. You'll find versions of all of these in this chapter.

There aren't many vegetables that don't find their way into a curry, or fruit for that matter: jackfruit, green mango and pineapple are all fine examples. There is a particularly good mango curry that I have adopted into my repertoire (see page 168), and I can still remember the unexpected delight of my first jackfruit curry (see page 143). I ate it while I was in Colombo doing a guest chef stint at a restaurant with more pasta than curry on the menu. The jackfruit curry was part of the staff meal and was more delicious than anything on the menu.

A lot of curry recipes, including the ones in this book, are fairly basic in terms of technique. They all have a similar rhythm: start with a fat, add spices, add curry powders, add bits, add the main thing and then finish with coconut. Onion, garlic, ginger, curry leaf and chilli form the base of most (I think I have chopped more onions in the LFS kitchen than the rest of my cooking career put together). The variety comes from the choice of spices and when and how they are used. The benefit of this is that once you get the hang of the method, it will be much easier for you to play around with flavours. I hope this chapter shows you just how many flavours and textures you can experiment with in curries.

When you are about to make a curry, have all your ingredients prepped and ready; this will ease the flow of constructing your dish and enable you to focus on the smells and flavours. The frying of the curry leaves and the aromas of the spices will help guide you, indicating when it's time for the next step. The other important thing to remember is that curries generally improve with time and it's often better to eat them after they have sat for a few hours or even a day. Something magical happens when the ingredients have the chance to mingle and the main protein, vegetable or fruit absorbs some of the gravy. It also takes the pressure off if you are cooking for a dinner party as nothing stressful needs to be done at the last minute.

# Kiri hodi

**SERVES 4**

The name translates to 'milk gravy', which is exactly what this is: a gentle dish that is more like a sauce than a curry. Kiri hodi is a great starter curry for kids or those in need of comfort, and is often served as an accompaniment to string hoppers, where its excellent sauciness soaks into the delicate strands. It's also really good with kottu roti (see page 100) or simply with a bowl of rice. Potato or boiled eggs are sometimes added and there are also lovely versions featuring tomatoes.

5 g (⅕ oz) fenugreek seeds

25 g (1 oz) coconut oil

4 g (⅛ oz) curry leaves

150 g (5½ oz) sliced brown onion

12 g (½ oz) finely chopped garlic

8 g (¼ oz) White curry powder (see page 42)

3 g (¹⁄₁₀ oz) turmeric powder

1 cinnamon quill

250 ml (8½ fl oz) coconut cream

4 x 5 cm (2 in) pieces pandan leaf

juice of up to 1 lime

salt flakes and freshly ground white pepper

Place the fenugreek seeds in a small bowl, add 75 ml (2½ fl oz) water and set aside.

Melt the coconut oil in a medium saucepan over a medium heat, add the curry leaves and cook, stirring for a minute or so until the leaves are fried. Add the onion and garlic and cook, stirring occasionally, for 4–5 minutes until the onion has softened.

Stir in the curry powder, turmeric and cinnamon and continue stirring for 1–2 minutes until the powder begins to catch on the bottom of the pan.

Add the coconut cream, pandan leaf, soaked fenugreek seeds and 600 ml (20½ fl oz) water. Bring the mixture just to the boil, then reduce the heat and simmer gently for 2–3 minutes until the sauce comes together. Season to taste with lime juice, salt and pepper. The flavour should be mild and sweet with just a hint of curry and pepper, and lime in the very background.

← **Pictured page 101**

# Jackfruit curry

**SERVES 6–8**

**This is an example of a fruit really shining in a curry; the texture of cooked jackfruit is soft and succulent, perfect for sucking up the flavour of the gravy. However, there are obstacles. Depending on where you are, sourcing an unripe jackfruit can be a challenge, and preparing the actual fruit is a sticky and time-consuming process. In addition, the fruit are usually quite large, which means you either have to make a lot of curry or waste a lot of fruit. If you can't source a green jackfruit there really isn't a suitable substitute. You can buy tinned jackfruit in brine but the result will be entirely different; you're much better off making a different curry. But if you can find a green jackfruit and are willing to give this dish a go, it's definitely worth it.**

600 g (1 lb 5 oz) unripe/green jackfruit

100 g (3½ oz) cooking salt

40 g (1½ oz) ghee

5 g (⅕ oz) curry leaves

6 g (⅕ oz) mustard seeds

4 g (⅛ oz) cumin seeds

200 g (7 oz) sliced brown onion

20 g (¾ oz) roughly chopped garlic

20 g (¾ oz) roughly chopped ginger

3 green bird's eye chillies, sliced into thin rounds

10 g (⅓ oz) Brown curry powder (see page 42)

40 g (1½ oz) jaggery, chopped

salt flakes and freshly ground black pepper

400 ml (13½ fl oz) coconut cream

20 g (¾ oz) tamarind concentrate

juice of 1–2 limes

Use a knife to peel the skin off the jackfruit and cut through the seeds into a square-ish 5 cm (2 in) chunks.

Mix together the cooking salt and 1 litre (36 fl oz) water in a bowl, add the jackfruit pieces and leave to brine for 30 minutes or so.

Melt the ghee in a large saucepan over a medium heat, add the curry leaves and mustard and cumin seeds and cook, stirring, for a minute or so until the curry leaves are fried and the spices are aromatic. Add the onion, garlic, ginger and chilli and cook, stirring occasionally, for 6–7 minutes until the onion has softened.

Add the curry powder and cook, stirring, for 1–2 minutes until it begins to catch on the bottom of the pan. Add the jaggery and stir for 1–2 minutes until it melts, then drain the jackfruit pieces and add to the pan, stirring well to coat. Season with salt and pepper.

Add the coconut cream, tamarind and 400 ml (13½ fl oz) water and give everything a good stir. Bring to a simmer, then reduce the heat to low and cover and cook gently, lifting the lid and stirring occasionally, for 1½ hours or until the jackfruit starts to soften. Remove the lid and cook, stirring occasionally, for another 25–30 minutes until the curry has thickened a little and the jackfruit pieces are just starting to fall apart.

By now the jackfruit should be sitting in a well-spiced, slightly sweet, slightly hot sauce with a good hit of tartness from the tamarind. Season to taste with salt, pepper and lime juice. Go easy on the lime – you just want it to cut through the richness rather than stand out as a flavour.

# Murunga curry

SERVES 6–8

approximately 480 g (1 lb 1 oz) murunga (drumstick)

30 g (1 oz) coconut oil

4 g (⅛ oz) curry leaves

250 g (9 oz) sliced brown onion

salt flakes and freshly ground white pepper

3 x 5 cm (2 in) pieces pandan leaf

35 g (1¼ oz) White curry powder (see page 42)

5 g (⅕ oz) fenugreek seeds

5 g (⅕ oz) mustard seeds

200 ml (7 fl oz) coconut cream

**This very mild curry is super simple to make but depends entirely on you being able to source one particular vegetable, which may be difficult. I have included the recipe anyway because it is such a quintessential Lankan curry. It is best eaten using your fingers as you need to split open the murunga lengths and use your teeth to scrape out the soft insides before discarding the outer layer.**

**If you can't find murunga, unfortunately there is nothing you can use as a substitute, so you will have to pick another curry. Don't worry, there are plenty to choose from in this chapter.**

Use a vegetable peeler or a spoon to scrape the skin off the murunga. Cut it into 8 cm (3¼ in) lengths and set aside.

Melt the coconut oil in a medium wide-based saucepan over a gentle heat, add the curry leaves and cook, stirring, for a minute or two until the leaves are fried. Add the onion and cook, stirring occasionally, for 2–3 minutes until it just starts to soften.

Stir in the murunga pieces, season with salt and pepper and cook for a minute or so. Add the pandan leaf, curry powder, fenugreek and mustard seeds and cook, stirring occasionally, for 4–5 minutes until the murunga starts to soften.

Pour in the coconut cream and 400 ml (13½ fl oz) water, gently bring to a simmer and cook, stirring every now and then, or 20–25 minutes until the murunga is nice and soft and almost collapsing.

Taste for seasoning. The gravy should be mild with only a touch of heat, and the flavour and texture inside the murunga should be almost asparagus like. Serve immediately.

# Cashew curry

SERVES 6-8

This delicate, creamy curry is distinctly Sri Lankan and a great one for your vegetarian and vegan friends. I suspect most of us won't have access to fresh cashews, or even the big and plump Sri Lankan variety, but make it with what you have. It will still be an excellent dish.

400 g (14 oz) raw cashews (see note)

40 g (1½ oz) coconut oil

4 g (⅛ oz) curry leaves

2 g (1/16 oz) cumin seeds

400 g (14 oz) sliced brown onion

25 g (1 oz) finely chopped garlic

20 g (¾ oz) finely chopped ginger

1 long green chilli, finely chopped

salt flakes and freshly ground white pepper

20 g (¾ oz) White curry powder (see page 42)

3 g (1/10 oz) turmeric powder

480 ml (16 fl oz) coconut cream

1 cinnamon quill

2 x 5 cm (2 in) pieces pandan leaf

juice of 1-2 limes

Soak the cashews in a bowl of cold water for 1 hour. Drain and set aside.

Melt the coconut oil in a medium saucepan over a medium heat, add the curry leaves and cumin seeds and cook, stirring, for a minute or so until the curry leaves are fried and the seeds are aromatic.

Add the onion, garlic, ginger and chilli and cook, stirring occasionally, for 4-6 minutes until the onion begins to soften. Lightly season with salt and pepper.

Add the curry powder and turmeric and cook, stirring, for 1-2 minutes until the powder begins to catch on the bottom of the pan.

Stir in the cashews to coat well, then add the coconut cream, cinnamon, pandan leaf and 280 ml (9½ fl oz) water. Reduce the heat to low and simmer gently, stirring occasionally, for 18-20 minutes until the sauce has reduced and thickened,

Season to taste with salt and pepper and squeeze in a little lime juice just before serving. The curry should be lovely and thick with a bit of pepper heat. Go easy on the lime – it's just there to cut through the richness rather than dominate.

NOTE If you are lucky enough to have access to fresh cashews, you don't need to soak them so skip that step.

# Cucumber curry

SERVES 6–8

Although technically a fruit, cucumber tends to be treated as a vegetable and is primarily used in salads and other cold dishes. But in Asia you occasionally see it in cooked preparations; and while the texture softens slightly in the pan, cooked cucumber still has a nice crunch to it. In this spiced curry the cooling characteristics of cucumber work beautifully with the heating properties of chilli. It's quite a dry curry so there won't be a lot of gravy.

3 large telegraph (long) cucumbers

60 g (2 oz) grated coconut

3 cardamom pods, bruised

6 g (⅕ oz) Brown curry powder (see page 42)

5 g (⅕ oz) chilli powder

7 g (¼ oz) curry leaves

200 g (7 oz) finely diced red onion

3 g (¹⁄₁₀ oz) fennel seeds

1 cinnamon quill

2 green bird's eye chillies, finely chopped

75 ml (2½ fl oz) coconut cream

salt flakes and freshly ground white pepper

juice of 1 lime

Peel the cucumbers a little unevenly, leaving some of the skin on; this adds to the overall texture and flavour of the dish. Slice them lengthways and remove the seeds, then cut them on a slight angle into 2 cm (¾ in) thick slices. Set aside.

Place the coconut, cardamom, curry and chilli powders and curry leaves into a medium saucepan over a gentle heat. Gently toast, stirring as you go, for 5–6 minutes until the coconut darkens to a golden-brown colour.

Add the cucumber, onion, whole spices, chilli, coconut cream and 150 ml (5 fl oz) water. Bring to a simmer over a medium heat and cook gently for 6–8 minutes until the cucumber has softened and the sauce has reduced and thickened slightly. Season well with salt, pepper and lime juice and serve.

# Garlic curry

SERVES 4–6

The first time I ate a garlic curry was at Palmyrah, a restaurant in the Hotel Renuka in Colombo that specialises in traditional Jaffna Tamil food. It's been around since the 1970s and is one of the places I always go whenever I'm in town. A garlic curry is distinctly Sri Lankan and a lot milder than you might think, as the slow cooking in coconut milk tames these pungent cloves. Even so, I wouldn't suggest you make this to eat on its own; it's much better enjoyed as part of a larger meal.

50 g (1¾ oz) ghee

3 g (¹⁄₁₀ oz) curry leaves

6 g (⅕ oz) coriander seeds

6 g (⅕ oz) mustard seeds

180 g (6½ oz) finely diced brown onion

1 green bird's eye chilli, finely chopped

salt flakes and freshly ground white pepper

6 g (⅕ oz) White curry powder (see page 42)

3 g (¹⁄₁₀ oz) chilli powder

3 g (¹⁄₁₀ oz) fenugreek seeds

300 g (10½ oz) garlic cloves, peeled (from 5–6 heads, preferably with similar-sized cloves; see note)

375 ml (12½ fl oz) coconut cream

2 x 5 cm (2 in) pieces pandan leaf

Preheat the oven to 150°C (300°F).

Melt the ghee in a medium ovenproof saucepan or flameproof casserole dish over a medium heat, add the curry leaves and coriander and mustard seeds and cook, stirring, for a minute or so until the curry leaves are fried and the spices are aromatic. Add the onion and chilli and cook, stirring occasionally, for 4–6 minutes until the onion begins to soften. Lightly season with salt and pepper.

Add the curry powder, chilli powder and fenugreek, and cook, stirring, for 1–2 minutes until the powder begins to catch on the bottom of the pan.

Add the garlic cloves and stir well to coat, then add the coconut cream, pandan leaf and 125 ml (4 fl oz) water. Bring to the boil, then take off the heat. Cover closely with a cartouche (a piece of baking paper cut to fit) and place in the oven. Bake for 35–40 minutes until the garlic has softened.

Taste and adjust the seasoning. The curry should be thick rather than saucy, with a gentle creaminess to it. The garlic should be soft and yielding with a mellow flavour and only the mildest hint of heat.

NOTE The only drawback with this curry is the labour-intensive task of peeling the garlic cloves. (You can use pre-peeled but generally I find the quality of these isn't the greatest.) One of the easiest ways is to separate the head into individual cloves and soak them in a bowl of warm water for a few minutes before peeling. If you have access to garlic scapes (the top stem and flowering part of the garlic) you can use these instead; just cut them into 4 cm (1½ in) lengths before cooking.

# An island built on coconuts

*Kalpa Vriksha: coconut in early Sanskrit, meaning*
*'tree that gives all that is necessary for living'*

A coconut palm, no matter what variety, is often referred to as a gift from the gods. And deservedly so.

We all know, don't we, that coconuts are actually a fruit (a drupe to be precise) and not really a nut at all? The trees generally start fruiting from six to eight years of age, producing between 30 and 80 coconuts a year, reaching their peak in their 20s but continuing up to the age of about 80.

There is some conjecture about their origin but it's safe to say coconut trees are native to Asia, with several varieties specific to Sri Lanka. The tree and all its applications have always been utilised in Sri Lanka, but it was the British who were responsible for commercialising production for export. During this time the process of drying the flesh to make desiccated coconut was discovered, which proved to be a useful way to store and ship this delicate product.

All of the coconut palm is useful, providing shelter, fuel ... none of it is wasted. And then there are all the ways to consume the fruit of this wondrous tree (also explored on pages 26–8).

The sap from the flower is extracted by toddy tappers, who scale the palm and use a large sickle-shaped knife to gently scrape a layer off the stalk of the coconut flower. A vessel is left underneath to collect the sap (tapped correctly, a stalk can produce sap for a whole month) and the tapper will move along to the next tree, usually via a thin rope strung between trees of a plantation for this very purpose. It is beautiful and slightly scary to watch these tappers at work. If used immediately, the sap can be made into a sweetener, either a palm sugar or treacle. Although the method for this is similar, it is not to be confused with kithul (see page 30). Once fermented, the sap becomes toddy, a slightly alcoholic drink which can then be used to make vinegar, distilled to make arrack and even turned into a delicious product called coconut amino, which is the fermented sap with added sea salt used to make an umami-rich seasoning sauce (you can even buy this at the supermarket these days).

The other liquid from this tree is known as the water. When it's from a mature coconut it can be used in cooking; the liquid from a young coconut is the drink we all know as coconut water, which I think is the perfect drink. The King coconut is a large orange fruit native to Sri Lanka that has a lower sugar content than many other varieties and produces a very delicious water. King coconuts grow wild and are also cultivated across the island.

The flesh of the fruit gives even more delights. Most commonly grated and used fresh, it can also be dried and turned into coconut oil, a fat that solidifies when cold and, depending how it's extracted, can be very healthful. Coconut milk and cream are made by processing the flesh with water; the only difference between the two is the fat content. Coconut butter is made by combining the oil and the milk. And there are even ways to turn coconut flesh into flour and sugar.

We are lucky that there is such a proliferation of these products made commercially, as in many places fresh coconuts are not that easy to come by. They also take up a lot of storage space and require knowledge and dexterity to open (I once tried using a hammer to get into a young coconut – it worked eventually but took a long time). You need a fair bit of muscle to remove the husk as it is dense and fibrous. To actually crack open a shell is fairly easy, ideally using the back of a cleaver. You need to find the seam in the middle and tap it as you roll the coconut around until the shell cracks and falls apart into two halves. Once opened you can prise out the flesh in pieces; I find

it easier to remove the thin brown skin, which can be quite firmly attached, if you freeze the flesh first.

The more traditional tool to extract the flesh is a type of grater: a flat length of metal with a rounded edge and serrated teeth along the outside. This is usually attached to a bench or even a plank of wood big enough for you to sit on. You place the halved coconut with the flesh up against the metal and scrape up and down, twisting your wrists around to get all of the flesh out. (There are slightly more modern versions with a handle to help turn the teeth.)

I have vague childhood memories of my father grating his own coconuts in the backyard, and I once went to a food market in Singapore where they had a coconut-grating machine, selling it freshly grated by weight. However you go about it, grated coconut is an essential ingredient in Sri Lankan cooking and you will need to get your hands on some if you want to make the most of this book (see pages 26–7 for more information).

## Things you can do with a coconut tree

**LEAVES** | Dried and thatched together to form mats (called cadjan), used to make walls, roofs and barriers, basically building you a home. Also used to make brooms and mats or trays to put things on or serve food on, or made into pretty coloured versions to sell to tourists.

**COIR** | These are the fibres on the husk of the fruit which are used to make broom heads, mats, brushes and as stuffing for mattresses. They can also be woven, made into string, rope and fishing nets. The eco shop where I buy my home cleaning products also makes a rather good scratchy coir sponge.

**SHELL** | Fashioned into spoons and bowls for cooking, eating and serving. They can also be made into musical instruments or you can clink two halves together to make the sound of a clip-clopping horse.

**HUSKS** | Used for burning as fuel and can be turned into a carbon product.

**TRUNK** | The hard wood with a beautiful grain is used to make furniture, canoes, frames for houses or anything else that requires wood.

**ROOTS** | Boiled down to make a dye

**FLESH** | Used to make soap, beauty products, candles, massage oil and medicine.

**WATER** | If you are desperate, in a jungle and have run out of saline solution for a drip, you can use the sterile water as a substitute as it has the same makeup as blood plasma; apparently it's safe to inject directly into the bloodstream (it's worked at least once anyway).

# Beetroot curry

SERVES 6–8

I don't think people immediately associate beetroot with tropical islands, but it actually arrived in Sri Lanka early on via trade routes and continues to thrive as it is one of the more heat-tolerant root vegetables. Its earthy flavour works well with strong spices and is a robust match for the creaminess of coconut milk, so it is not surprising that beetroot curry is a common and popular Lankan dish.

50 g (1¾ oz) ghee

8 g (¼ oz) curry leaves

6 g (⅕ oz) mustard seeds

3 g (1⁄10 oz) coriander seeds

1 cinnamon quill

180 g (6½ oz) diced brown onion

25 g (1 oz) roughly chopped garlic

20 g (¾ oz) roughly chopped ginger

2 long red chilli, finely chopped

salt flakes and freshly ground black pepper

30 g (1 oz) Brown curry powder (see page 42)

400 g (14 oz) beetroot, peeled and cut into thick julienne or batons (see note)

200 ml (7 fl oz) coconut cream

2 x 5 cm (2 in) pieces pandan leaf

Melt the ghee in a large saucepan over a medium heat, add the curry leaves and whole spices and cook, stirring, for a minute or so until the curry leaves are fried and the spices are aromatic. Add the onion, garlic, ginger and chilli and cook, stirring occasionally, for 4–6 minutes until the onion starts to soften. Season well with salt and pepper.

Add the curry powder and cook, stirring, for 1–2 minutes until it begins to catch on the bottom of the pan. Add the beetroot, stir well to coat and cook for 2–3 minutes.

Add the coconut cream, pandan leaf and 200 ml (7 fl oz) water, then reduce the heat to low and simmer gently, stirring occasionally, for 16–18 minutes until the beetroot has softened and started to take on the flavours of the sauce. Taste and adjust the seasoning if necessary. The curry will be only mildly hot with a sweet, earthy flavour.

NOTE Cutting the beetroot into nice even batons can be a little time-consuming but it's important to ensure it all cooks at the same rate, and there is something delightful about the texture of eating it in strips. However, you can cut the beetroot into chunks if preferred; simply increase the cooking time a little.

# Potato curry

SERVES 4-6

There are as many versions of potato curry as there are types of potato. This particular one has a sharp hit of mustard combined with a little chilli, giving it a deep heat with a vinegary tang. It has a strong flavour and makes for a substantial, slightly heavy curry.

40 g (1½ oz) ghee

8 g (¼ oz) curry leaves

240 g (8½ oz) sliced brown onion

40 g (1½ oz) finely chopped garlic

40 g (1½ oz) finely chopped ginger

20 g (¾ oz) finely chopped lemongrass, white part only

1 long green chilli, cut into thin rounds

salt flakes and freshly ground white pepper

30 g (1 oz) Brown curry powder (see page 42)

2 g (1/16 oz) turmeric powder

850 g (1 lb 14 oz) dutch cream potatoes, peeled and cut into 3 cm (1¼ in) chunks (see note)

240 ml (8 fl oz) coconut cream

3 x 5 cm (2 in) pieces pandan leaf

40 g (1½ oz) Sri Lankan mustard (see page 31)

Melt the ghee in a large saucepan over a medium heat, add the curry leaves and cook, stirring, for a minute or so until the leaves are fried. Add the onion, garlic, ginger, lemongrass and chilli and cook, stirring occasionally, for 4–6 minutes until the onion starts to soften. Lightly season with salt and pepper.

Add the curry powder and turmeric powder and cook, stirring, for 1–2 minutes until the powder begins to catch on the bottom of the pan.

Add the potato and stir well to coat, then add the coconut cream, pandan leaf and 240 ml (8 fl oz) water. Reduce the heat to low and simmer gently, stirring occasionally, for 30–35 minutes until the sauce has reduced and thickened.

Just before serving, stir through the mustard and have a final taste for seasoning.

NOTE Waxy potatoes work best in this recipe as they hold their shape and are firm enough to stand up to the hefty sauce. A floury variety will result in a mushy curry. You want the potatoes to be nicely cooked through and tender enough to suck up the flavour of the sauce, but not so soft that they are falling apart.

# Pumpkin curry

SERVES 4–6

12 g (½ oz) rice (any variety)

40 g (1½ oz) grated coconut

50 g (1¾ oz) ghee

5 g (⅕ oz) mustard seeds

180 g (6½ oz) diced brown onion

salt flakes and freshly ground
black pepper

3 green bird's eye chillies

40 g (1½ oz) Sri Lankan mustard
(see page 31)

4 g (⅛ oz) coriander seeds

4 g (⅛ oz) cumin seeds

10 g (⅓ oz) curry leaves

20 g (¾ oz) Maldive fish flakes
(see note)

14 g (½ oz) Brown curry powder
(see page 42)

600 g (1 lb 5 oz) Jap pumpkin
(squash), mostly peeled and cut into
3 cm (1¼ in) chunks (see note)

200 ml (7 fl oz) coconut cream

4 x 5 cm (2 in) pieces pandan leaf

**This curry is an excellent example of the way Maldive fish is used to season a dish. The dried fish adds a little texture to this mild, creamy curry, and brings a savoury, slightly smoky note without actually tasting fishy. The result is a lovely balance of sweet, tangy and earthy flavours.**

Tip the rice into a small frying pan and gently toast over a low heat for 1–2 minutes until it just begins to colour. Transfer to a bowl and set aside to cool.

Add the coconut to the pan and toast, stirring constantly so it doesn't burn, for 2–3 minutes until it is an even dark brown colour. Add to the bowl with the rice.

Melt 20 g (¾ oz) of the ghee in a small saucepan over a medium heat, add the mustard seeds and cook until they start to pop. Add the onion, season with salt and pepper and cook, stirring occasionally, for 5–6 minutes until softened. Set aside to cool to room temperature.

Using a mortar and pestle, pound the rice, coconut and chillies to a coarse paste. Add the onion mix and pound – you won't get it completely smooth but you can break down the onion quite a lot. This can get a little messy and you may need to do it in batches. Stir in the mustard.

Melt the remaining ghee in a large wide-based saucepan over a medium heat, add the coriander and cumin seeds and fry for a minute. Add the curry leaves and Maldive fish, reduce the heat to low and cook gently for 2 minutes, stirring occasionally.

Stir in the curry powder, then add the pumpkin and mix well to coat. Add the coconut cream, pandan leaf and 500 ml (17 fl oz) water, and season again with salt and pepper. Bring to the boil, then reduce the heat to low and stir through the pounded onion mixture. Simmer for 16–18 minutes until the pumpkin is cooked through and the gravy has thickened.

Taste both the pumpkin and the sauce before serving. This curry can easily veer into 'too sweet' territory so add salt to taste; it also benefits from plenty of black pepper.

NOTES This is also tasty without the Maldive fish, if you want to make a vegetarian dish. You will just need to season it more heavily.

If you are using a different type of pumpkin, make sure it is a firm dry one; anything too watery will make the curry a little insipid. Don't worry about removing every scrap of skin when peeling the pumpkin – a little skin here and there is fine.

# Fish curry

SERVES 4–6

A lot of Sri Lankan fish curries are made with oily fish, and have a strong flavour and dark colour due to the addition of goraka. This recipe goes down a different route, using a white-fleshed fish and a gentle cooking method to give a delicate texture. The mildly spiced gravy is cooked separately, with the fish added at the very end.

500 g (1 lb 2 oz) skinless and boneless snapper fillet (see note)

40 g (1½ oz) coconut oil

4 g (⅛ oz) curry leaves

220 g (8 oz) sliced brown onion

20 g (¾ oz) finely chopped garlic

15 g (½ oz) finely chopped ginger

15 g (½ oz) finely chopped lemongrass, white part only

1 long green chilli, cut into thin rounds

30 g (1 oz) Brown curry powder (see page 42)

8 g (¼ oz) fennel seeds

4 g (⅛ oz) fenugreek seeds

400 ml (13½ fl oz) coconut cream

4 x 5 cm (2 in) pieces pandan leaf

salt flakes and freshly ground white pepper

Start by slicing the fish into bite-sized pieces. Much will depend on the size of your fillet, but try to make the slices about 1.5 cm (½ in) thick. The main thing is to cut them into similar-sized pieces for even cooking. Set aside in the fridge.

Melt the coconut oil in a medium saucepan over a medium heat, add the curry leaves and cook, stirring, for a minute or so until the leaves are fried. Add the onion, garlic, ginger, lemongrass and chilli and lightly season with salt and pepper. Cook, stirring occasionally, for 6–7 minutes until the onion has softened.

Add the curry powder and fennel and fenugreek seeds and cook, stirring, for 1–2 minutes until the curry powder begins to catch on the bottom of the pan. Season again.

Add the coconut cream, pandan leaf and 500 ml (17 fl oz) water and bring to the boil, then reduce the heat and simmer gently for about 10 minutes until everything is cooked and you can no longer taste a sharpness from the ginger.

Add the fish pieces and simmer gently until cooked. The cooking time will depend on the size of your pieces but start checking from about 5 minutes. Alternatively, cool the curry base and store in the fridge alongside the fish, then combine the two and gently simmer when you are ready to serve. Either way, be sure to taste the curry again once the fish is cooked and season as required.

NOTE Most varieties of white-fleshed fish will work here, though I would recommend one with large flakes that is not too delicate.

# Prawn curry

SERVES 6–8

Sri Lanka is rife with prawns, small and large, freshwater and salt. Their sweet, firm flesh holds up well to strong flavours and they are curried all along the coastline. However, I have often found that the time it takes a prawn to absorb enough flavour from a curry sauce does not tally with its optimal cooking time. At Lankan Filling Station we get around this by making the curry base and letting it cool, then adding the prawns and letting them have a good soak in the sauce overnight. From there it's just a matter of cooking them briefly the next day.

50 g (1¾ oz) ghee

10 g (⅓ oz) curry leaves

350 g (12½ oz) sliced red onion

35 g (1¼ oz) finely chopped garlic

25 g (1 oz) finely chopped ginger

25 g (1 oz) finely chopped lemongrass, white part only

6 red bird's eye chillies, finely chopped

freshly ground white pepper

115 g (4 oz) Red curry powder (see page 43)

600 ml (20½ fl oz) coconut cream

5 x 5 cm (2 in) pieces pandan leaf

60 g (2 oz) tamarind concentrate

150 g (5½ oz) coriander (cilantro), well washed, leaves picked, stems and roots finely chopped

800 g (1 lb 12 oz) medium cleaned prawns (shrimp), peeled and deveined, tails intact (see note)

salt flakes

juice of 1–2 limes

Melt the ghee in a medium saucepan over a medium heat, add the curry leaves and cook, stirring, for a minute or so until the leaves are fried. Add the onion, garlic, ginger, lemongrass and chilli and cook, stirring occasionally, for 6–7 minutes until the onion has softened. Lightly season with pepper.

Add the curry powder and cook, stirring, for 1–2 minutes until it begins to catch on the bottom of the pan.

Add the coconut cream, pandan leaf, tamarind and 600 ml (20½ fl oz) water and stir well. Reduce the heat to low and gently simmer, stirring occasionally, for 10–12 minutes until the sauce has reduced and thickened. Stir in the coriander stem and root.

Allow your curry base to cool completely, then mix in the prawns. Transfer to an airtight container and place in the fridge overnight.

When you are ready to finish cooking the curry, remove it from the fridge – it will have thickened considerably. Scoop it into a medium saucepan and gradually bring to a simmer over a gentle heat, stirring every now and then.

Once the sauce starts to simmer, season to taste with salt and more pepper if needed. Cook the prawns until they are just cooked, about 9–12 minutes, depending on size. The curry will have quite a lot of thick sauce, very hot and sour, but you should be able to detect the sweetness of the prawns. Season to taste with a little lime juice before serving.

NOTE The way you prepare a prawn curry depends on how you like to eat your prawns. Do you like peeling the shells as you go, sucking on the heads, or do you prefer the convenience of eating a peeled prawn? This is entirely subjective and the ease of eating a peeled prawn can outweigh the messiness of peeling or the extra flavour a prawn head gives. There is also the option of removing the heads and cooking them in the sauce along with the bodies to have the best of both worlds. It's a matter of personal preference, so choose your favourite prawn and do it your way.

Pictured pages 268 & 276 →

# Fried egg curry

SERVES 6–8

There are many variations of boiled egg curries, all of which I love, but this one is based on a recipe that my mum makes only occasionally. The boiled eggs are rolled in turmeric and deep-fried before they go in the sauce. Preparing the eggs in this way gives them a slightly chewy, tofu-like skin, which works well with this rather robust sauce. It is a little more time-consuming to prepare, but very much worth it.

12 eggs, at room temperature

100 g (3½ oz) plain (all-purpose) flour

11 g (⅓ oz) turmeric powder

10 g (⅓ oz) cooking salt

vegetable oil, for deep-frying

40 g (1½ oz) coconut oil

7 g (¼ oz) mustard seeds

6 g (⅕ oz) curry leaves

200 g (7 oz) sliced red onion

40 g (1½ oz) finely chopped garlic

20 g (¾ oz) finely chopped ginger

20 g (¾ oz) finely chopped lemongrass, white part only

2 long red chillies, finely chopped

salt flakes and freshly ground black pepper

70 g (2½ oz) jaggery, chopped

20 g (¾ oz) Red curry powder (see page 43)

10 g (⅓ oz) chilli powder

400 ml (13½ fl oz) coconut cream

25 g (1 oz) tamarind concentrate

juice of 1–2 limes

**NOTE** When you boil the eggs for this recipe you need to make sure the yolk is firmly encased in the whites; any poking out will cause spitting when you try to fry them. The best way to ensure this is to use the freshest possible eggs and swirl them gently in the water when boiling.

Bring a large saucepan of water to a simmer, then gently lower the eggs into the water. Cook at a very low simmer for 9 minutes, stirring to create a little whirlpool a few times in the first couple of minutes (to help centre the yolks). Remove the eggs, cool in a bowl under running water and then peel. I find it helps to peel the eggs while they are submerged in water. Drain the peeled eggs on paper towel.

Mix together the flour, turmeric and cooking salt in a bowl. Wearing prep gloves if you want to avoid yellow hands, add each egg to the bowl and turn to coat quite heavily in the seasoned flour.

Pour vegetable oil into a large heavy-based saucepan to a depth of 4–6 cm (1½–2½ in) (the oil should come no more than two-thirds of the way up the pan). Place over a high heat and heat to 170°C (340°F). If you don't have a thermometer you can check by dipping in the tip of an egg; if it sizzles immediately, the oil is ready.

Working in small batches, fry the eggs for 3–4 minutes until they are a golden colour, gently swishing them around so they cook evenly. Lift them out with a slotted spoon and drain on a wire rack. Give the oil a moment to heat up again before you fry the next batch. Set the fried eggs aside.

Melt the coconut oil in a medium saucepan over a medium heat, add the curry leaves and mustard seeds and cook, stirring, for a minute or so until the curry leaves are fried and the seeds are aromatic. Add the onion, garlic, ginger, lemongrass and chilli and cook, stirring occasionally, for 6–7 minutes until the onion has softened. Lightly season with salt and pepper.

Add the jaggery and cook for 3–4 minutes until it has melted, darkened and caramelised. Add the curry powder and chilli powder and cook, stirring, for 1–2 minutes until the powders begin to catch on the bottom of the pan. Season again.

Stir in the coconut cream, tamarind and 250 ml (8½ fl oz) water, then add the fried eggs. Increase the heat and bring the sauce to the boil, then reduce to a very low simmer. Cook gently for 4–5 minutes until the sauce has thickened slightly and some fat has split out.

The curry sauce should be thick and look a bit oily, with a strong flavour that is fairly hot, tangy and a little sweet – a lovely foil to the creaminess of the boiled eggs. Season to taste with lime juice before serving.

**Pictured overleaf** →

**Fried egg curry →**

# Green mango curry

**SERVES 6–8**

You will need to source firm sour green mangoes for this recipe. Once cooked, they become almost fudgy, with an excellent stringy texture when you eat the flesh from the seeds. This version is based on a curry cooked for me by my friend Dinaseeka, who runs an eco-lodge in Sigiriya with her husband Wageesha. It uses black curry powder, lots of sugar and is extremely hot and sweet, with a background tang of tamarind and a burst of fresh lime at the forefront. There is an extra step at the end which, while not strictly necessary nor traditional, does make the texture of the mango even more fudgy, and the sauce more intense, succulent and sticky.

4 sour green mangoes

100 g (3½ oz) cooking salt

40 g (1½ oz) ghee

5 g (⅕ oz) curry leaves

300 g (10½ oz) eschalot, finely sliced

20 g (¾ oz) finely chopped garlic

15 g (½ oz) finely chopped ginger

15 g (½ oz) finely chopped lemongrass, white part only

2 long red chillies, finely chopped

salt flakes and freshly ground black pepper

30 g (1 oz) Black curry powder (see page 43)

20 g (¾ oz) chilli powder

6 g (⅕ oz) cardamom seeds

180 g (6½ oz) jaggery, chopped

14 g (½ oz) tamarind concentrate

juice of 1–2 limes

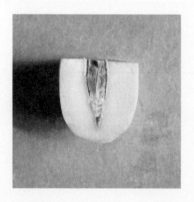

Peel the mangoes, then use a cleaver to chop each one in half lengthways and then in half widthways to give you four nice chunks. Chop straight through the seed as it stays in as you cook.

Mix together the cooking salt and 1 litre (36 fl oz) water in a bowl until dissolved, then add the mango pieces and leave to brine for about an hour.

Melt the ghee a wide-based saucepan large enough to hold all the mango over a medium heat, add the curry leaves and cook, stirring, for a minute or so until the leaves are fried. Add the eschalot, garlic, ginger, lemongrass and chilli and cook, stirring occasionally, for 4–5 minutes until the eschalot has softened. Lightly season with salt and pepper. Add the curry and chilli powders and the cardamom seeds and cook, stirring constantly, for 4–5 minutes until the chilli powder darkens considerably. Try not to breathe in too much of the spice. Add the jaggery and cook, stirring, for 2–3 minutes until melted and starting to caramelise.

Drain the mango pieces, add to the pan and stir well to coat. Stir in the tamarind and another 1 litre (36 fl oz) water. Bring to the boil, then reduce to a simmer and cook, stirring occasionally, for 12–14 minutes until the mango has softened and a nice sauce has developed. At this stage, you can season the curry with lime juice and serve if you like. For those who want to take that optional last step, read on.

Preheat the oven to 150°C (300°F) and line a baking tray with baking paper. Remove the mango pieces from the gravy and lay them all out, seed side down, on the tray. Season lightly with salt and pepper.

Bring the gravy back to the boil, then let it simmer for 18–20 minutes until it has reduced by half and thickened considerably. Remove from the heat. Using a pastry brush, brush the sauce over the mango pieces. Place in the oven and bake for 50–60 minutes, basting another four or five times during this time, leaving the remaining gravy in the pan. The outer layer of mango will start to form a sticky shell.

Transfer the baked mango pieces to a serving bowl. Reheat the gravy in the pan – there won't be a lot left but what is there will be rich, thick and glossy. Season well with lime juice then spoon the sauce over the mango pieces; you may have more sauce than is needed.

# Crab curry

SERVES 4–6

Crab curry was the first curry I learnt to make and has always been my favourite. For years I cooked it with a brown curry powder but recently I've been trying different versions, like the black one in this recipe. I usually use blue swimmer crabs as they have lovely sweet meat and I enjoy the battle you have to go through to get to their flesh. The rich, ample flesh of mud crabs is also good here, and will make it a more decadent dish. When we make this at Lankan Filling Station we prepare and cool the curry base the day before, then add the raw crabs and leave them to sit overnight. But by all means make it all in one go if preferred – it will still be delicious.

6 blue swimmer crabs (250–300 g (10½ oz) each) or 2–3 muddies, depending on their size (see note)

100 g (3½ oz) ghee

10 g (⅓ oz) curry leaves

500 g (1 lb 2 oz) diced red onion

70 g (2½ oz) finely chopped ginger

25 g (1 oz) finely chopped garlic

20 g (¾ oz) finely chopped lemongrass, white part only

5 red bird's eye chillies, finely chopped

salt flakes and freshly ground black pepper

40 g (1½ oz) Black curry powder (see page 43)

9 g (⅓ oz) chilli powder

60 g (2 oz) jaggery, chopped

2 x 5 cm (2 in) pieces pandan leaf

30 g (1 oz) tamarind concentrate

juice of 3–4 limes

NOTE The size of the crabs you use doesn't matter greatly as the sauce will be enough to take these variances into account. You may just need to adjust your cooking time.

First, prepare the crabs (do this over a bowl to collect the juices). Pull off and discard the top shell, making sure you keep any nice juicy bits from the top shell. Remove and discard the feathery gills. Cut the crabs in half from top to bottom, then place them in the fridge until needed, reserving the juices in the bowl.

If you are using mud crabs, you will need to put them in the freezer for about 45 minutes to induce insensibility, then, using a cleaver, quickly cut them straight through the middle. Follow the preparation method above, making an extra cut so the body of each crab is cut into quarters. Also, lightly crack the big claw with a pestle or the back of a knife.

Melt the ghee a large wide-based saucepan over a medium heat, add the curry leaves and cook, stirring, for a minute or so until the leaves are fried. Add the onion, ginger, garlic, lemongrass and chilli and cook, stirring occasionally, for 6–8 minutes until the onion has softened. Lightly season with salt and pepper.

Add the curry and chilli powders and cook, stirring, for 1–2 minutes until they begin to catch on the bottom of the pan. Add the jaggery and cook, stirring, for 4–5 minutes until melted and starting to caramelise.

Add the pandan leaf and 220 ml (7½ fl oz) water and bring to the boil. Stir in the tamarind, then reduce the heat to low and simmer gently for 8–10 minutes until it has reduced a little. Season with black pepper.

If you want to cook the crabs immediately, add them now, along with any reserved crab juices, and season generously with salt. Stir well, then cover and cook, stirring occasionally, for 15–20 minutes until the crabs are cooked through and have turned orange. Add an extra 8–10 minutes to the cooking time if you are using mud crabs. Season with more salt and lots of lime juice, then serve immediately.

If you want to rest the sauce overnight, take it off the heat after you've added the pepper and cool to room temperature. Stir in the reserved crab juices and leave to cool completely. Arrange the crabs in a single layer in a shallow container and pour over the cooled sauce, using a large spoon to spread it evenly through the crab. Cover and rest in the fridge overnight.

The next day, preheat the oven to 220°C (430°F). Remove the container from the fridge and bring the crabs and sauce to room temperature.

Transfer the curry to a baking dish large enough to fit the crab pieces in a single layer, season with salt and stir well to coat the crabs in the sauce. Place in the oven and bake for 6 minutes. Remove and give everything a stir, then bake for another 5–6 minutes until cooked through. Add an extra 6–8 minutes to the cooking time if you are using mud crabs. Season with more salt and lots of lime juice. The sauce should be a little thick, salty and very hot, with a nice sweetness to it and a good tang of sour lime. Serve immediately.

**Pictured page 279** →

# Chicken curry

**SERVES 6–8**

Chicken curry is very common as it's the one meat that every race and religion on the island can eat – at least those that eat meat. It's always better cooked on the bone as chicken is quite a delicate meat and needs all the extra flavour it can get. As a child it was one of the first curries I was willing to try, and my ~um's version is still the one I aspire to. This recipe is based ~hose memories: it's hot and oily, tangy with tomatoes and ~ly spiced with cardamom and cloves. Traditionally you ~ see any Sri Lankan curries cooked in the oven, but ~d works quite well.

~hop each chicken thigh across the bone into ~, depending on size. Set aside.

~ prepare the pounded rice mix, which will ~ck. Tip the rice into a small frying pan ~ow heat for 2–3 minutes until it just begins ~ a bowl and set aside to cool.

~t to the pan and toast, stirring constantly so it ~or 2–3 minutes until it is an even dark brown colour. ~ bowl with the rice.

~g a mortar and pestle, pound the rice, coconut, chilli, ~amom and cloves to a fine consistency. Add a splash of water ~ear the end to make a paste. Rub this mix through the chicken and let it sit in the fridge for an hour or so.

Combine the spice mix ingredients, massage into the chicken and set aside for another hour. You can do this the day before and leave it overnight in the fridge if preferred. If you are just leaving it for an hour, room temperature is fine.

Preheat the oven to 160°C (320°F).

Mix all the remaining ingredients through the chicken, making sure you season well with salt and pepper. Transfer to a shallow baking dish or casserole dish that is large enough to fit everything snugly in a single layer.

Cover closely with a layer of baking paper, then seal with foil or a lid, and place in the oven. Bake for 1 hour 20–30 minutes until the chicken is cooked through, checking it every half hour and giving it a good stir.

~bottom

stem, li~

1 pandan le~

200 ml (7 fl oz) ~eam

600 g (1 lb 5 oz) tin~d peeled tomatoes

salt flakes and freshly ground black pepper

## POUNDED RICE MIX

12 g (½ oz) rice (any variety)

8 g (¼ oz) grated coconut

2 green bird's eye chillies

3 cardamom pods

5 whole cloves

## SPICE MIX

24 g (⅞ oz) Red curry powder (see page 43)

8 g (¼ oz) fenugreek seeds

7 g (¼ oz) mustard seeds

4 g (⅛ oz) chilli flakes

4 g (⅛ oz) chilli powder

4 g (⅛ oz) sweet paprika

3 g (1/10 oz) salt flakes

# Pork belly curry

SERVES 6–8

This dish is straight thievery from my mother; the recipe is almost exactly as she showed me. It all came about because of a cazuela that she bought in Spain and made me carry around the world for months. Back home it became her favourite dish to cook in, and was the reason this slightly dry pork belly curry came to be cooked in the oven. This is a rich, very slow-cooked fatty curry; the pork belly is unctuous and meltingly tender with a little sauce that is hot and a touch sweet.

1 kg (2 lb 3 oz) piece pork belly, skin on, chilled

30 g (1 oz) coconut oil

340 g (12½ oz) diced red onion

2 long red chillies, finely chopped

20 cm (8 in) pandan leaf, tied into a knot

4 g (⅛ oz) curry leaves

30 g (1 oz) finely chopped garlic

20 g (¾ oz) finely chopped ginger

40 g (1½ oz) Red curry powder (see page 43)

14 cardamom pods, bruised

3 star anise

2 cinnamon quills

salt flakes and freshly ground black pepper

25 g (1 oz) tamarind concentrate

150 ml (5 fl oz) coconut cream

Preheat the oven to 150°C (300°F).

Cut the pork belly into 5 x 1.5 cm (2 x ½ in) slices and set aside. It is easier to do this when the meat is cold.

Melt the coconut oil in a large flameproof casserole dish or baking dish over a medium heat. Add the onion and cook for about 5 minutes, stirring occasionally. Add the chilli, pandan and curry leaves and continue cooking and stirring for another minute or so. Stir in the garlic and ginger, then turn up the heat before adding the curry powder and whole spices. Keep cooking until the spices darken and start to stick to the pan, about 3–4 minutes.

Add the pork and stir to coat and brown the meat for about 6–8 minutes. Season with salt and pepper.

Mix the tamarind and 450 ml (15 fl oz) water, then pour this into the dish with the pork and use a spoon to scrape the edges and the bottom of the pan. Add the coconut cream and bring to a simmer for about 5 minutes, then remove from heat, cover with lid or foil and place it in the oven to cook for 3 hours, removing it to stir a few times.

After 3 hours, turn the oven down to 110°C (230°F) and remove the lid or foil. By this stage, the gravy should be mostly dried out. Let the pork cook for a further 50–60 minutes uncovered, stirring once or twice. Once it's cooked the pork pieces will be looking nicely roasted, there will be little gravy left in the pan and the whole dish will have a lovely oiliness to it.

# Goat curry

**SERVES 4–6**

This is a dark curry made with a profusion of sweet spices and no coconut milk, so it's dry and a little oily rather than saucy. It works very nicely with pork, lamb or mutton, and one of my favourite versions of it was made with wild boar. Whichever meat you choose, I find shoulder is best, preferably with a nice amount of fat.

500 g (1 lb 2 oz) goat shoulder, cut into 2 cm (¾ in) dice, at room temperature

20 g (¾ oz) ghee

4 g (⅛ oz) curry leaves

60 g (2 oz) eschalot, finely sliced

salt flakes

bottom 6 cm (2½ in) of 1 lemongrass stem, lightly bruised

juice of 3–4 limes

**SPICE MIX**

3 g (⅒ oz) chilli powder

20 g (¾ oz) long red chillies, finely chopped

7 g (¼ oz) finely chopped garlic

5 g (⅕ oz) finely chopped ginger

6 g (⅕ oz) fenugreek seeds

11 g (⅓ oz) Black curry powder (see page 43)

**TEMPER**

3 g (⅒ oz) chilli powder

20 g (¾ oz) ghee

4 g (⅛ oz) curry leaves

60 g (2 oz) eschalot, finely sliced

3 g (⅒ oz) Black curry powder (see page 43)

2 g (1/16 oz) cardamom seeds

For this recipe you need to first toast the chilli powder used for both the spice mix and temper. Place it all in a small saucepan over low heat and toast for 4–5 minutes until dark but not burnt, keeping a very close eye on it as it can catch easily. This process is fraught with danger and will cause coughing if you breathe in too much of the spice. Set aside to cool before halving to add to the spice mix and temper.

Combine the spice mix ingredients, massage into the diced goat and set aside at room temperature for at least an hour. You can do this the day before and leave it overnight in the fridge if preferred – just make sure you take it out an hour before cooking so it returns to room temperature.

Preheat the oven to 220°C (430°F).

Melt the ghee in a large flameproof casserole dish or baking dish over a medium heat, add the curry leaves and cook, stirring, for a minute or so until the leaves are fried. Add the eschalot and cook, stirring occasionally, for 7–8 minutes until softened.

Add the goat meat, increase the heat to high and season well with salt. Cook, stirring, for 8–9 minutes until the meat becomes quite dark and almost fried. Throw in the piece of lemongrass about halfway through this cooking time. Cover with a lid or foil, then place in the oven and bake for 20 minutes.

Meanwhile, make the temper. Melt the ghee in a medium frying pan over a medium–high heat, add the curry leaves and cook, stirring, for a minute or so until the leaves are fried. Add the eschalot and cook, stirring occasionally, for 4–5 minutes until they start to caramelise. Add the curry and chilli powders and cardamom seeds and cook, stirring, for another 2 minutes. Set aside.

Take the dish out of the oven and reduce the heat to 200°C (390°F). Give the goat mixture a little stir, then return to the oven for another 20 minutes.

Take the curry out again and stir in the temper. Have a taste – it should be almost cooked by this stage. Cover and return to the oven for a final 10–15 minutes until the meat is dark and crusty but tender to the bite.

Remove the curry from the oven and season generously with lime juice and more salt. The flavour should be aromatic with sweet spice and quite hot, with a good tang of lime.

# Beef smore

SERVES 6–8

This Burgher dish was a revelation when my nan first cooked it for me. Based on the idea of a European pot roast, the meat is cooked in one large piece with the usual curry suspects, then sliced and served with the sauce spooned over the top. Technically it's not really a curry, but it is such an anomaly, it doesn't quite fit into any category. There is also a Malaysian beef smore dish, which is quite different, but also takes inspiration from European cooking methods. This is my nan's recipe (mostly).

1.5 kg (3 lb 6 oz) piece beef brisket or chuck, at room temperature (see note)

20 g (¾ oz) coconut oil, plus extra for rubbing

salt flakes and freshly ground black pepper

6 g (⅕ oz) curry leaves

200 g (7 oz) red onion, sliced

20 g (¾ oz) finely chopped garlic

15 g (½ oz) finely chopped ginger

35 g (1¼ oz) Black curry powder (see page 43)

16 g (½ oz) chilli powder

1½ pickled limes (see page 224), pulp removed, skin cut into medium fine dice

30 g (1 oz) grated coconut

12 g (½ oz) fine rice flour

30 g (1 oz) tomato paste (concentrated puree)

10 g (⅓ oz) caster (superfine) sugar

juice of 1–2 limes

Rub the beef with a little coconut oil and season well all over. Heat a saucepan large enough to hold the beef over a medium heat, then add the meat and sear on all sides until nicely browned. Remove from the pan and set aside. There should be some fat left behind, but also add the remaining 20 g (¾ oz) coconut oil.

Add the rest of the ingredients except the lime juice and cook, stirring, for 2 minutes. Pour in 750 ml (25½ fl oz) water and bring to a simmer, then reduce the heat to low.

Return the beef to the pan. Cover and cook gently for 3½–4 hours, until the meat is cooked through and very tender (see note), turning it every 30 minutes or so for even cooking. Remove the meat from the pan and set aside in a warm spot to rest for a good 20 minutes.

Turn up the heat under the cooking liquid and simmer until it has reduced to the consistency of a thick gravy. This should take about 10 minutes. Season to taste with lime juice – you're looking for a nice spicy flavour with a hint of sweetness and a noticeable sharpness from the pickled limes.

Cut the rested beef into 1 cm (½ in) thick slices and arrange on a platter. Spoon the gravy over the top and serve.

NOTE Both cuts of meat work well here; it basically comes down to how fatty you like your meat. I always go for the brisket as I prefer a fatty cut. The cooking time will vary, depending on the shape and cut of the meat you choose, but you want the end result to be tender, unctuous and starting to give way.

පරිප්පු, මැල්ලුම් සහ එළවළු

# All the Side Bits: Dhal, Mallungs & Vegetables

ஏனைய பக்க உணவுகள்

*No man is an island,
entire of itself; every man
is a piece of the Continent,
a part of the main*

John Donne

This section covers other essential cooked dishes that are not classified as curries. They are all designed to be eaten alongside a rice and curry meal and, like the curries, most of them focus on one main ingredient (mainly vegetables). Some are saucy, some dry, some are made to be eaten hot, but most are happy at room temperature.

The most essential side dish is dhal (see page 186), also referred to as a dhal curry, which falls into the yellow curry category (see page 139). With its various spellings, dal/daal/dhal/dahl is a term used to describe dried split pulses, a large category which in this case usually means lentils, peas and beans. However, the word has also become synonymous with the dish of the same name.

In India, the types of dhal vary from region to region as different types of pulses are used; some hold their shape despite long cooking, while others break down more readily. In Sri Lanka there is a fairly standard red lentil version found throughout the island. Within this, of course, there are variations: you can cook it with chilli; you can make it thicker or thinner, usually depending on the other dishes it is being served with; very occasionally the recipe will include a vegetable, perhaps a green leaf; others have a temper stirred through at the end for extra flavour; and sometimes fried onion is added for texture. However it's cooked, you will find a dhal included in almost every rice and curry meal.

A mallung (or mallum; see pages 188–9) is a lightly cooked dish, almost like a Sri Lankan version of a salad, offering a clean, refreshing counterpoint to a rich curry. The word means 'to mix up' and the dish is generally a shredded green leafy vegetable mixed with grated coconut, often turmeric but not too many other spices, and sometimes Maldive fish. The dish is briefly cooked without added fat and seasoned with pepper, lime and sometimes chilli. Mallungs often feature native greens that are not easily sourced elsewhere, such as passionfruit leaves, murunga leaves, or the leaves and flowers of kathurumurunga (the hummingbird tree). These flowers are also used in Thai cooking. Like salad, mallung is a very broad term and can accommodate many more variations than I have just described here. Although not strictly traditional, at Lankan Filling Station we include wok-fried vegetable dishes cooked in ghee or coconut oil in this category; you'll find a few of the recipes in this chapter.

There are other terms that refer more to a cooking style, and not just for vegetables, that fit here too; for example, a thel dala (sometimes called a devilled dish; see page 57), which means a dry-fried dish. Things get a little hazy here as these terms are sometimes interchangeable with certain dishes, but can also veer off in completely different directions. Just to add to the confusion, Sri Lankan potato thel dala is strikingly similar to a South Indian masala potato dish, but at least this hints at the origins of this cooking method. Have a look at the recipe for the potato pan roll filling on page 76 for an example of this.

The terms pahi and moju generally refer to a way of cooking eggplant (although I have found recipes for pork moju), both creating a slight pickled flavour. Inevitable exceptions and variations aside, they are side dishes, often fried and made without coconut milk, with a chilli heat and distinct vinegary sourness. The mustard eggplant from the Lamprais recipe on page 130 is an example of this, and the eggplant recipe on page 202 also fits into this category, but is less traditional.

Finally, there are the dishes that are simply referred to as a vegetable, such as the snake bean dish on page 200. If I was served this as part of my meal and asked what it is, I would be told it is a snake bean vegetable. Not a curry, not a mallung, not a thel dala; simply a vegetable. It makes sense really, no?

# Dhal

SERVES 4–6

A good dhal is a thing of beauty and comfort. Cheap, nutritious and simple to make, it appears as a side to most meals, though really a bowl of rice and dhal on its own is enough to warm the heart and fill the belly. You can add a temper at the end to fancy it up a bit, or make it wetter or drier to suit your purposes. This dhal is based on the recipe my mum taught me. Creamy, mild and very savoury, this is exactly the way we cook it at Lankan Filling Station.

75 g (2¾ oz) coconut oil

5 g (⅕ oz) curry leaves

550 g (1 lb 3 oz) brown onions, cut into medium dice

18 g (⅔ oz) finely chopped garlic

15 g (½ oz) finely chopped ginger

salt flakes and freshly ground black pepper

7 g (¼ oz) black mustard seeds

5 g (⅕ oz) turmeric powder

1 cinnamon quill

4 x 5 cm (2 in) pieces pandan leaf

bottom 5 cm (2 in) of 1 lemongrass stem, lightly bruised

525 g (1 lb 3 oz) red lentils, thoroughly washed

450 ml (15 fl oz) coconut cream

Melt the coconut oil in a medium saucepan over a medium heat, add the curry leaves and cook, stirring, for a minute or so until the leaves are fried. Add the onion, garlic and ginger and cook, stirring occasionally, for 6–7 minutes until the onion has softened. Lightly season with salt and pepper.

Add the mustard seeds, turmeric and cinnamon and cook, stirring, for 1–2 minutes until the turmeric begins to catch on the bottom of the pan.

Add the pandan leaf, lemongrass and lentils and give everything a good stir to combine. Pour in the coconut cream and 1 litre (36 fl oz) water and mix well, then reduce the heat to low and simmer gently for 10–15 minutes, stirring occasionally. The dhal is ready when all the lentils have just given away and turned yellow, while still retaining a little texture. Re-season with salt and pepper and serve hot.

# Mallungs

**EACH SERVES 4**

There are so many types of mallung it would be impossible to cover them all. Here are a few very different versions to give you the idea.

## Cabbage mallung

This is one of the simplest dishes on the menu at Lankan Filling Station and a surprising favourite with our customers, many of whom don't usually like cabbage. I have a special fondness for this vegetable, and this is a great way to use it. The ingredients are traditional but the way it's cooked is not; the ghee and wok cooking give it a richness and smokiness you wouldn't find in a more conventional mallung.

30 g (1 oz) ghee

14 g (½ oz) black mustard seeds

6 g (⅕ oz) curry leaves

300 g (10½ oz) white cabbage, finely sliced

salt flakes and freshly ground black pepper

4 g (⅛ oz) turmeric powder

50 g (1¾ oz) grated coconut

Melt the ghee in a wok or wide-based frying pan over a high heat, add the mustard seeds and curry leaves and cook for a minute or so until the seeds start to pop and the leaves are fried.

Add the cabbage, season generously with salt and pepper and give everything a good mix. Cook, stirring, for 1–2 minutes, then add the turmeric and cook for another minute. While you need to keep the cabbage moving in the high heat of the wok, allow for some moments of stillness to encourage a little char.

Add the coconut and taste again for seasoning, then cook for another 2–3 minutes until the cabbage has wilted but still has a little crunch. This dish will be dry, the flavour a little buttery with hints of smoky char, rounded out by the soft sweetness of the coconut. Serve hot or at room temperature.

Pictured overleaf →

## Green papaya mallung

This is a more traditional mallung recipe as it doesn't use any fat and is much gentler in flavour. Light yet still with a chilli kick, it works well as a foil for strongly flavoured curries, adding crunch and contrast. It's the quintessential quiet achiever: on its own it doesn't stand out, but as part of a group it plays an important role.

260 g (9 oz) green papaya, julienned and washed under cold water

75 g (2¾ oz) eschalot, finely sliced

2 long green chillies, finely chopped

3 g (⅒ oz) freshly ground black pepper

3 g (⅒ oz) turmeric powder

130 g (4½ oz) grated coconut

salt flakes

juice of 1–2 limes

Combine the papaya, eschalot, chilli, pepper, turmeric and 70 ml (2¼ fl oz) water in a medium wide-based saucepan over a medium heat and cook, stirring occasionally, for 2–3 minutes until the papaya has started to soften.

Stir in the coconut, season to taste with salt and cook for another minute or so until the papaya is soft but still has a little crunch to it.

Remove from the heat and squeeze in some lime juice. The mix should be quite dry with a distinct heat from the chilli and pepper. Serve at room temperature.

Pictured page 272 →

# Cavolo nero mallung

This is another less traditional version but the flavour of this dark green leaf works really well with curries. It's tough, sturdy and extremely good for you, with an earthiness that provides a wonderful platform for the pops of spice and mild chilli heat.

40 g (1½ oz) ghee

4 g (⅛ oz) coriander seeds

3 g (1/10 oz) cumin seeds

100 g (3½ oz) brown onion, cut into medium dice

300 g (10½ oz) shredded cavolo nero leaves

6 g (⅕ oz) turmeric powder

3 g (1/10 oz) chilli flakes

75 g (2¾ oz) grated coconut

salt flakes and freshly ground black pepper

Melt the ghee in a wide-based saucepan over a medium heat, add the coriander seeds and cumin seeds and cook, stirring, for a minute or so until they start to darken. Add the onion and cook, stirring, for 2–3 minutes until it begins to soften.

Add the cavolo leaves and give everything a good mix, then cook, stirring, for another 2–3 minutes. Add the turmeric and chilli and cook for another minute before adding the coconut.

Season with salt and pepper and cook for another few minutes, stirring to make sure the mix doesn't stick to the bottom of the pan. It's ready when the cavolo nero is soft but still has a bit of bite. Serve hot or at room temperature.

**Pictured page 275** →

# Leek mallung

This gently cooked mallung is similar in flavour to a European buttered leek dish and looks like it should be quite mild, but it has a surprise heat from the green chilli.

400 g (14 oz) whole leek

40 g (1½ oz) ghee

6 g (⅕ oz) mustard seeds

4 g (⅛ oz) coriander seeds

6 g (⅕ oz) curry leaves

3 green bird's eye chillies, finely chopped

salt flakes and freshly ground black pepper

3 g (1/10 oz) chilli powder

2 g (1/16 oz) turmeric powder

60 g (2 oz) grated coconut

juice of 1 lime

Cut the leek in half lengthways and finely slice into half-moons until just after you hit the green part. Wash well in water and set aside to drain in a colander. It's good for the leek to still be a little wet when you add it to the pan.

Melt the ghee in a wide-based saucepan over a medium heat, add the mustard seeds and coriander seeds and cook, stirring, for a minute or so until the mustard seeds start to pop. Add the curry leaves and green chilli and cook, stirring, for a minute or so.

Add the leek and season well, then cook, stirring occasionally, for 3–4 minutes until softened. Stir in the chilli powder and turmeric, then add the coconut and cook, stirring, for another minute or two.

Remove from the heat, squeeze in a little lime juice and season well with salt and pepper. Serve hot or at room temperature.

**Pictured page 278** →

↑ Cabbage mallung

# Water spinach

SERVES 2–4

Water spinach (kangkung) is a popular ingredient in many southeast Asian cuisines, often simply stir-fried with garlic. This recipe has a little more to it and is based on a dish introduced to me by Dinaseeka, she of the green mango curry (see page 168). The spinach is cooked until soft and yielding, with a strong, savoury sauce redolent of Maldive fish and chilli. I always feel extra healthy when I eat this dish. This makes a smaller serve than most of the other dishes but only because if you are cooking in a wok you won't be able to fit much more in. If you want to double the quantities, go right ahead – you'll just need to cook it in a large saucepan instead.

30 g (1 oz) ghee

80 g (2¾ oz) red onion, cut in half and then across the grain into medium slices

1 long green chilli, cut into thin rounds

100 g (3½ oz) green tomato, quartered and cut into medium slices

22 g (⅞ oz) Maldive fish flakes

salt flakes and freshly ground black pepper

200 g (7 oz) water spinach (see note)

3 g (1/10 oz) turmeric powder

3 g (1/10 oz) chilli flakes

Melt the ghee in a wok or a wide-based frying pan over a low heat, add the onion, chilli, tomato and Maldive fish, season well and cook, stirring gently, for 2–3 minutes until the dried fish and onion have softened.

Increase the heat to high and stir in the water spinach. Add the turmeric and chilli flakes and cook for another 1–2 minutes. Add 100 ml (3½ fl oz) water and check the seasoning. This dish will take a lot of salt – taste a piece of the spinach as well as the liquid to get a better idea of flavour.

Cook, stirring, for another 2–3 minutes until the water spinach is soft and you are happy with the flavour. Remove from the heat. You want to have a nice puddle of sauce so add a splash more water if needed and toss through. Serve hot.

NOTE If water spinach is unavailable most other leafy greens can be used instead. At LFS this dish has been cooked with various greens, including combinations of warrigal greens, saltbush, pumpkin tendrils and cavolo nero.

# Carrot

SERVES 4–6

Carrots are another vegetable I wouldn't really associate with a tropical island but they have been cultivated in Asia for many centuries, so who am I to question? I have eaten carrot sambols in Sri Lanka but never came across this dish. I discovered it in written form on my hunt for recipes and liked the sound of the flavours. So here is my version.

20 g (¾ oz) coconut oil

3 g (¹⁄₁₀ oz) fennel seeds

6 g (⅕ oz) curry leaves

18 g (⅔ oz) finely chopped garlic

12 g (½ oz) finely chopped ginger

100 g (3½ oz) eschalot, finely sliced

400 g (14 oz) peeled carrot, cut into large matchsticks

40 g (1½ oz) grated coconut

salt flakes and freshly ground black pepper

3 g (¹⁄₁₀ oz) turmeric powder

2 g (¹⁄₁₆ oz) chilli flakes

1 g (¹⁄₃₂ oz) ground star anise

coconut vinegar (see page 28), to season

Melt the coconut oil in a wok or large frying pan over a medium heat, add the fennel seeds and cook for a minute until they start to change colour. Add the curry leaves and cook briefly to crisp up, then add the garlic, ginger and eschalot. Cook, stirring, for 2–3 minutes until the eschalot starts to soften.

Add the carrot and coconut and give everything a good stir. Season with salt and pepper and cook, stirring occasionally, for 2–3 minutes.

Stir in the spices and season to taste with a splash of vinegar. Cook for another 2–3 minutes until the carrot is tender but still has a little crunch and holds its shape. Taste and check the seasoning – there should be a slight tang from the vinegar, a little chilli heat, with the star anise at the forefront. Serve hot or at room temperature.

# Pineapple

SERVES 6–8

I know the question of whether pineapple should be cooked can be very divisive, but I am firmly in the yes camp. As are our Sri Lankan friends, who use this fruit in curries and chutneys. This dish sits somewhere in between: the spice, mustard and chilli flavours are similar to those in a curry, but the pineapple is cooked without coconut milk, giving a drier result. It's an excellent side dish – sweet, hot and tangy.

1 small pineapple (approximately 750 g/1 lb 11 oz; see note)

45 g (1½ oz) coconut oil

15 g (½ oz) mustard seeds

10 g (⅓ oz) fennel seeds

5 g (⅕ oz) curry leaves

160 g (5½ oz) eschalot, finely sliced

15 g (½ oz) jaggery, chopped

4 g (⅛ oz) chilli powder

2 g (1/16 oz) ground star anise

salt flakes and freshly ground black pepper

70 g (2½ oz) Sri Lankan mustard (see page 31)

To prepare your pineapple, start by taking all the skin off. Make sure you do this carefully, maintaining its natural curves so it doesn't start to look like a square. If you are feeling clever, use a paring knife on an angle to cut out the eyes, which will leave you with a lovely angled pattern and beautifully shaped pineapple. Otherwise, remove the eyes by simply cutting off the skin in a thicker layer; it will just mean more wastage.

Cut the pineapple crossways into 1.5 cm (½ in) thick rounds, then halve each round and cut each half into 6 even triangles. Don't worry about cutting out the core. Set aside.

Melt the coconut oil in a wide-based saucepan over a medium heat, add the mustard seeds and fennel seeds and cook, stirring, for 1–2 minutes until they begin to colour and pop. Add the curry leaves and cook briefly, then add the eschalot and cook, stirring occasionally, for 6–7 minutes until softened.

Add the jaggery and cook, stirring, for 2–3 minutes until it melts and starts to caramelise. Stir in the ground spices, then add the pineapple pieces and season with salt and pepper. Cook, stirring occasionally, for 10–15 minutes until the pineapple is nicely tender but still holding its shape.

Stir in the mustard, then give it few moments to warm through. Depending how juicy your pineapple is you may need to add a little splash of water to make sure everything is nicely coated. Serve just warm or at room temperature.

NOTE Look for pineapple that is ripe, but only just. If it's too ripe the flavour can be overly sweet and fermenty, and will also mess with the texture of the dish.

# Beetroot

SERVES 4–6

Although beetroot is often used in traditional Sri Lankan vegetable dishes and curries, this side dish is not one of them. It is actually based on a Stephanie Alexander recipe from *The Cook's Companion,* which I have adapted to include some Sri Lankan flavours. Laden with vinegar, yet buttery and earthy, it expertly cuts through the heat and richness of curries.

60 g (2 oz) ghee

5 g (⅕ oz) mustard seeds

4 g (⅛ oz) curry leaves

400 g (14 oz) beetroot, grated on the largest holes of a grater

salt flakes and freshly ground black pepper

3 g (¹⁄₁₀ oz) chilli flakes

50 ml (1¾ fl oz) coconut vinegar (see page 28)

Melt the ghee in a wide-based saucepan over a medium heat, add the mustard seeds and cook, stirring, for a minute until they start to pop. Add the curry leaves and cook briefly to crisp up.

Add the beetroot and stir to thoroughly coat it in the ghee. Season generously with salt and pepper and stir in the chilli flakes. Cook, stirring occasionally, for 4–5 minutes until the beetroot starts to soften. Pour in the vinegar and cook, stirring, for another 3–4 minutes.

Taste and check the seasoning. The beetroot should still have a hint of crunch to it, with a small puddle of deep red liquid in the base. This is best eaten warm but it will still taste good served cold or hot. I like to eat it on toast.

# Snake bean

SERVES 4

Snake beans are used all over southeast Asia, and in Sri Lanka they're often cooked in a curry, the soft beans soaking up the flavours of the gravy. This dish is from the restaurant and could almost be considered a curry. Maldive fish is usually added as a background seasoning but here it's just as important as the beans, bringing both flavour and texture to the dish.

| |
|---|
| 80 g (2¾ oz) ghee |
| 300 g (10½ oz) sliced brown onion |
| 10 g (⅓ oz) cumin seeds |
| salt flakes and freshly ground white pepper |
| 65 g (2¼ oz) Maldive fish flakes |
| 500 g (1 lb 2 oz) snake beans, cut into 5 cm (2 in) lengths |
| 8 g (¼ oz) turmeric powder |
| 350 ml (12 fl oz) coconut cream |

Melt the ghee in a medium saucepan over a medium–low heat, add the onion and cumin seeds and season with a little salt and pepper. Cook, stirring occasionally, for 4–5 minutes until the onion has softened but hasn't coloured. Add the Maldive fish and cook, stirring occasionally, for another minute or so until it starts to soften.

Add the snake beans and turmeric and give everything a good stir. Cook for another minute or so to coat, stirring to make sure the turmeric doesn't stick to the bottom of the pan.

Pour in the coconut cream and 350 ml (12 fl oz) water and simmer gently for 10–12 minutes until the beans have softened but still hold their shape. Season as you go; this dish will take quite a lot of salt.

To test if it's ready, taste a bean: you're looking for the moment the beans go from being relatively tasteless to suddenly soft, unctuous and flavourful, and the sauce has thickened. Serve hot or warm.

NOTE If snake beans are unavailable you can use long green beans, but they won't soak up the sauce quite as well. Also, keep an eye on how they're cooking; with these beans there's a very fine line between tender and too mushy.

# Eggplant

SERVES 4

**Eggplant is native to India and Sri Lanka and has always been popular in curries and side dishes. This recipe is based on one my mum cooks; it loosely fits the definition of a pahi (a sweet and sour pickled dish) but after the long cooking time it morphs into a darker, oilier, saucier dish than the traditional version.**

700 g (1 lb 9 oz) eggplants (aubergines)

13 g (½ oz) turmeric powder

4 g (⅛ oz) cooking salt

25 g (1 oz) coconut oil

8 g (¼ oz) coriander seeds

8 g (¼ oz) mustard seeds

5 g (⅕ oz) curry leaves

300 g (10½ oz) finely sliced red onion

50 g (1¾ oz) finely chopped garlic

30 g (1 oz) finely chopped ginger

2 long red chillies, sliced into thin rounds

salt flakes and freshly ground black pepper

30 g (1 oz) jaggery, finely chopped

350 g (12½ oz) ripe tomatoes, quartered or chopped into 4 cm (1½ in) dice

7 g (¼ oz) chilli flakes

14 g (½ oz) tamarind concentrate

vegetable oil, for deep-frying

Cut the tops off your eggplants, slice them down the middle and then cut each half into angular chunks about 8–10 cm (3¼–4 in) long and 3 cm (1¼ in) at the widest point, making sure each piece has some skin on it. Don't get too caught up in exact measurements; the pieces just need to be big enough to retain their shape and hold up in the sauce. I suggest angular pieces because when fried, the pointy bits add to the overall texture of the dish.

Place the eggplant chunks in a mixing bowl and sprinkle over the turmeric and cooking salt. Put on a pair of prep gloves to prevent staining, then give it all a good mix to make sure all the eggplant pieces are evenly coated. (My mum's trick is to combine the salt and turmeric in a plastic bag and add a few eggplant pieces at a time, shaking every batch.) Once coated, place the eggplant pieces in a colander and set aside for at least 30 minutes.

While the eggplants are soaking up the spice, start your sauce.

Melt the coconut oil in a wide-based saucepan over a medium heat, add the coriander seeds and mustard seeds and cook, stirring, for a minute until they start to pop. Add the curry leaves and cook briefly to crisp up.

Add the onion, garlic, ginger and chilli, season with salt and pepper and cook, stirring occasionally, for 8–10 minutes until the onion has softened. Add the jaggery, increase the heat a little and cook, stirring occasionally, for 5–6 minutes until melted and slightly caramelised. Add the tomato, chilli flakes and tamarind and stir well, then reduce the heat to medium and simmer gently for 5 minutes until the tomato pieces just start to break down. Add 180 ml (6 fl oz) water and cook for another 5 minutes until the sauce is rich and thick. Taste and check your seasoning.

Pour vegetable oil into a large heavy-based saucepan to a depth of 4–6 cm (1½–2½ in) (the oil should come no more than two-thirds of the way up the pan). Place over a high heat and heat to 180°C (350°F). If you don't have a thermometer you can check by dipping a little bit of eggplant into the oil; if it sizzles immediately, the oil is ready. Add the eggplant pieces in small batches and swish them around so they cook evenly. You need to fry each batch for longer than you think as you want them really dark, almost black, and nearly dried out; 8–9 minutes should do it. Lift them out and drain on a wire rack. Give the oil a moment to heat up again before you fry the next batch. Give the last batch at least 5 minutes to rest on the rack.

Add the fried eggplant to the sauce and carefully mix it through. Heat gently over a very low heat for 5 minutes. The flavour should be tangy and sour with a good hit of heat, the dark bitter crust of the eggplant giving way to an unctuous centre when you bite into it.

This dish is best eaten slightly warm or just hot. Taste before serving as you may need to season it with a little more salt.

# Sprats

SERVES 4–6

This dish is a thel dala and is an excellent addition to a rice and curry spread. My mum cooks it a lot; she told me her recipe over the phone one day, obviously without proper measurements, so this is my take on it. It's also extremely good in a sandwich made with soft white supermarket bread and lots of butter, or, better still, in a jaffle. It's sticky, crunchy, hot, tangy, a little bit sweet and incredibly moreish.

vegetable oil, for deep-frying

300 g (10½ oz) dried sprats (see note)

40 g (1½ oz) coconut oil

6 g (⅕ oz) curry leaves

300 g (10½ oz) sliced red onion

20 g (¾ oz) finely chopped garlic

15 g (½ oz) finely chopped ginger

1 long red chilli, finely chopped

salt flakes and freshly ground black pepper

8 g (¼ oz) chilli powder

4 g (⅛ oz) sweet paprika

30 g (1 oz) jaggery, chopped

300 g (10½ oz) roma (plum) tomatoes, cut into rough 2 cm (¾ in) chunks

7 g (¼ oz) tamarind concentrate

Pour vegetable oil into a large heavy-based saucepan to a depth of 4–6 cm (1½–2½ in) (the oil should come no more than two-thirds of the way up the pan). Place over a high heat and heat to 160°C (320°F). If you don't have a thermometer you can check by dropping a sprat into the oil; if it sizzles immediately and pops straight up to the top, the oil is ready.

Add the sprats in small batches and fry for 3–4 minutes until they crisp up and turn a dark shade of brown. Lift them out with a slotted spoon and drain on a wire rack. Give the oil a moment to heat up again before you fry the next batch. Once cooled, make sure they are very crisp; if not, fry them for a little longer and drain again.

Melt the coconut oil in a large frying pan over a high heat, add the curry leaves and cook, stirring, for a minute or so until the leaves are fried. Add the onion, garlic, ginger and chilli, season with a little salt and pepper and cook, stirring regularly, for 7–8 minutes until the onion is soft and starting to caramelise.

Add the chilli powder and paprika and cook, stirring, for 1–2 minutes until they begin to catch on the bottom of the pan. Add the jaggery and cook, stirring, for another minute until melted.

Add the tomato and tamarind and mix well. Reduce the heat to medium and simmer for 5–6 minutes until the tomato pieces just start to break down. Stir in the fried sprats, then increase the heat to high and cook, stirring occasionally, for a final 2 minutes. Season generously with more pepper and taste to see if you need any more salt. Serve hot or at room temperature.

**NOTE** Dried sprats can be found at most Asian grocers; just be aware that the quality will vary, and some will taste stronger and more fishy than others. Sprats are a type of fish but the word is also applied to any small oily fish in the herring family, such as sardines and anchovies, which can be used as a substitute.

සම්බෝල වැනි දේවල

# Sambols
# &
# Such Like

சம்பலும் சம்பல் போன்றவையும்

This is an important chapter as it covers the interesting and exciting little extra bits that add flavour, spice and texture to a meal. Some are extremely hot, others have a cooling effect, and some are almost salad like. In the same way that we wouldn't cook a meal without using salt and pepper, a Sri Lankan meal would never be served without at least one or two of these delights.

Let's start by talking about what a sambol actually is. In fact, the common definition of 'sambal' (Sri Lankans are the only ones who spell it with an 'o' instead of an 'a') is a chilli-based condiment found in southern Indian, Malaysian and Indonesian cookery. It doesn't mention Sri Lanka at all, or come close to covering the many Lankan dishes the word sambol is applied to. A condiment is an easy descriptor but it still doesn't feel like enough. In terms of origin, while the name and some characteristics are shared, it seems Sri Lankan sambols are in a category of their own.

In Sri Lanka, the term covers a wide range of recipes: a simple chilli relish, such as katta sambol (see page 222); an array of fresh coconut-based sides, others cooked, almost like a relish; pickled things; and some even more salad-like in preparation. Pol and seeni are two of the more common ones and give a good indication of how varied they can be. Pol sambol (see page 214) is coconut-based, usually quite hot, made with Maldive fish and a perfect blend of Lankan flavours, fresh and tangy with lime. Seeni sambol (see page 228) is completely different: caramelised onion fragrant with curry leaves, ginger and garlic, soured with tamarind. What they have in common is chilli heat and savoury notes of Maldive fish, but apart from that they are two very different preparations. If you were to make all the sambols in this book you'd have an even clearer idea of the range. So, you see, one word, many things.

Just like in India, there is also a whole world of fruit chutneys: green mango, date and tamarind, all usually sweet, but still scented with spice and chilli. Chutneys, like pickles, were originally a means of preservation and, with the abundance of tropical fruit found on the island, the variations are profuse and necessary. (I apologise in advance if chutneys are your thing as you will only find one recipe here, on page 234, but they are still on my list of things to explore.) You will also find a couple of acharu recipes (see page 230), which are more pickle like than the simple versions of fruit and chilli powder we spoke of in the street food chapter (see page 58).

A friendly word of warning about the salady versions of sambol. If you are in Sri Lanka, eating a spread of rice and curry and your mouth is burning from heat, you may spy a cucumber sambol (see page 218) and imagine sweet relief. Be careful: there is every chance it will be as hot as Hades, and cause your mouth to burn even more.

While there are a lot of accepted influences in Sri Lankan food, what is less talked about and a little more speculative is what I see as similarities between this island's food and that of Thailand. The history of Buddhism and the folk stories that go with it are shared by these two countries, and there is in fact a long documented history of Buddhist monks travelling between them, teaching and learning from each other.

This connection can be detected in both the flavour and the make-up of the food. As with many Asian cuisines, they share the idea that a meal is made up of an array of dishes, balancing flavour, texture, heat and spice levels, with a mind to healthfulness: sweet (Sri Lankan jaggery and Thai palm sugar); sour (both cultures use tamarind and lime to season); fresh (an abundance of coconut, bitter greens and lightly cooked ingredients); umami (Maldive fish is used in much the same way as fish sauce in Thai cooking); and hot (they both started using pepper but quickly and easily integrated fresh chillies to give a searing heat). The taste of many of the sambols illustrate these shared flavour profiles.

# Pol sambol

SERVES 8–10

**Meaning coconut sambol, this is the most ubiquitous sambol in Sri Lanka. During any given day on the island you would be hard pressed to not eat a version of it at some stage. It's the first sambol my mum taught me to make. The flavour is perfectly balanced: sweet from the coconut, smoky and umami from the Maldive fish, hot from the chilli and pepper, and sour from the lime. This recipe makes more than you need for an average meal (about 450 g/1 lb) but it will keep for a good week in the fridge and is delicious on many things. I like it on toast with butter, particularly if there is a poached egg involved.**

300 g (10½ oz) grated coconut

100 g (3½ oz) eschalot, finely sliced

3 small green chillies, finely chopped

20 g (¾ oz) Maldive fish flakes, ground

5 g (⅕ oz) chilli powder

3 g (¹⁄₁₀ oz) freshly ground black pepper

3 g (¹⁄₁₀ oz) sweet paprika

juice of 1–2 limes

salt flakes

Place all the ingredients, apart from the lime juice and salt, in a bowl and firmly mix them together with one hand, using a squeezing and kneading motion. This not only combines the ingredients, it also helps release the oils from the coconut. Keep going until the texture of the sambol is almost a little sticky.

Season to taste with lime juice and a generous amount of salt, mixing and squeezing again. Serve at room temperature.

# Green pol sambol

SERVES 8–10

The origin of this sambol is south Indian, although this recipe is the one we use at Lankan Filling Station and is definitely my take on it. It's zesty, fresh and coconutty with just a hint of heat, and makes excellent use of coriander leaf, which is sometimes overlooked in Sri Lankan food. It makes about 400 g (14 oz) but will keep in the fridge for four days or so. You may find that it loses a little colour and zest over time, but you can freshen it up with a splash of extra lime juice.

100 g (3½ oz) diced green tomato

95 g (3¼ oz) coriander (cilantro) leaves and stems, finely chopped

45 g (1½ oz) eschalot, finely sliced

4 g (⅛ oz) finely chopped ginger

3 g (1/10 oz) finely sliced garlic

1 long green chilli, cut into thin rounds

salt flakes and freshly ground white pepper

200 g (7 oz) grated coconut

grated zest and juice of 1 lime

Using a mortar and pestle, pound the tomato, coriander, eschalot, ginger, garlic and chilli to a fine, juicy paste. Add a little salt here to help things along. You may need to do this in batches, depending on the size of your mortar.

Transfer the paste to a bowl and mix with the coconut and lime zest. Return to the mortar, in batches if necessary, and pound to a uniform green paste.

Season with lime juice, a generous amount of white pepper and salt to taste. Serve at room temperature.

# Cucumber raita

SERVES 6–8

Firmly Indian in origin, raita is actually a term that covers a wide range of condiments using vegetables, fruits and sometimes even pulses. What they all have in common is their role as a cooling accompaniment to a curry. This version is very simple, which I generally prefer as there is usually so much going on in a curry meal that it's a relief to have something gentle to cool the palate and balance the flavours. This also makes quite a lot (about 450 g/1 lb) but it will keep in the fridge for up to a week.

1 medium telegraph (long) cucumber

7 g (¼ oz) salt flakes

4 g (⅛ oz) cumin seeds

300 g (10½ oz) thick Greek yoghurt

Using the second finest grade on a box grater, grate the cucumber, skin and all, into a bowl. Add the salt and mix through. Transfer the cucumber mix to a fine strainer and leave to drain over a bowl for at least an hour.

Meanwhile, place the cumin seeds in a small frying pan over a medium heat and toast, stirring, for 1–2 minutes until fragrant. Tip into a bowl and allow to cool, then grind to a coarse powder.

Transfer the drained cucumber to a bowl and mix through the yoghurt and cumin. Serve cold.

# Cucumber sambol

**SERVES 4–6**

1 telegraph (long) cucumber

2 small green tomatoes

100 g (3½ oz) eschalot, finely sliced

3 green bird's eye chillies,
finely chopped

salt flakes and freshly ground
black pepper

juice of 1–2 limes

**This is my version of a super-simple sambol that is crisp and refreshing and makes an excellent accompaniment to curries. But don't be fooled – like many things in Sri Lanka, it's also laden with chilli. Instead of the more traditional red tomatoes, I use green ones as I like the extra tang and crunch they bring, but if red is all you have, don't let that stop you. It will be just as delicious.**

Peel the cucumber, cut it in half lengthways and scrape out the seeds. Cut the cucumber halves into 3 mm (⅛ in) thick half-moons and place in a bowl.

Cut the green tomatoes into a small (about 1 cm/½ in) dice and add to the bowl with the cucumber.

Add the eschalot and chilli and season generously with salt, pepper and lime juice. This is best served on the day you make it – if you let it sit for too long it will release a lot of liquid and lose its crunch.

# Bitter gourd sambol

**SERVES 4–6**

2 bitter gourd

12 g (½ oz) turmeric powder

15 g (½ oz) cooking salt

2 Lebanese (short) cucumbers

70 g (2½ oz) eschalot, finely sliced

salt flakes and freshly ground black pepper

vegetable oil, for deep-frying

2 green bird's eye chillies, finely chopped

40 ml (1½ fl oz) coconut vinegar (see page 28)

10 g (⅓ oz) picked round mint leaves

8 g (¼ oz) picked gotu kola (pennywort) leaves

5 g (⅕ oz) picked coriander (cilantro) leaves

**This is one of my mum's favourite sambols and one of the best ways to use this vegetable. Aside from being good for your digestion, bitter gourd has a unique flavour that I love, and this sambol does an excellent job of cutting through richness and making it easier to eat just a little more of everything; the gotu kola sambol (overleaf) is in this realm too. This is a non-traditional version of this dish.**

Cut the bitter gourd in half lengthways and scrape out the seeds with a spoon. Slice the gourd into half-moons about 3 mm (⅛ in) thick and place in a mixing bowl. Add the turmeric and cooking salt and thoroughly mix through. Set aside for about an hour.

Meanwhile, peel the cucumbers, cut them in half lengthways and scrape out the seeds. Cut them into 1.5 cm (½ in) chunks. (I like to do an angled half roll cut, but it's up to you. Just make sure they are a similar size.)

Place the cucumber and eschalot in a large bowl, season lightly with salt flakes and set aside.

Pour vegetable oil into a large heavy-based saucepan to a depth of 2–3 cm (the oil should come no more than two-thirds of the way up the pan). Place over a high heat and heat to 160°C (320°F). If you don't have a thermometer you can check by dropping a piece of gourd into the oil; if it sinks to the bottom and pops straight back up again, the oil is ready.

Working in small batches, fry the gourd for 4–5 minutes until they are a dark brown colour, gently swishing them around with a slotted spoon so they cook evenly. Lift them out and drain on a wire rack. Make sure that the oil stays at about the same temperature while frying.

Check the cucumber mixture and drain off any liquid that has collected in the bowl. Add the gourd, chilli and coconut vinegar and mix well. Have a taste; it should be salty enough but please do add some pepper.

Once you are happy with the flavour, roughly chop the fresh leaves and gently mix them through. This is best served on the day you make it – you can keep it in the fridge for up to 2 days, but the sambol will lose some of its freshness.

# Gotu kola & herb sambol

SERVES 6–8

A gotu kola sambol is usually made with finely sliced gotu kola, chilli and coconut, but this version is nothing like a traditional one and actually veers more into salad territory. Herbaceous, bitter and refreshing, it makes an excellent little side to a curry. This sambol should be mostly about the herbs so make sure you dress and season with great restraint. As long as you have the gotu kola in there, you can mix up the other herbs at your whim.

100 g (3½ oz) eschalot, sliced into 2 mm (1/12 in) thick rounds (preferably with a mandolin)

50 g (1¾ oz) picked watercress

20 g (¾ oz) picked gotu kola (pennywort) leaves

20 g (¾ oz) picked flat-leaf parsley leaves

20 g (¾ oz) picked round mint leaves

small splash of coconut vinegar (see page 28)

small splash of mild extra virgin olive oil

salt flakes and freshly ground white pepper

Rinse the sliced eschalot in cold water, then let it soak in a fresh bowl of cold water for about 30 minutes. This will take the edge off the sharp raw onion flavour.

Drain the eschalot, squeezing out the excess liquid, and place in a mixing bowl.

Roughly chop the fresh leaves and add to the bowl. Dress with a little coconut vinegar and olive oil and season with salt and pepper, then gently mix together and serve immediately.

# Katta sambol & lunu miris

Each serves 4–6

I have grouped these recipes together as there is much conjecture about the difference between them, and whether they are in fact versions of the same thing with different names. The direct translation of lunu miris is onion chilli, which gives a good indication of ingredients, though some say the difference between the two is that lunu miris doesn't have onion, while katta sambol does. But surely that doesn't make any sense? The best explanation I have come across is that the difference lies in the method rather than the ingredients. Lunu miris is more of a paste, pounded using a mortar and pestle, whereas katta sambol is made with cut ingredients. (However, I use a mortar and pestle when I make katta sambol. Extra confusion.) Basically they are both a form of chilli relish, made with or without Maldive fish. But look, if anyone has a better explanation I would love to hear it.

## Katta sambol

This is based on the Lankan Filling Station version, which we leave out at room temperature to ferment slightly. It's fine out of the fridge for a good week or so, but if you find it's getting too fermenty whisk it into the fridge, where it will keep for weeks and weeks. This sambol is slightly crunchy with a fresh, very hot flavour and possibly a little tang, depending on how long you ferment it for.

| | |
|---|---|
| 3 long red chillies, cut into thin rounds | |
| 80 g (2¾ oz) eschalot, finely sliced | |
| 12 g (½ oz) salt flakes | |
| 8 g (¼ oz) chilli flakes | |
| 3 g (¹⁄₁₀ oz) freshly ground black pepper | |
| juice of 1 lime | |

Using a mortar and pestle, pound the long red chillies and eschalot until the eschalot begins to break down but still retains a little texture. You want an amalgamated mix with visible pieces of chilli and onion.

And the remaining ingredients and use the pestle to mix through. You can eat it immediately, or leave it to ferment slightly at room temperature before using. Either way, it should be served at room temperature.

## Lunu miris

This version is more paste like and slightly fierier than the katta sambol, with an extra punch from the Maldive fish flakes. Not for the faint hearted.

| | |
|---|---|
| 22 g (⅞ oz) Maldive fish flakes | |
| 4 g (⅛ oz) chilli flakes | |
| 4 g (⅛ oz) salt flakes | |
| 3 long red chillies, cut into thin rounds | |
| 70 g (2½ oz) eschalot, finely sliced | |
| 3 g (¹⁄₁₀ oz) freshly ground black pepper | |
| 4 g (⅛ oz) chilli powder | |
| juice of 2 limes | |

Using a mortar and pestle, pound the Maldive fish, chilli flakes and salt until the fish flakes are finely ground.

Add the long red chillies and eschalot and pound to a paste-like consistency; it doesn't have to be super smooth.

Mix through the pepper and chilli powder and season to taste with lime. Serve at room temperature.

Katta sambol ↓

← Lunu miris

# Lime pickle

FILLS A 1 LITRE (36 FL OZ) JAR

These little beauties are a sharp, tangy, mouth-puckering delight in the same vein as preserved lemon, but the limes are slightly dried (traditionally in the sun), and there's vinegar involved. My nan always had a batch on hand but her method was to dry one or two limes as needed and add them to the base of the lime pickle jar she had on the go, almost like a constant ferment. I think this is why hers were so good. Lime pickle is most commonly used in sambols, but really, you can use it anywhere you would otherwise add preserved lemon.

15 medium limes (see note)

approximately 350 g (12½ oz) rock salt

3 small dried chillies

approximately 600 ml (20½ fl oz) white vinegar

**NOTES** Unwaxed limes are ideal here if you can source them. You can also use imperfect or slightly discoloured limes as they are going to be dried out anyway.

If you happen to have a dehydrator, use this instead of an oven.

At LFS we actually keep the pulp from our lime pickle (without the seeds) and blitz to puree to use as a seasoning paste. It is super salty and tangy, but can add a great flavour if used judiciously.

Preheat the oven to its lowest possible setting.

Wash the limes and, if waxed, use an abrasive kitchen sponge to gently scrape it away.

Cut the limes into quarters from the top, leaving 1.5 cm (½ in) attached at the base so the limes hold together. Balance them on a wire rack inside a baking tray and pack the inside of the limes with as much rock salt as they will hold.

Place the tray in the oven for 12–24 hours. The time will depend on your oven and how juicy your limes are; you want them to dry out enough to turn the skins brown with some salt still inside them, but not to the point of being completely dry and hard.

When the limes are brown enough, pack them into a 1 litre (36 fl oz) sterilised jar, along with the dried chillies. Discard any liquid that has pooled in the bottom of your tray. Top up the jar with vinegar, tap it down to remove any air bubbles and secure the lid.

Now leave the limes to pickle at room temperature. My nan told me to keep the jar somewhere warm and turn it every couple of weeks. The limes will be ready to use in as little as 2 months, but they will get better and better over time. The unopened jar will keep for years; once opened, store it in the fridge.

Prepare the limes exactly as you would a preserved lemon – remove the pulp and use the skin (see note).

**Pictured overleaf →**

# Lunu dehi

**SERVES 10–12**

When your lime pickle is ready you'll be able to make this excellent sambol. If you don't have the patience, don't worry: most Sri Lankan grocers sell ready-made lime pickle in jars. This sambol has a strong, rather sharp flavour, but it keeps very well in the fridge for at least a few weeks. There are versions that add tomatoes and/or sugar and chilli, but I like the pure tang of this one.

3 whole pickled limes (see opposite)

approximately 80 g (2¾ oz) eschalot

juice of up to 1 lime

Cut out and discard the inner pulp from the limes and finely dice the skin.

Finely dice the eschalot. You're aiming to have equal amounts of lime and eschalot.

Combine the pickled lime and eschalot in a bowl. The sambol should just hold together and be a little sticky rather than wet, with a nice little crunch. Season with a small amount of lime juice and serve at room temperature.

↑ **Lime pickle**

# Seeni sambol

SERVES 10–12

Along with pol sambol, this is the other sambol found everywhere. The name translates to sugar sambol, but it has the perfect balance of sweet, hot, smoky, sour and umami. It is a great accompaniment to most Lankan meals, particularly egg hoppers, but also anywhere you would want caramelised onion. Because of this versatility, and the fact that it keeps well, this is a good one to make in larger batches (this recipe makes just under 800 g/1 lb 12 oz). The cooking method is key to get the onions to the right texture – we want them caramelised but still holding their shape with a nice little crunch.

50 g (1¾ oz) ghee

1 kg (2 lb 3 oz) red onions, sliced with the grain to a 2 mm (1/12 in) thickness

24 g (⅞ oz) finely chopped garlic

18 g (⅔ oz) finely chopped ginger

8 g (¼ oz) curry leaves

40 g (1½ oz) Maldive fish flakes, ground

20 g (¾ oz) Seeni sambol spice mix (see page 47)

50 g (1¾ oz) jaggery, chopped

40 g (1½ oz) tamarind concentrate

salt flakes

Warm the ghee in a large shallow saucepan over a high heat until it starts to smoke.

Add one-third of the onion, give it a good stir to coat with the ghee, then leave to sit undisturbed for 30 seconds or so. Repeat this method of stirring and sitting for 4–5 minutes until the onion has softened.

Add half the remaining onion, along with the garlic, ginger and curry leaves, and continue with the stir, sit method for another 3–4 minutes.

Add the rest of the onion and cook in the same way for another 3–4 minutes.

Mix in the dried fish and spice mix and stir constantly for 1–2 minutes to combine well and to make sure the onion doesn't catch. By now it should be nicely softened and starting to caramelise.

Stir in the jaggery and tamarind. Give these two ingredients time: the jaggery needs to melt and caramelise slightly and the tamarind needs be thoroughly incorporated into the mix. Cook, stirring, for 3–4 minutes until the onion mix is dark, caramelised and looking sticky.

Remove from the heat and have a taste; you should only need a bit of salt for seasoning. Set aside to cool and serve at room temperature.

NOTE If you want to keep some aside for longer storage, transfer to sterilised jars while the sambol is still hot. It will keep in your pantry for up to 2 months. Otherwise, it will be just as happy in the fridge for several weeks.

# Acharu

EACH FILLS 3 X 500 ML
(17 FL OZ) JARS

Here we have two types of an acharu (pickled dish). Both versions are more appropriate with a meal than some of the simpler types eaten as a street food. One is traditional, the other less so.

In both of these recipes the size and shape of the cut vegetables is important. The weights given are for the prepared vegetables so I would suggest starting off with a little extra of each to allow for wastage.

## LFS acharu

This a staple on the Lankan Filling Station menu and one of the dishes that we start our banquet with (I've always loved a pickle to whet the appetite). We make it in big buckets and let it sit for a few weeks to ferment slightly. Our version is more of a standard pickle, but with familiar Sri Lankan flavours. The hot liquor is poured over the raw vegetables, ensuring the final product has a satisfying crunch, and the pineapple provides a subtle sweetness to balance the heat from the pepper and chilli.

250 g (9 oz) peeled ripe pineapple (about ½ small one), prepped weight

260 g (9 oz) red onion, prepped weight

240 g (8½ oz) carrots, prepped weight

240 g (8½ oz) cauliflower, prepped weight

### PICKLING LIQUOR

8 g (¼ oz) mustard seeds

6 g (⅕ oz) black peppercorns

12 g (½ oz) chilli powder

12 g (½ oz) turmeric powder

375 ml (12½ fl oz) cider vinegar

75 g (2¾ oz) caster (superfine) sugar

22 g (⅞ oz) cooking salt

To prepare your pineapple, start by taking all the skin off. Make sure you do this carefully, maintaining its natural curves so it doesn't start to look like a square. If you are feeling clever, use a paring knife on an angle to cut out the eyes, which will leave you with a lovely angled pattern and beautifully shaped pineapple (see picture on page 196; otherwise, remove the eyes by simply cutting off the skin in a thicker layer – it will just mean more wastage). Cut the pineapple crossways into 1.5 cm (½ in) thick rounds, then halve each round and cut each half into six even triangles. Don't worry about cutting out the core. Place in a large mixing bowl.

Peel the onions and cut the very edge off the top and bottom, leaving a little core to help the onion wedges stay slightly intact. Cut into quarters or sixths, depending on the size. The wedges should only be slightly larger than the pineapple pieces. Add to the mixing bowl.

Peel your carrots and use a roll cut to chop them into pieces similar in size to the pineapple. Add to the bowl.

Cut your cauliflower into florets, again about the same size as the pineapple. Try your best to follow the natural florets, using the tip of your knife to flick them off rather than cut pieces away. Add to the bowl and give everything a quick stir to combine.

Transfer the pickle mix to appropriate storing containers. If you are planning for long-term storage use sterilised jars; if you will be eating it as soon as it's ready any type of storage vessel is fine, either one large or several small. Just make sure the pickle mix is packed in well.

To prepare the pickling liquor, place the mustards seeds and peppercorns in a small frying pan over a low heat and gently toast for 2–3 minutes. Use a mortar and pestle to coarsely grind to break up the peppercorns.

Tip the pepper mix into a large saucepan and add the remaining ingredients along with 600 ml (20½ fl oz) water. Place over

a medium heat and slowly bring to the boil. Simmer for 5 minutes, to allow the flavours to mingle, then remove from the heat and set aside for 2 minutes.

Pour the liquor over the prepared vegetables to completely cover, making sure the spices go in. (Reserve any leftover liquor and turn it into a salad dressing or use some to make a Sri Lankan version of a dirty martini.)

If you have chosen storage jars, seal the lids tightly, making sure there are no air bubbles. The pickles will need to sit for about 1 month to reach their optimum flavour but will last for years unopened.

If you are more impatient and want to eat the pickles as soon as they ready, make a cartouche (a piece of baking paper cut to fit) to sit on top and use some sort of weight, such as a small ramekin or plate, to submerge it slightly. Let the acharu sit for 1–2 weeks, depending on the temperature. Taste after a week to get an idea of the flavour; they will become less sweet and more fermenty over time. Let your personal taste guide you on this one. When you're happy with it, transfer the acharu to the fridge, where it will keep happily for months.

Serve at room temperature with a generous spoon of the liquor over the top.

# Malay pickle

**This is my version of a dish that fits into the acharu category, its name a clear indication of its origins, although it is also called Sinhala or lata pata acharu. ('Lata pata' is one of my favourite terms; loosely translated it means bits and pieces or clutter.) The flavour should be savoury and a little hot with a hint of sweetness, and the vegetables should be yielding but still have some crunch.**

250 g (9 oz) red eschalot, peeled (see note)

200 g (7 oz) long green beans, topped and halved on a slight angle

200 g (7 oz) cauliflower, cut into small florets

200 g (7 oz) carrot, peeled and cut into strips (similar size to the beans)

10 dates, deseeded and quartered lengthways

12 green bird's eye chillies, split, seeds scraped and discarded

400 ml (13½ fl oz) cider vinegar

5 g (⅕ oz) cooking salt

**MUSTARD PASTE**

40 g (1½ oz) mustard seeds

15 g (½ oz) black peppercorns

30 g (1 oz) cooking salt

20 g (¾ oz) finely chopped garlic

15 g (½ oz) finely chopped ginger

100 g (3½ oz) caster (superfine) sugar

9 g (⅓ oz) turmeric powder

Prepare the vegetables, dates and chillies and have them ready.

To make the paste, use a mortar and pestle to pound the mustard seeds, peppercorns and salt. Once ground, add the garlic and ginger and continue pounding to a paste.

Place the vinegar and salt in a medium saucepan over a high heat and bring to the boil. Blanch the eschalot for 1 minute, then scoop them out with a slotted spoon and place in a large mixing bowl. Individually blanch the remaining vegetables, dates and chillies in the same way, for 30 seconds each, adding to the bowl with the eschalot as you go.

Once all the vegetables are blanched, add the mustard paste to the vinegar along with the sugar and tumeric and bring to the boil, then reduce the heat and simmer for 5 minutes. Remove and set aside to cool for 5 minutes.

Pour the pickling liquid over the vegetable mix and give it a good stir. Leave at room temperature for an hour or so, stirring every now and then. There shouldn't be a huge amount of liquid.

Pack the pickle and liquor into jars, gently pressing down as you go to remove any air bubbles. Seal and allow the pickle to sit at room temperature for 24 hours before you use it. Once ready, this pickle can be stored in the fridge and will last for a good few months.

**NOTE** This recipe uses those excellent tiny red Thai eschalots, so do your best to source them. Of course you can use other types of eschalot, but you will need to chop them smaller (to a similar size to the cauliflower florets) and it won't be quite the same.

# Pineapple chutney

**SERVES 8–10**

1 small sweet pineapple (approximately 750 g/1 lb 11 oz)

200 g (7 oz) jaggery, chopped

6 g (⅕ oz) chilli powder

5 g (⅕ oz) salt flakes

3 g (¹⁄₁₀ oz) freshly ground black pepper

1 whole star anise

4 g (⅛ oz) cardamom powder

**Although fruit chutneys aren't generally my thing, we do make this one sometimes at Lankan Filling Station. It's not based on a traditional recipe, but the hot, sweet and spicy flavours fit very comfortably into a Lankan meal. This will last for ages in the fridge, but can also be jarred and stored at room temperature.**

Peel your pineapple and roughly chop, core and all, into small triangles or 2 cm (¾ in) chunks. Don't worry too much about the shape as it all gets chopped again – it's more important to ensure they are a similar size.

Place the pineapple in a bowl, add the remaining ingredients and mix well so the jaggery almost melts and coats the pineapple.

Heat a large frying pan (preferably non-stick) over a high heat, then spoon in enough of the pineapple mix to form a single layer no more than 2 cm (¾ in) high. Leave it to sit undisturbed for 2–3 minutes until the jaggery starts to catch and the pineapple has taken on a bit of colour. Continue cooking for another 7–8 minutes, stirring every now and then, until the mixture starts to look almost burnt.

Transfer the charred pineapple to a clean bowl and repeat with the remaining mixture, including any liquid that has pooled in the bottom of the bowl.

Set aside all the cooked pineapple until it is cool enough for you to touch it and remove the star anise. Turn it out onto a chopping board (it should be sticky and a little saucy) and run a knife or cleaver through it. Chop it to your preferred consistency, but keep it reasonably chunky.

Be warned: this can get messy and you may need to do it in batches.

Taste the chutney and adjust the seasoning if necessary. You want to be able to taste all the spices, particularly the black pepper, and the sweetness should be tempered by a darker charred flavour.

It's now ready to eat, or you can transfer it to sterilised jars for longer storage. Serve at room temperature.

පැණිරස කෑම

# Sweet Things

இனிப்புவகைகள்

While the western idea of a dessert after a meal isn't the traditional way of eating in Sri Lanka there is certainly no shortage of sweet delights. In fact, I would say the tendency for a sweet tooth is actually quite strong. There is a veritable bounty of tropical fruits to choose from; these are consumed throughout the day and often appear after a meal. If you are a banana or mango lover, you are in luck as there are many varieties to choose from, along with the sweetest of pineapples. There are also the stronger fragrant flavours of less common fruits like jackfruit and wood apple. Natural sweetness abounds.

Another category of sweet morsels are the sweetmeats, tiny delights that incorporate more unusual textures and flavours: pulses, chickpeas, rice flours, sesame, cashews, green gram, tapioca, cassava, yam, semolina and the ever-present coconut. I am unfamiliar with many of these, but there are some that I love. Thala guli (see page 242) are small, not-too-sweet balls of sesame seeds pounded with coconut and jaggery and rolled in more sesame seeds. They are Indian in origin, although the Lankan version is usually softer and less toffee like. Then there is kalu dodol (see page 247), a dodol being an Indonesian sweet that arrived courtesy of Malay migrants. Made with palm sugar, rice flour and coconut, this sticky treat has been thoroughly adopted on the island and is served as part of Sinhala New Year's Eve celebrations. Most countries have some version of a toffee and my childhood favourite is Lankan milk toffee (see page 244), made with milk or condensed milk and often cashews. Cut into small squares, it is a little crumbly in texture, rather than sticky or firm.

There are also a few deep-fried treats. Kokis are a beautiful star-shaped biscuit, Dutch in origin, made from a batter and cooked in coconut oil. Konda kavum is oily and sweet, and more like a little cake. Among others, these fried delights usually appear at festivals and celebrations.

Another sweet thing that needs a mention is a faluda (see page 260), a rose milkshake affair. Made with rose syrup, vanilla ice cream, milk, basil seeds and usually a semolina or cornflour noodle, this used to be my mum's childhood after-school favourite. She would often describe it to me but for years I remained unconvinced. This almost dessert-like drink trickled into Sri Lanka via India via Persia, and its name comes from one of the ingredients, basil seeds (also known as folooda seeds). While the drink is far from healthy, according to Ayurveda the seeds are classified as cooling. Its popularity has spread and there are versions all over southeast Asia, but the place to find them in Sri Lanka is in an Indian or Bombay sweet shop. Finally, on one trip, I decided it was time to see what all the fuss was about. I went to a little shop that I was told made one of the best in Colombo. I was hot and tired as I'd spent the day in hideous traffic, trying to track down various things for Lankan Filling Station. The owner of the shop let me watch as he constructed it and told me the secret was in the brand of rose syrup you use. Much to my surprise, it was truly delicious. Definitely on the sickly sweet side, but the sugar was a welcome afternoon pick-me-up, and the basil seeds lived up to their reputation of being wonderfully cooling.

From our Malaysian friends we have another popular sweet treat, this one more along the lines of a traditional dessert. Wattalappam (see page 252) is a cooked custard made with jaggery, giving it a dark appearance, and sometimes containing cashews or sultanas. The custard is steamed or baked until firm, so is often cut into slices like you would a cake. Traditionally this dessert was served at Eid al-Fitr celebrations to mark the end of Ramadan but it's since been adopted all over the island.

The Portuguese influence can still be seen in less common desserts that I have only found reference to in Charmaine Solomon's *The Complete Asian Cookbook*. One is the bolo folhado, a layered pastry dessert with cashews, and the other is foguete, a deep-fried pastry shaped into hollow tubes and filled with sweetened avocado cream. The Portuguese also kickstarted baked goods on the island, which were developed and adapted by the following European settlements.

This influence is clearly illustrated by a few of the Burgher favourites, such as breudher, a sweet yeasted bread made with butter, which is Dutch in origin and traditionally eaten at Christmas with Edam cheese. This has been firmly adopted into our family, although breudher is hard to come by (every year it's on my list of things to make but so far no luck) so instead we start Christmas Day with panettone, more cakey but a good substitute. We have it toasted and buttered with Edam cheese, pol sambol (see page 214) and usually a bowl of cherries on the side. It might sound a little strange, but it is most delicious.

Two cakes in particular are a big part of the Burgher community: love cake and Christmas cake, both of which have acquired an almost mythical status. Sri Lankan love cake (see page 254) is dense, weighty and fudgy, made with semolina, chopped cashews, butter, honey, pumpkin preserve, lots of eggs and heaps of sugar, and seasoned with almond, rose and spices. There is also a Persian love cake which shares some similarities, including the backstory of being so delicious they were the clincher in making people fall in love and decide to marry. Love cake ingredients are richer and more expensive than normally found in Sri Lankan sweets so it is regarded as a special occasion treat. The recipe is usually a closely guarded secret.

Luckily for me, my nan taught me her version, which is a staple on the LFS menu.

I was also fortunate enough to be given the original handwritten recipe of her sister's, Aunty Sweetie's, Christmas cake (see page 256). This cake arrived in Sri Lanka courtesy of the British, and it is a close cousin of traditional fruit cake; the main differences are the use of semolina instead of flour and the way the dried ingredients are chopped, resulting in a more fudge-like texture. Sri Lankan ingredients crept in, and the cake was woven into the Burgher Christmas rituals so thoroughly that stories of making and eating it are deeply entrenched in the history of the community.

Aunty Sweetie was one of my nan's older sisters from the second bed (an excellent Lankan term for a second marriage), along with Aunty Sivim and Aunty Savi – a quartet of women, who, apart from Nan, all remained in Sri Lanka. I only visited Aunty Sivim and Aunty Savi a couple of times, in their once-grand old house in Kandy, but I spent a little more time with Aunty Sweetie. I often ring her daughter, Bernadette, with food questions and she will dig up old family recipes and tell me what I need to know. Bernadette's daughter, Odette, is also a good friend and helped me set up LFS, keeping me entertained with excellent impressions of Sri Lankan aunties.

My mum has great stories of the Christmas cake rituals. Months before Christmas all the aunties would descend on the house and, with the help of the children, spend the day hand chopping and mincing vast quantities of dried ingredients (there was always a lot as you never made just one cake). This communal undertaking was also a chance for the sisters to spend the day gossiping. Nan would put the base of dried fruits, preserves, spices and essences in large Horlicks or Nestle milk jars, then add extra brandy over time and turn the jars to help it soak through.

Closer to Christmas there would be another day of aunties. This time it was all about hand whisking the excessive amount of eggs and sugar for the cakes and mixing that with the booze-soaked fruit. Cake tins would be lined with newspaper (an important step that we still follow), filled with the heavy, dense mixture and tapped down. Because most kitchens didn't have ovens, they would form a procession and take the cakes to the local baker with precise instructions on how to bake them. The cooked cakes would be cooled, perhaps topped up with a little brandy, and then cut into small pieces and wrapped in wax paper and cellophane. Each house had its own special way of folding the paper as a signature of the maker.

In the lead up to Christmas, whole households would spend the day visiting and eating too much. At each house you would be offered cake, and it was acceptable to eat a piece there and pop one in the handbag for later. All the 'for later' pieces would be kept and unwrapped when there was another gathering of the aunties, this time to taste and dissect each piece to determine whose was better this year, whose wasn't up to scratch and all the many reasons why ...

So, carry on and try some of these sweet recipes, safe in the knowledge that you will be spared such intense judgement.

# Thala guli

MAKES 28 BALLS

Indian in origin, this sweet is essentially a sesame paste sweetened with sugar. The Sri Lankan versions tend to be slightly softer than the Indian ones, which are more like a hard toffee. These little balls are just the thing when you want a not-too-sweet morsel with a cup of tea. The method is easy but does require a bit of hefty pounding. You will need a large mortar and pestle to fit all the mixture, or a small blender. You can use a normal blender but that is usually only effective if you make a bigger batch – they do last a good month in the fridge though.

100 g (3½ oz) white sesame seeds

45 g (1½ oz) grated coconut

good pinch of salt flakes

90 g (3 oz) jaggery, chopped into small pieces

120 ml (4 fl oz) kithul

### SEED COATING

20 g (¾ oz) white sesame seeds

20 g (¾ oz) black sesame seeds

a little kithul

Preheat the oven to 150°C (300°F).

Spread out the white sesame seeds in a small baking tray and place in the oven for 12–15 minutes until lightly toasted (or you can toast them in a small frying pan). Jiggle them a couple of times for even cooking.

Place the coconut into a small frying pan and cook over a medium heat, stirring fairly constantly for 3–4 minutes until golden brown in colour and toasted. Set aside.

Using a mortar and pestle, pound the toasted sesame seeds and salt for 4–5 minutes to form a smooth paste. Add the jaggery and pound again to combine. Add the toasted coconut and again pound until combined. Transfer to a bowl.

Place the kithul in a small saucepan and warm over high heat until it comes to the boil. Let it boil until it reduces by half, then add it into the sesame mix. Mix with a wooden spoon for 2–3 minutes until cool enough to touch.

Using clean hands, take about 10 g (¼ oz) of the mix and roll it into a small ball. Repeat with all the mixture, then set aside.

To make the coating, place the white and black sesame seeds in a small frying pan and toast over a medium heat until the white seeds begin to colour. Tip onto a plate and cool slightly.

Slightly moisten each ball with kithul, then roll in the seeds to completely cover. Place on a tray in a single layer.

You can either eat them immediately or refrigerate until they firm up a bit. Serve straight from the fridge or at room temperature.

# Milk toffee

MAKES 52 SQUARES

200 g (7 oz) cashews

2 x 395 g (14 oz) tins condensed milk

400 g (14 oz) caster (superfine) sugar

220 g (8 oz) butter, diced

5 g (⅕ oz) Sweet spice mix (see page 47)

salt flakes

**Made with condensed milk, this toffee was my favourite treat from my nan when I was a child. It is super sweet, but this version includes cashews and a little extra spice for added flavour and texture. Like the kalu dodol on page 247, it's not difficult to make but does need constant stirring on the stove.**

Preheat the oven to 150°C (300°F).

Spread out the cashews on a baking tray and toast for 15–20 minutes until they are uniformly pale golden, giving them a jiggle every 5 minutes to ensure they are cooking evenly. Set aside to cool, then very roughly chop.

Line a rectangular cake tin (approximately 28 cm x 18 cm/11 in x 7 in) with baking paper.

Place the cashews, condensed milk, sugar, butter and spice mix in a wide-based saucepan and stir over a high heat until melted and combined. A wooden spoon is fine but a heatproof spatula is better.

Reduce the heat to low and keep stirring, gently and evenly, as it can catch very easily. It will take about 20 minutes to cook. It's ready when it darkens and you start to see patches that look a little foamy.

Carefully turn out the mix into the prepared tin and spread it out evenly with your spatula, gently pressing it down as you go. Tap the tin firmly on a hard surface a few times to compress the mixture a little and make it easier to cut. Finish with a nice sprinkle of salt flakes and gently press them down with the spatula.

Allow to cool to room temperature, then turn out the toffee slab and cut it into 3 cm (1¼ in) squares. A ruler is a helpful tool here if you want to be precise. You may find that bits crumble off but that's OK. If it's too hard and crumbly it can be a sign that you have cooked it a little too much; if it doesn't set to firm, the mix is slightly undercooked.

Milk toffee can be stored at room temperature for up to a month, although I find it rarely lasts that long.

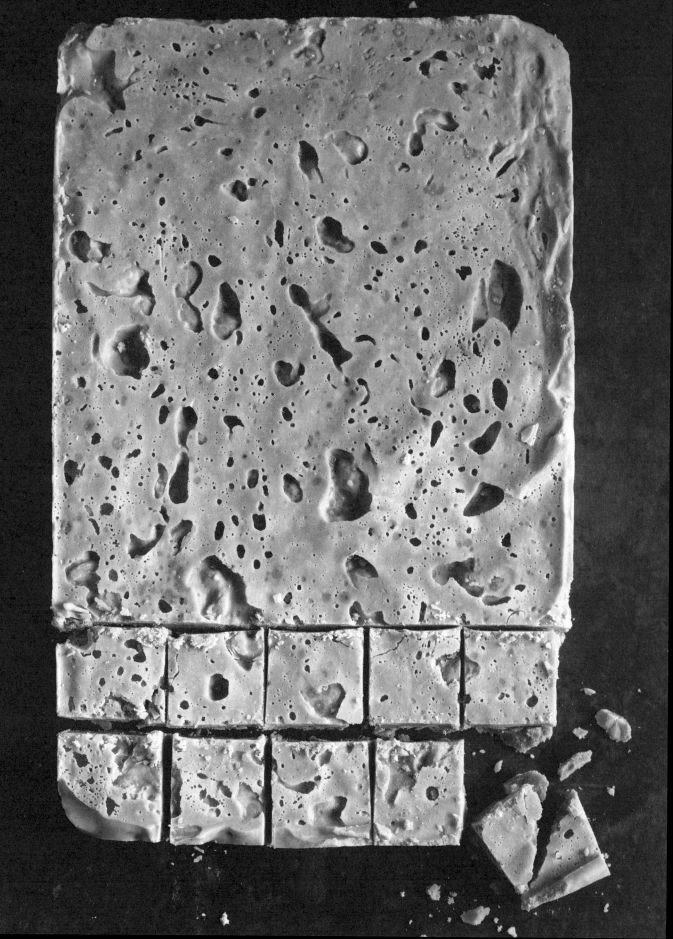

# Kalu dodol

MAKES 27 PIECES

When cooked correctly, this little dessert is a textural delight – chewy, sticky and sweet but not overly so, with a hint of smoke and spice. It's sort of a cross between jelly, Turkish delight and mochi. While it's very easy to make, the process is time-consuming as you need to stand over the pan, stirring constantly for over an hour. Perhaps find a good podcast to listen to? It does make rather a lot, but keeps well for a good week at room temperature, longer if you store it in the fridge. Just be sure to let it come to room temperature before eating.

75 g (2¾ oz) cashews

1.35 litres (46 fl oz) coconut cream

650 g (1 lb 7 oz) jaggery, chopped

200 g (7 oz) regular rice flour

3 g (¹⁄₁₀ oz) cardamom powder

2 g (¹⁄₁₆ oz) freshly ground black pepper

1 g (¹⁄₃₂ oz) salt flakes

Preheat the oven to 150°C (300°F).

Spread out the cashews on a baking tray and toast for 15–20 minutes until they are uniformly pale golden, giving them a jiggle every 5 minutes to ensure they are cooking evenly. Set aside to cool, then roughly chop.

Line a rectangular cake tin (approximately 28 cm x 18 cm/11 in x 7 in) with baking paper.

Place the coconut cream, jaggery and rice flour in a wide-based saucepan over a gentle heat and whisk until the jaggery has melted. Increase the heat slightly and continue whisking for another 8–10 minutes or so until the mix has thickened.

Add the cashews, cardamom, pepper and salt, and swap your whisk for a heatproof spatula.

Now you need to keep stirring as the mix slowly cooks, scraping up the sticky bits caught on the base and mixing them through. After about 25 minutes the coconut oil will start to separate from the mix, although this can depend on the brand of coconut cream, as some will split out earlier than others. Once it does start splitting be careful as you don't want to be splashed by the hot oil.

By about the 1-hour mark (from when everything first goes into the pan) you should be able to wrangle your pan and carefully pour out any excess fat. You can do this earlier if your mix is super fatty; if there's not much, don't be alarmed as it should still work OK.

After a total cooking time of 1 hour 10 minutes or so you should be left with a dark sticky mass, having drained off as much coconut oil as possible. This final 10 minutes of cooking is critical as it's when the mixture fully darkens and caramelises enough to make it set properly. Don't be tempted to stop at an hour. Carefully turn out the mix into the prepared tin and spread it out evenly with the spatula.

Allow to cool to room temperature and set, and then use a knife to cut the dodol into rectangles, about 6 cm x 3 cm (2½ in x 1¼ in). Traditionally it is served wrapped in a banana leaf but you can store it between layers of baking paper.

# Pani pol pancakes

MAKES 10

Made with jaggery and cardamom, pani pol is an excellent coconut mix that's almost like a sweet coconut sambol. It's good as a filling inside a pol roti, but here it's wrapped inside a pancake, tinted yellow with a little turmeric. This popular treat is simple to make, and while you can prepare the pani pol in advance, it's best to make the pancakes fresh.

## PANI POL

120 g (4½ oz) jaggery, grated

200 g (7 oz) grated coconut

3 g (1/10 oz) cardamom powder

salt flakes and freshly ground black pepper

## PANCAKES

125 g (4½ oz) plain (all-purpose) flour

3 g (1/10 oz) cooking salt

1 g (1/32 oz) turmeric powder

225 ml (7½ fl oz) full-cream (whole) milk

2 eggs

vegetable oil, for pan-frying (optional)

For the pani pol, place the jaggery and coconut in a medium frying pan over a medium heat and stir with a wooden spoon until the jaggery starts to melt. Add the cardamom. Cook, stirring occasionally, for 5–6 minutes until the jaggery is nicely caramelised and the mixture is sticky and dark brown in colour. Season generously with salt and pepper and set aside to cool.

To make the pancakes, sift the flour into a mixing bowl and add the salt and turmeric. Whisk together the milk, eggs and 25 ml (1 fl oz) water in a jug. Gradually whisk the milk mixture into the flour, taking care to avoid any lumps forming. Once you have a nice smooth batter, vigorously whisk for another minute or so, then let it rest at room temperature for half an hour. (Alternatively, place all the ingredients in a blender and blitz until smooth.)

Now it's time to test your pancake-making skills. If you are using a non-stick pan you will not need any oil; if not, use a bit of paper towel dipped in oil to season your pan between pancakes.

Heat a 20 cm (8 in) non-stick frying pan or crepe pan over a medium heat, pour in approximately 50 ml (1¾ fl oz) of batter and swirl it around to evenly cover the base, forming a nice thin pancake. Cook until almost entirely cooked through on the base, then flip over and cook for just 10 seconds on the other side. Slide the pancake out of the pan and onto a plate or tray to start a stack. Repeat with the remaining batter.

Once all your pancakes are cooked you can start the filling and rolling.

Place one pancake flat in front of you, then put approximately 20 g (¾ oz) of the filling in the middle of the bottom third of the pancake, spreading it slightly so it reaches almost the top of the pancake. Fold up the bottom so it covers the pani pol, fold in the two sides, then tightly roll it up to form a log.

Set aside, seam side down, and repeat with the remaining pancakes and filling to make 10 rolls.

Eat immediately at room temperature with a cup of tea, although they will happily sit for a good few hours and still be delicious. Leftovers can be placed in the fridge and slightly warmed to eat later (if there are any left).

# Pineapple & pepper

SERVES 4

1 small very ripe pineapple

freshly ground black pepper

salt flakes

This isn't so much a recipe as a suggestion to put a couple of simple ingredients together. Like the curd and kithul below, this is something you would be offered as a dessert or perhaps for breakfast. You will need a nice ripe pineapple for this; the salt works to draw out and balance the sweetness of the fruit, while the pepper adds a pleasing spice. While the magic of this dish lies in its simplicity, a splash of olive oil, a little chilli powder or some ground toasted fennel seeds are all good additions.

To prepare the pineapple, start by taking all the skin off. Make sure you do this carefully, maintaining its natural curves so it doesn't start to look like a square. If you are feeling clever, use a paring knife on an angle to cut out the eyes, which will leave you with a lovely angled pattern and beautifully shaped pineapple (see picture on page 196). Otherwise, remove the eyes by simply cutting off the skin in a thicker layer; it will just mean more wastage.

Cut the pineapple crossways into 1 cm (½ in) thick rounds. Don't worry about cutting out the core.

Arrange the pineapple rounds on a tray and generously season with pepper and a judicious amount of salt. Eat with your fingers.

# Curd & kithul

Again, I would hardly call this a recipe; it's more of a classic pairing of ingredients. This simple but excellent combination is eaten for dessert or breakfast all over the island. Unfortunately, the two ingredients you need can be hard to find outside Sri Lanka, so although you can put together a lovely approximation, to get the true flavour you need to eat it there.

The taste of buffalo curd comes from both the milk and the clay pots it's made in. The curd is thick, firm and rich, due to the high fat content of buffalo milk, but it has a good sour tang to it that veers almost into fermented territory. You can substitute top-quality yoghurt, the thicker the better.

Kithul is fairly easy to source at Sri Lankan grocers or online, but many of the commercial varieties have added sugar, which masks the flavour of the kithul. True organic kithul is dark and thick with a strong smoky flavour, its sweetness balanced by a slight savoury molasses tone.

As for the 'recipe':

Put some buffalo curd in a bowl. Pour over kithul. Eat.

# Wattalappam

SERVES 10

This recipe is almost exactly the same as the one Nan taught me; the one thing I have changed is the cooking method. Traditionally this dessert is steamed or baked until very firm, to the point where it can be cut, and forms tiny air holes which trap little pools of sugar syrup. Because I am not fond of this texture, at Lankan Filling Station we cook it until it is just set, giving it a silky texture similar to a soft creme caramel. It is a rich spiced custard, with a dark, more savoury sweetness from the jaggery. Usually served unadorned, we make a praline to sprinkle on top for added crunch.

360 g (12½ oz) jaggery, grated

400 ml (13½ fl oz) coconut cream

6 eggs

10 ml (⅓ fl oz) vanilla essence

10 ml (⅓ fl oz) rose essence

4 g (⅛ oz) cardamom powder

2 g (1/16 oz) cinnamon powder

1 g (1/32 oz) freshly grated nutmeg

2 g (1/16 oz) salt flakes

### CASHEW PRALINE

200 g (7 oz) cashews

180 g (6½ oz) caster (superfine) sugar

salt flakes

For the cashew praline, preheat the oven to 150°C (300°F).

Spread out the cashews on a baking tray and toast for 15 minutes until they are uniformly pale golden, giving them a jiggle every 5 minutes to ensure they are cooking evenly. Set aside to cool. Tip the cashews onto a lined heatproof tray just large enough to fit the nuts snugly in a single layer.

Combine the sugar and 180 ml (6 fl oz) water in a small saucepan over a medium heat and boil to a very dark caramel. Allow a good 6–7 minutes for this – you want to take it to the very edge of burnt. Quickly and evenly pour the caramel over the cashews and season the top with a sprinkle of salt. Set aside to cool.

Once cooled, use a mortar and pestle to crush the praline into fine-ish chunks; a little bit powdery is good. Set aside. (You can make this ahead of time if you like and store in an airtight container until needed. It will keep for months.)

Place the jaggery and 250 ml (8½ fl oz) water in a small saucepan over a low heat and allow the jaggery to melt. Add the coconut cream and whisk to combine. Bring to a simmer, then take the pan off the heat and leave to cool to room temperature

Whisk together the eggs, essences, spices and salt until just combined. Pour in the jaggery mix, whisking as you go, until smooth and well combined. Strain and allow to sit for 30 minutes.

Preheat the oven to 170°C (340°F). Line a large roasting tin with a tea towel (dish towel).

Give the custard a good mix to disperse the spices and pour evenly into 10 shallow ovenproof bowls.

Place the bowls in the prepared tin (the tea towel will provide a more secure base) and pour enough hot water into the tin to come halfway up the side of the bowls. Cover the bowls with a sheet of baking paper, then tightly cover the tin with foil, securing it firmly.

Carefully place in the oven and bake for 40–60 minutes. The cooking time will depend on the bowls you use, so start checking from the 40-minute mark. You want the custard mix to be just set with a tiny jiggle in the middle. If not, put the tin back in the oven for a few more minutes and check again.

When ready, remove the tin from the oven, take off the foil and allow the wattalappam to cool in the water bath. When the water reaches room temperature, remove the custards. You can eat them straight away at room temperature or refrigerate and serve chilled. Top with a spoonful or two of the praline just before serving.

# Love cake

SERVES 12–16

**This is one of those dishes that people speak of in hushed tones. It is as much about the texture as it is the flavour. It should be dense, really moist and almost fudge like in the middle, surrounded by a layer that is slightly more cooked, and topped with a thin crust. It has a strong, rich cashew flavour, fragrant with spice and the essence of rose. My nan's version was particularly fine – it always had the right texture and her recipe was much sought after. I'm certain that part of her secret was the newspaper she used to line the tins.**

225 g (8 oz) coarse semolina

225 g (8 oz) butter, diced, at room temperature

finely grated zest of 1 lemon

9 egg yolks

225 g (8 oz) caster (superfine) sugar

1 g (1/32 oz) freshly grated nutmeg

5 egg whites

### SPICED CASHEW MIX

225 g (8 oz) cashews, finely chopped

110 g (4 oz) pumpkin preserve (see page 31), finely chopped

15 g (1/2 oz) honey

5 ml (1/5 fl oz) rose essence

5 ml (1/5 fl oz) vanilla essence

3 ml (1/10 fl oz) almond essence

5 g (1/5 oz) cardamom powder

3 g (1/10 oz) cinnamon powder

pinch of salt flakes and freshly ground white pepper

**NOTES** Cooking this cake to the correct texture can involve time and patience and a good knowledge of your oven. I prefer to bake it in a conventional oven but if you only have fan-forced try reducing the temperature to about 140°C (275°F). If you are unsure of doneness, I would err on the side of slightly under.

Store leftover egg whites in the freezer, or why not make a pavlova?

For the spiced cashew mix, combine all the ingredients in a bowl. Cover and leave to sit at room temperature at least overnight. This allows all the flavours to soak into the cashews and mingle nicely.

Preheat the oven to 180°C (350°F). Line a rectangular cake tin (approximately 28 cm x 18 cm/11 in x 7 in) with six layers of newspaper. The best way to do this is to cut out the appropriate size, as you would with baking paper, then hold the newspaper under running water until it's quite damp before fitting it into the tin. Oil this paper and then line with a layer of baking paper. Set aside.

Spread out the semolina on a baking tray and place in the oven for 10–15 minutes until it starts to colour slightly, stirring it around a few times to ensure even toasting. (Alternatively, you can toast it in a large frying pan over a medium heat, stirring often.) Add the butter and lemon zest and mix it through the semolina until fully melted and combined. Set aside.

Reduce the oven temperature to 160°C (320°F). Pour 400 ml (13½ fl oz) water into an oven-proof container and place in the base of your oven. This will add a little moisture to the cooking process.

While the semolina is toasting, place the egg yolks, sugar and nutmeg in a stand mixer fitted with a whisk attachment and beat for 10–12 minutes on a high speed. The best way to tell when the yolks are ready is to turn the mixer off and look for slow volcanic bubbles forming in the mix. Transfer to a mixing bowl large enough to hold all the ingredients and set aside.

In a clean bowl, whisk egg whites to form stiff peaks. Set aside.

Working in alternate batches, gradually add the cashew mix and buttery semolina to the whipped yolks, ensuring each batch is thoroughly incorporated before adding the next. When the cake batter is thoroughly mixed, gradually add two-thirds of the egg whites, again in batches and mixing well. Spoon the batter into the prepared tin and spread it out evenly. Holding the tin with both hands, tamp it down by firmly tapping the tin on a bench.

Now, with clean and slightly damp hands, spread the remaining egg whites evenly over the cake.

Bake for 40–50 minutes, turning the cake halfway through, until a skewer inserted in the centre comes out clean, but only just.

Remove from the oven and allow to cool. Wrap the cake in beeswax wrap (or plastic wrap) and leave to sit for at least a day, a week is even better. This is a long-lasting cake and I have heard tales of it being kept for months and months.

# Christmas cake

**SERVES 20–25**

This boozy fruit cake is wonderfully soft and fudgy, with a rich flavour sharpened by sweet spices. This recipe is Aunty Sweetie's version, kindly given to me by her daughter Berna. When I read through it I was struck by the similarity in method and tone to Nan's love cake recipe (see page 254). You need to start this recipe well in advance as the soaked fruit only gets better over time. To achieve the perfect texture it's best to hand chop all the ingredients, which isn't too tiresome if you're only making one cake, but can get a bit much if you are making several. In this case, my best advice would be to use a mincer and grind the ingredients as coarsely as you can.

165 g (6 oz) coarse semolina

165 g (6 oz) butter, diced, at room temperature

8 eggs, separated

300 g (10½ oz) caster (superfine) sugar

80 g (2¾ oz) glace cherries, finely chopped

### FRUIT AND NUT MIX

165 g (6 oz) raisins, finely chopped

165 g (6 oz) sultanas (golden raisins), finely chopped

165 g (6 oz) pumpkin preserve (see page 31), finely chopped

165 g (6 oz) dates, pitted and finely chopped

165 g (6 oz) cashews, finely chopped

160 g (5½ oz) ginger preserve (see page 29), finely chopped

160 g (5½ oz) chow chow preserve (see page 26), finely chopped

80 g (2¾ oz) candied peel, finely chopped

130 g (4½ oz) fruit jam (your favourite flavour)

110 ml (4 fl oz) brandy

50 g (1¾ oz) honey

12 ml (½ fl oz) vanilla essence

12 ml (½ fl oz) rose essence

7 ml (¼ fl oz) almond essence

finely grated zest of 1 lime

2 g (1/16 oz) Sweet spice mix (see page 48)

For the fruit and nut mix, place all the ingredients in a bowl and stir until very well combined. This mix needs to be covered and stored at room temperature for at least a few days, and can be made up to 6 months in advance. If you happen to have a vacuum sealer, this is a good time to use it to help speed up the process.

Preheat the oven to 180°C (350°F).

Line a rectangular cake tin (approximately 38 cm x 28 cm/15 in x 11 in) with six layers of newspaper. The best way to do this is to cut out the appropriate size, as you would with baking paper, then hold the newspaper under running water until it's quite damp before fitting it into the tin. Oil this paper and then line with a layer of baking paper. Set aside.

Spread out the semolina on a baking tray and place in the oven for 10–15 minutes until it starts to colour slightly, stirring it around a few times to ensure even toasting. (Alternatively, you can toast it in a large frying pan over a medium heat, stirring often.) Add the butter and mix it through the semolina until fully melted and combined. Set aside.

Reduce the oven temperature to 160°C (320°F); if you have a fan-forced oven see the note on page 254. Pour 400 ml (13½ fl oz) water into a small metal bowl or container and place in the base of your oven. This will add a little moisture to the cooking process.

While the semolina is toasting, place the egg yolks and sugar in a stand mixer fitted with a whisk attachment and beat for 10–12 minutes on a high speed. The best way to tell when the yolks are ready is to turn the mixer off and look for slow volcanic bubbles forming in the mix. Transfer to mixing bowl large enough to hold all the ingredients and set aside.

In a clean bowl, whisk the egg whites to form stiff peaks. Set aside.

Working in alternate batches, gradually add the fruit and nut mix, glace cherries and buttery semolina to the whipped yolks, ensuring each batch is thoroughly incorporated before adding the next.

When the cake batter is thoroughly mixed, gradually add two-thirds of the egg whites, again in batches and mixing well.

Spoon the batter into the prepared tin and spread it out evenly. Holding the tin with both hands, tamp it down by firmly tapping the tin on a bench.

Now, with clean and slightly damp hands, spread the remaining egg whites evenly over the cake.

Bake for 1 hour 45 minutes, turning the cake every 30 minutes or so, until a skewer inserted in the centre comes out clean.

Remove from the oven and allow to cool. Tightly wrap the cake in beeswax wrap (or plastic wrap) and leave to sit for at least a week before serving. Stored correctly, it will keep for at least 3 months.

---

**NOTE** As with the love cake, the texture of this cake is part of its beauty but getting it correct is a matter of understanding your oven.

If you want to get fancy, lightly brush your cake with a little extra brandy every week for a few weeks before serving.

---

**Pictured overleaf →**

↑ **Christmas cake**

# Faluda

MAKES ABOUT 10

This drink can have many variations, often including noodles and jelly, but it can also be as simple as milk, ice cream, rose syrup and basil seeds. At Lankan Filling Station we make a glutinous pandan noodle, but this recipe is a simplified version using a rice vermicelli noodle. The flavour is like a sweet rose milkshake with extra textural delight and a background note of pandan. All the bits make enough for about 10 serves but most of them can or should be made at least a day in advance and stored in the fridge. They'll keep for a good week, ready for the urge for a faluda to hit you.

70 g (2½ oz) rice vermicelli noodles, cut up into approximately 5 cm (2 in) lengths

30 g (1 oz) basil seeds

30 g (1 oz) tapioca

### PANDAN SYRUP

300 g (10½ oz) caster (superfine) sugar

10 ml (¼ fl oz) pandan essence (see notes)

### FOR EACH GLASS

30 ml (1 fl oz) Delicious rose syrup (see notes)

ice cubes

1 scoop vanilla bean ice cream

100 ml (3½ fl oz) full-cream (whole) milk

Prepare the pandan syrup, noodle strands, tapioca and basil seeds a day early.

For the syrup, combine the sugar and 400 ml (13½ fl oz) water in a small saucepan over a high heat and bring to a boil until the sugar dissolves. Remove from the heat and cool to room temperature, then stir through the pandan essence.

Decant the syrup evenly into two separate containers.

In a pot of boiling slightly salted water, blanch your noodle strands for 5 minutes. Strain, run under cold water, then add to one of the containers of pandan syrup and leave in the fridge overnight.

Cook the tapioca in 2 litres (68 fl oz) of boiling water for 14–15 minutes until just translucent. Drain and run under cold water, then place in the other container of pandan syrup and leave it in the fridge overnight.

Combine the basil seeds and 350 ml (12 fl oz) water in a small container and leave to soak in the fridge overnight.

When you're ready for your faluda, pour the rose syrup into a milkshake glass (or other large glass) and add a handful of ice.

Add 2 tablespoons each of the basil seeds, tapioca pearls and soaked noodle strands, along with a little of the pandan syrup. Layer in a scoop of ice cream and top the glass with milk.

Serve with a thick straw and a spoon. Give the drink a good stir before you sip as you don't want to end up with a mouthful of rose syrup on its own.

NOTES Pandan essence can be found at Asian grocers.
I have given you the name of rose syrup I like best as flavour and quality can vary greatly from brand to brand.

# Things to drink

*... all food needs drink but not all drink needs food.*

Allegra McEvedy, *The Good Cook*

One of Sri Lanka's best-known exports is tea. Considered to be among the finest in the world, it's grown in the breathtakingly beautiful hill country, a landscape incongruous with the rest of the island and one of the few spots where you could ever possibly be cold. If you are offered tea in Sri Lanka, you will either be presented with a strong milky brew sweetened with an inordinate amount of sugar, which I don't like, or a strong black tea, often just as sweet with a lime cheek floating on top. I am very fond of this version, especially when it comes with a little slice of love cake (see page 254) or a few ginger biscuits for afternoon tea.

What is less well known is that Sri Lanka also had a thriving but relatively short-lived moment of coffee production. Coffee shrubs were introduced to the island sometime in the 17th century, but it wasn't until British occupation that they were grown commercially to make coffee. Production quickly flourished, bringing with it a large Tamil workforce to cope with this new industry, but it fell into disarray in the late 1880s, decimated by a virulent coffee fungus.

This is when tea stepped in, accompanied by an increase in imported labour, creating a new minority of people referred to as hill or up-country Tamils (as opposed to the Sri Lankan Tamils). Tea production has been a great boon for the island, commonly represented in tourist images by rolling green hills dotted with Tamil women in beautifully coloured saris. This is no doubt very appealing; rather less appealing is the harsh reality that these people worked, and continue to work, under dreadful conditions. One would hope this situation is gradually improving as tea continues to be profitable, and coffee production is also starting to see a resurgence.

Fruit juices and drinks are everywhere. The most common is the ever-present thambali (liquid from young coconuts) and my other favourite, a lime juice combination made with fresh juice, water, sugar and a pinch of salt. I find both of these most refreshing. Other mixed fruit juices are often thick like a lassi, particularly the wood apple and avocado 'juice' both made by blending the fruits with condensed milk. Faluda (see page 260) is technically a drink, but I think it's so much more than that. And of course there is a roaring trade in soft drinks, both local and imported; there are several versions of locally made ginger beer, which are also very sweet but have an extra kick from the strongly flavoured Sri Lankan ginger.

When it comes to booze, we need to segue once again to religion. As a predominantly Buddhist country there isn't a huge culture of drinking, except sometimes when there is, and it becomes a problem. Poya day is a public holiday in line with the Buddhist lunar calendar and occurs at every full moon. Traditionally it is a day of fasting but in modern terms it is a day when the whole island shuts down and the sale of meat and alcohol is prohibited. There is also an archaic law from the 1950s banning women from both buying and selling alcohol, although it is not strictly enforced. Women working in hotels or restaurants are required to have a permit to serve alcohol, but as a tourist you would never be prevented from buying booze (although I've been given a few funny looks whenever I have visited a local bottle shop and I have rarely seen another women inside). As recently as 2018, the government passed a reform to do away with this law, but the president stepped in and blocked it, supposedly due to pressure from the monks in the Buddhist community. This is a sad reflection

of the discrimination woman still face at the hands of what is outwardly seen as a very tolerant religion, and it also shows how much power the monks continue to have over the island. More significantly, it has created a drinking culture in Sri Lanka that is essentially the purview of men, although this is more applicable to rural areas than modern city life. This is not to say women don't drink at all; a nip of brandy sometimes – the female equivalent of a man's scotch on the rocks.

Despite this, alcohol is still made in the country. Beer production is a thriving industry, an obvious drink for a tropical country and an excellent match for a spicy curry. There is no wine industry at all and if you do want to purchase some on holidays you will pay a very high price for it. Toddy, or palm wine, is the simplest form of alcohol, cheap and easy to obtain but not terribly alcoholic. It does become stronger the longer it ferments and is very easily turned into a moonshine version of arrack – a popular drink in rural areas, and one that can easily become a problem. It is super strong, unregulated, and if you drink too much it can easily send you a little doolally. When distilled properly, arrack can be a very fine spirit, made in the same way as a whisky. The popularity of arrack has risen and fallen with changes in the political climate; in times of occupation it was looked down upon as an inferior local product, and imported alcohol was imbibed not only for its taste, but also for the status it conveyed. As a result, scotch whisky remains a drink of choice for Sri Lankan gentleman to this day. Gin too had its moment, particularly in the times of the British, and honestly, who doesn't enjoy a gin and tonic with a tropical sunset? Britain even granted local distilleries a license to make gin.

There is also an interesting little drink called milk wine, a Burgher speciality made with arrack as the base. It generally appears at Christmas celebrations and is usually drunk by the aunties. We make it at Lankan Filling Station using Aunty Sivim's recipe; it's a delicious sweet-spiced infusion that takes months to complete and involves many steps, some of which are almost witchy. But we do not question the recipe – we just follow it. Arrack is first infused with spices and citrus zest, then strained and combined with both sugar and a caramel, along with a boiled mix of water and condensed milk. This mixture is curdled with citrus juice and left to sit, then strained, left to sit again, then strained one last time. It may sound a little strange, but the result is a delicately flavoured clear amber liquid which smells like spice and Christmas. I guess this just goes to show that there is *nothing* Lankans won't add spice to.

කෑම වේල

# WHAT GOES WITH WHAT

எது எதனுடன் ஒத்துப்போகும்

*It is perfectly correct to have a serving of everything on your plate at one time.*

Charmaine Solomon, *The Complete Asian Cookbook*

We have talked about the kind of traditional meals you would expect to have and the way to eat them, and if you look ahead you will see some photo spreads showing examples of various meal ideas. The easy option would be to recreate these meals, but perhaps you'd like some more tips on how to do it yourself?

◆ Pick one or two curries that you want to base your meal around and then match flavours based on the ingredients.

◆ Always have more vegetable dishes than meat or fish.

◆ Think about colours and make sure your meal has several of them.

◆ Have a variety of dry and saucy dishes.

◆ Choose at least two or three sambols.

◆ Dhal and rice always.

These ideas work just as well for planning a small meal or a celebratory banquet. The short eats can come into play as starters, although the array you find in a meal may make them unnecessary. Curd and kithul (see page 251) or fruit would be enough for dessert, but if you are feeling fancy then try wattalappam (see page 251).

If it's breakfast you're looking for, curd and kithul with fruit is also great, but here are some other ideas.

◆ Pol sambol (see page 214) + toast + poached eggs

◆ Pol roti (see page 96) + katta sambol (see page 222) + dhal (see page 186) + hard-boiled eggs (one of my favourite simple ways to start the day, especially if you have some dhal leftover – peel the boiled eggs and add them to the pan with watered-down dhal)

◆ Hoppers (see page 108) + seeni sambol (see page 228) + sprats (see page 204)

◆ String hoppers (see page 106) + kiri hodi (see page 147) + pol sambol (see page 214)

And then there are some dishes that stand by themselves.

◆ Kola kanda (see page 118) is enough for breakfast.

◆ Kiri bath (see page 120) also makes a great breakfast, either with a sambol or two, or go the sweet option with banana and kithul.

◆ Lamprais (see page 127) are the perfect one-packet lunch or dinner (you may even want two).

◆ Kottu roti (see page 100) is an excellent light dish to be eaten at any time of the day.

◆ Biryani (see page 123) is good for a celebratory dinner – although you could add a couple of sambols and perhaps a side too.

← Prawn curry

↓ Seeni sambol

↑ Dhal

Pol sambol →

Lunu miris →

# A hopper breakfast or dinner

↑ Egg hoppers

↑ Plain hoppers

Dhal ↓

↑ Fish curry

↑ Pol sambol

↑ Seeni sambol

# Small rice & curry meal

↓ Beetroot

↓ Steamed samba rice

← Snake beans

↓ Pork belly curry

Katta sambol ↓

↑ Green pol

Green papaya mallung ↑

Cashew curry ↑

# Medium rice & curry meal

↓ Dhal

↓ Steamed red rice

Moru chillies ↓

↑ Water spinach

↓ Pappadums

← Murunga curry

↑ Dhal

← Carrot

Pumpkin curry ↑

# Large rice & curry meal

Cavolo nero mallung →

← Fragrant yellow
rice (sans egg)

↑ Chicken curry

Eggplant →

↑ Cucumber sambol

Lunu dehi →

← Pol sambol

Gotu kola & herb sambol ↑

Prawn curry →

Fragrant yellow rice ↑

← Pappadums

Raita ↓

← Malay pickle

↓ Pol sambol

Pineapple
chutney
↓

# Extra fancy
rice & curry meal

← Cucumber curry

Dhal ↑

↑ Garlic curry

Cabbage mallung ↓

← Green mango curry

Sprats →

277

← Steamed samba rice

Bitter gourd sambol
↓

Dhal ↑

Lunu dehi →

↑ Leek mallung

← Beetroot curry

# Crab curry meal

↑ Crab curry

← Pineapple

↓ Godhamba roti

↑ Pol sambol

කියවීමේ ලැයිස්තුව
# READING LIST
புத்தகங்கள்

- *The Complete Asian Cookbook*,
  **Charmaine Solomon**
  Because she did it first and it's still an excellent
  book after all these years.

- *Ceylon Cookery*, **Chandra Dissanayake**
  A very dated but useful book; it even talks you
  through how to set up your Sri Lankan kitchen.
  (Also, her grandson attempted to teach me
  salsa one night in a club in Colombo.)

- *Spice Notes*, **Ian Hemphill**
  All you need to know about spices.

- *Serendip*, **Peter Kuruvita**
  A cookbook by an Australian Sri Lankan chef
  which has many lovely recipes.

- *Reef*, **Romesh Gunesekera**
  My favourite of the many books written by
  this Sri Lankan–born British author. His books
  speak of a particular time in Sri Lanka's history
  and weave beautiful stories with politics.

- *Running in the Family*, **Michael Ondaatje**
  A Sri Lankan–born Canadian writer and poet
  who is also prolific; this particular book feels
  like a remembering of childhood and history.

- *The Road from Elephant Pass*, **Nihal De Silva**
  Set during the civil war, this is a love story
  between a soldier in the Sri Lankan army and
  person defecting from the Tamil Tigers.

- *The Jam Fruit Tree*, **Carl Muller**
  A fairly explicit tale of a Burgher family
  and their madness.

- *Funny Boy*, **Shyam Selvadurai**
  This book has all the issues – family, growing
  up, class, ethnicity, sexuality and the impending
  civil war – told with great humour.

- *Upon a Sleepless Isle*, **Andrew Fidel Fernando**
  An unsentimental and very amusing travel
  book that gives a real sense of what the country
  is like now.

- *Elephant Complex*, **John Gimlette**
  A more in-depth travel book that looks into the
  politics of the country.

- **Islandsmile.org**
  A food blog that seems to always have the
  Sri Lankan recipes that I need to check for
  reference with good explanations.

- **karunacollective.sl on Instagram**
  A female-led collective of young Sri Lankan
  women; their mission is to 'spotlight and uplift
  Sri Lankan stories' by celebrating history and
  learning from diverse voices.

**O Tama Carey** first learnt to cook the food of her Sri Lankan heritage at her mother and grandmother's side but for many years this remained separate to her cooking career. She started working in kitchens quite by accident as a teenager after landing a job in a restaurant in London's Notting Hill. Since then, she has cooked French at Bistro Moncur, Chinese at Billy Kwong and Italian – her version – at Berta where she was head chef. In 2018 she opened Lankan Filling Station, her first solo venture in Sydney's inner-city Darlinghurst. It's here that she spends most of her time, cooking, pounding spices, working the floor and trying to keep a restaurant alive through a pandemic.

පිළිගැනීම

# ACKNOWLEDGEMENTS

நன்றி

A book full of recipes doesn't sit alone. It's made up of years spent tasting things, the people who have helped along the way, places travelled to, the staff who do much of the hard work, the ideas stolen and made your own, meals eaten and the memories of flavours.

To Muu the most, because he is my love, and supports and helps with everything I do – even the ridiculous things.

To both my grandmothers, Ranee and Pat, as they were and are both very fine women and excellent cooks who spawned other equally fine humans and cooks, so the traditions live on.

To the chefs who have trained me and to the people I have worked alongside who have taught me just as much.

To my friends in Sri Lanka, who have looked after me, fed me, entertained me and have become like family. Jane, who was first, always there when I arrived, the loveliest, most generous and welcoming, and who made me feel like I was home. It will never quite be the same without her there. Through her there were so many others. Tilak, who took me on adventures; their beautiful children, Misha and Tarik. Mary, her mum, for the gin and tonics, card games and particularly for the night of casinos in Colombo. To West Winds, where I feel safe. To Nimanthi, who has held my hand, led me places and become my friend, and Padma, her mum, who is a great cook. Also to Ushi and Jeevan, who housed me, partook in many hopper-eating excursions and helped uncover the mystery of the plaster of Paris.

To Nickos and Odette for being there at the inception of Lankan Filling Station.

To Jemma for many reasons. She was the first head chef of Lankan Filling Station and helped from the beginning, researching, writing recipes, finding staff, setting up systems, chopping more onions faster than anyone and keeping me sane. But also because we have cooked side by side since she was a teenager and she still appears whenever I need her.

To my team at Lankan Filling Station, those who are there and those who have passed through, because they help make the restaurant run and without it this book wouldn't exist. Eliott, who was there from the start and now runs the kitchen calmly. Clare and Coco, who are the backbone of the kitchen and also very fine recipe testers. Eddie, because he runs the floor and does all the things all the time. Stu-bear, who works the floor, knows all the customers and also re-upholsters the stools. (A special mention also to Pasi, who was the most over-qualified hopper maker ever and helped navigate the chaos of opening.)

To Jane for wanting to publish the book and giving me good pep talks and generally being fabulous. To Hardie Grant for making it happen, Rachel for helping with the words, Alex for the quotes, Todd for making the gold cover happen, and particularly Em, who managed it all and was such a delight to work with.

To Daniel for his design, Anson for his photos and Steve for his styling. Not only did they help create this, but they also made for an excellent shoot team, notably for the judicious use of props and for shadows made from sprigs of curry leaves.

To Wendy and Scruff for Giragirga, a beautiful space for me to create a self-made writer's retreat, and for the cups of tea and chocolate brownies.

And to the spirit of Bosco. She hovers within these pages.

ආකාරාදිය

# INDEX

அட்டவணை

Published in 2022 by Hardie Grant Books,
an imprint of Hardie Grant Publishing

Hardie Grant Books (Melbourne)
Wurundjeri Country
Building 1, 658 Church Street
Richmond, Victoria 3121

Hardie Grant Books (London)
5th & 6th Floors
52–54 Southwark Street
London SE1 1UN

hardiegrantbooks.com

A catalogue record for this
book is available from the
National Library of Australia

Lanka Food
ISBN 978 1 74379 725 9

10 9 8 7 6 5 4 3 2 1

Publishing Director: Jane Willson
Project Editor: Emily Hart
Editor: Rachel Carter
Design Manager: Kristin Thomas
Designer: Daniel New
Typesetters: Hannah Schubert and Daniel New
Stylist: Steve Pearce
Food Assistants: Jemma Whiteman, Elliott Hodgkinson
and Georgia Lahif
Production Manager: Todd Rechner
Production Coordinator: Jessica Harvie

Colour reproduction by Splitting Image Colour Studio
Printed in China by Leo Paper Products LTD.

The paper this book is printed on is from FSC®-certified forests and
other sources. FSC® promotes environmentally responsible, socially
beneficial and economically viable management of the world's forests.